Lecture Notes in Computer Science 10578

Commenced Publication in 1973
Founding and Former Series Editors:
Gerhard Goos, Juris Hartmanis, and Jan van Leeuwen

More information about this series at http://www.springer.com/series/7407

Xuanhua Shi · Hong An
Chao Wang · Mahmut Kandemir
Hai Jin (Eds.)

Network and
Parallel Computing

14th IFIP WG 10.3 International Conference, NPC 2017
Hefei, China, October 20–21, 2017
Proceedings

Springer

Editors
Xuanhua Shi
Huazhong University of Science
  and Technology
Wuhan
China

Hong An
University of Science and Technology
  of China
Hefei
China

Chao Wang
University of Science and Technology
  of China
Hefei
China

Mahmut Kandemir
Pennsylvania State University
University Park, PA
USA

Hai Jin
Huazhong University of Science
  and Technology
Wuhan
China

ISSN 0302-9743   ISSN 1611-3349 (electronic)
Lecture Notes in Computer Science
ISBN 978-3-319-68209-9   ISBN 978-3-319-68210-5 (eBook)
DOI 10.1007/978-3-319-68210-5

Library of Congress Control Number: 2017954908

LNCS Sublibrary: SL1 – Theoretical Computer Science and General Issues

Printed on acid-free paper

This Springer imprint is published by Springer Nature
The registered company is Springer International Publishing AG
The registered company address is: Gewerbestrasse 11, 6330 Cham, Switzerland

Message from the NPC 2017 Chairs

Welcome to the proceedings of the 14th IFIP International Conference on Network and Parallel Computing (NPC 2017)!

The goal of the NPC conferences is to establish an international forum for engineers and scientists to present their excellent ideas and experiences in system fields of distributed and parallel computing.

High-performance computing and big data are two main areas where NPC 2017 provided a dynamic forum to explore, discuss, and debate state-of-the-art technology issues and challenges. High-performance computers and big-data systems are tied inextricably to the broader computing ecosystem and its designs and market adoption. They also highlight information security needs and economic competitiveness in ways that distinguish them from most other scientific instruments. We strongly believe that the stakes are high, and it is far beyond the boundaries of nations and continents, and should strongly encourage a broad international participation.

For their contribution toward a successful conference, we would like to thank the reviewers for the amazing service that they provided for the NPC conference to ensure that submissions (88 for the conference) received the consideration and attention that they deserve. As the NPC chairs, we especially appreciate the timely completion of reviews for the final selection phases. Each paper was reviewed by three to five expert reviewers ensuring that review details were considered in the decision-making of the final acceptance of 21 full papers (slightly below 24%), including 12 papers published as Special Issue papers of the *International Journal of Parallel Programming*, and nine papers published as LNCS proceedings. A number of strong papers that could not be accepted to the full papers track were considered for the short paper tracks. Finally, we selected 11 short papers (for an acceptance rate of 12.5%). These papers cover traditional areas of network and parallel computing, including parallel applications, distributed algorithms, parallel architectures, software environments, and distributed tools.

We sincerely appreciate the work and effort of the authors in preparing their submissions for review, and addressing the reviewers' comments before submitting the camera-ready copies of their accepted papers, and attending the conference to present and discuss their work.

We also want to thank every member of the NPC 2017 Organizing Committee and Steering Committee for their help in putting together such an exciting program. Finally, we thank all the attendees.

August 2017

Xuanhua Shi
Hong An
Chao Wang
Mahmut Kandemir
Hai Jin

Organization

Organizing Committee

General Co-chairs
Michael Gschwind   IBM, USA
Weisong Shi   Wayne State University, USA

Organization Chair
Guohua Cheng   Hangzhou Jianpei Technology Co., Ltd., China

Program Co-chairs
Hong An   University of Science and Technology of China, China
Mahmut Kandemir   Pennsylvania State University, USA

Publications Chair
Xuanhua Shi   Huazhong University of Science and Technology, China

Local Arrangements Chair
Yu Zhang   University of Science and Technology of China, China

Publicity Co-chairs
Yong Chen   Texas Tech University, USA
Guangzhong Sun   University of Science and Technology of China, China
Keiji Kimura   Waseda University, Japan
Stephane Zuckerman   University of Delaware, USA

Registration Chair
Chao Wang   University of Science and Technology of China, China

Web Chair
Hui Sun   Anhui University, China

Steering Committee

Kemal Ebcioglu (Chair)   Global Supercomputing USA
Hai Jin (Vice Chair)   Huazhong University of Science and Technology, China
Chen Ding   University of Rochester, USA
Jack Dongarra   University of Tennessee, USA
Guangrong Gao   University of Delaware, USA

Jean-Luc Gaudiot	University of California Irvine, USA
Tony Hey	Science and Technology Facilities Council, UK
Guojie Li	Institute of Computing Technology, China
Yoichi Muraoka	Waseda University, Japan
Viktor Prasanna	University of Southern California, USA
Daniel Reed	University of Iowa, USA
Weisong Shi	Wayne State University, USA
Ninghui Sun	Institute of Computing Technology, China
Zhiwei Xu	Institute of Computing Technology, China

Program Committee

Meena Arunachalam	Intel, USA
Nachi Nachiappan	Apple, USA
Myoungsoo Jung	Yonsei University, Republic of Korea
Mahmut Kandemir	Pennsylvania State University, USA
David Abramson	University of Queensland, Australia
Pavan Balaji	Argonne National Laboratory, USA
Taisuke Boku	University of Tsukuba, Japan
Sunita Chandrasekaran	University of Delaware, USA
Barbara Chapman	Stony Brook University, USA
Robert Harrison	Brook University, USA
Miron Livny	University of Wisconsin at Madison, USA
Keiji Kimura	Waseda University, Japan
Kise Kenji	Tokyo Institute of Technology, Japan
Xiaosong Ma	Qatar Computing Research Institute
Yuefan Deng	Stony Brook University, USA
Hong An	University of Science and Technology of China, China
Wenguang Chen	Tsinghua University, China
Yeching Chung	National Tsinghua University, Taiwan
Chen Ding	University of Rochester, USA
Qing Yi	University of Colorado at Colorado Springs, USA
Zhihui Du	Tsinghua University, China
Xiaobing Feng	Institute of Computing Technology, CAS, China
Kai Lu	National University of Defense Technology, China
Yutong Lu	Sun Yat-sen University, China
Yun Xu	University of Science and Technology of China, China
Yifeng Chen	Peking University, China
Yingwei Luo	Peking University, China
Yong Chen	Texas Tech University, USA
Xuanhua Shi	Huazhong University of Science and Technology, China
Weiguo Wu	Xi'an Jiaotong University, China
Yungang Bao	Institute of Computing Technology, CAS, China
Weihua Zhang	Fudan University, China
Yunquan Zhang	Institute of Computing Technology, CAS, China
Li Shen	National University of Defense Technology, China

Chao Yang	Institute of Software, CAS, China
Dongrui Fan	Institute of Computing Technology, CAS, China
Chunyuan Zhang	National University of Defense Technology, China
Di Wu	Sun Yat-sen University, China
Jinlei Jiang	Tsinghua University, China

Contents

SCMKV: A Lightweight Log-Structured Key-Value Store on SCM

Zhenjie Wang, Linpeng Huang$^{(\boxtimes)}$, and Yanmin Zhu

Department of Computer Science and Engineering,
Shanghai Jiao Tong University, Shanghai, China
{zhenjie.wang,lphuang,yzhu}@sjtu.edu.cn

Abstract. Storage Class Memories (SCMs) are promising technologies that would change the future of storage, with many attractive capabilities such as byte addressability, low latency and persistence. Existing key-value stores proposed for block devices use SCMs as block devices, which conceal the performance that SCMs provide. A few existing key-value stores for SCMs fail to provide consistency when hardware supports such as cache flush on power failure are unavailable. In this paper, we present a key-value store called SCMKV that provides consistency, performance and scalability. It takes advantage of characteristics of key-value workloads and leverages the log-structured technique for high throughput. In particular, we propose a static concurrent cache-friendly hash table to accelerate accesses to key-value objects, and maintain separate data logs and memory allocators for each worker thread for achieving high concurrency. To reduce write latency, it tries to reduce writes to SCMs and cache flushing instructions. Our experiments show that SCMKV achieves much higher throughput and has better scalability than state-of-the-art key-value stores.

Keywords: Storage Class Memory · Key-value store · Memory management · Log structure

1 Introduction

Emerging Storage Class Memory (SCM) technologies such as phase-change memory (PCM) [15], spin-torque transfer RAM (STT-RAM) [10] and resistive RAM (ReRAM) [11] have been gaining great attentions from both academia and industry. They have both DRAM-like and disk-like features, such as byte addressability, low latency and persistency. The most promising solution to integrating SCMs into current computer systems is to attach them directly to the memory bus along with traditional DRAM. Thus it is possible to access SCMs through regular load/store instructions. Such hybrid volatile/non-volatile memories offer an opportunity to build more effective and voluminous storage systems such as file systems and databases.

© IFIP International Federation for Information Processing 2017
Published by Springer International Publishing AG 2017. All Rights Reserved
X. Shi et al. (Eds.): NPC 2017, LNCS 10578, pp. 1–12, 2017.
DOI: 10.1007/978-3-319-68210-5_1

Nowadays, key-value stores such as LevelDB [9], and Dynamo [6] have been very important applications in many Internet companies like Google and Amazon. Many data-intensive services provided by these companies rely on fast access to data. However, today's state-of-the-art key-value stores are optimized for block-based devices (e.g. disks and SSDs). These stores rely on file systems to persist data to devices. There exist file systems designed for SCM such as PMFS [7] and NOVA [17]. However, this will introduce some overheads caused by the software layer of file systems and lost the chances to improve the performance of key-value stores by directly accessing SCMs via load/store instructions.

Many researchers have focused on in-memory key-value caches. Memcached [8] and MICA [12] are popular key-value caches. They act as lookaside caches, keep a small part of workloads in DRAM for fast access, and rely on key-value stores to hold all data. Figure 1 shows different roles key-value caches and stores play in today's software stack. These cache systems can't act as key-value stores on SCMs because they are designed for different purpose and don't consider differences between SCMs and DRAM and data inconsistency due to system crashes.

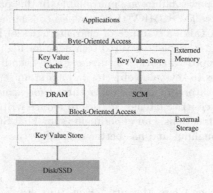

Fig. 1. Various key value systems on different storage devices

One of the most challenging problems for SCM key-value stores is consistency. Modern memory systems keep recently updated data on CPUs' caches and reorder stores to memory for performance. It may lead to inconsistency of data in the face of system crashes. To ensure key-value objects stored on SCM are consistent after recovery, writings of key-value objects must survive unexpected crashes. A simple method to persist data is to flush CPUs' caches explicitly and use memory barriers (e.g. sfence) to enforce write orders. However, frequently flushing CPUs' caches can introduce significant overheads and degrade the performance of the system. In this paper, we present a key-value store named SCMKV that takes advantage of characteristics of key-value workloads and adapts the log-structured technology to maximize throughput of SCMs while providing good scalability and consistency. SCMKV adapts conventional log-structured approach to manage memory, and appends new data to the sequentially written logs. It uses per-thread logs to avoid overheads caused by synchronization primitives and lock-free data structures to provide high concurrency. It uses cache flushing instructions to persist metadata, and data corruption is detected by checksums when SCMKV recovers. Thus the number of cache flushing instructions is reduced greatly. Some information such as *next version number* and *current active log usages* can be constructed from the key-value store when SCMKV recovers. Thus they are allocated to DRAM and omitted from key-value store to reduce accesses to SCM.

The contributions of this paper are summarized as follows.

- It adapts existing log-structuring technology to SCMs and exploits the characteristics of key-value workloads to develop a key-value store.
- It designs a memory allocator for SCMs that moves some information to DRAM that reduces accesses to SCMs.
- It shows that SCMKV outperforms existing in-memory key-value cache and block-device optimized key-value store.

The remainder of the paper is organized as follows. Section 2 provides an overview of SCMKV Design. Section 3 gives details of SCMKV's implementation. Section 4 evaluates this work. Section 5 presents related work and Sect. 6 concludes.

2 Overview of SCMKV

SCMKV is a log-structured key-value store optimized for SCMs while taking advantage of the key-value workloads characteristics. Log-structuring technology is first introduced to build a file system to maximize disk bandwidth [14]. We adapt it to SCMs to offset the performance and wear out weaknesses of SCM and achieve more concurrency.

We designed SCMKV based on following observations. First, because the recently updated data are always appended to logs, the corruption of data due to power failure can only occur at the tail of logs. Thus it is easy to recover key-value store to the consistent state by scanning few logs. Second, there is only single log on storage systems based on disk because of the limited ability of disk sequential addressing. SCMs support random access, thus using multiple logs can achieve more concurrency. Third, a log of 2 MB can contain more than 4,000 key-value objects, if the size of each key-value object is less than 500 bytes. So we fix the size of the log and use small logs, thus it is easy to reserve contiguous free regions for garbage cleaning. Finally, according to [1], the sizes of key-value objects show strong modalities. Over 90% of SYS's keys are less than 40 bytes, and values sizes around 500 B take up nearly 80% of the entire cache's values. So given the size of an SCM device, we estimate the number of key-value objects it can contain.

Based on these observations, we have the following design decisions in SCMKV.

Maintaining Logs in SCM. SCMKV appends key-value objects to logs and inserts them into a hash table. Both logs and the hash table are located in SCM. It doesn't cache updated key-value objects in DRAM as LevelDB. As we observed, the throughput of LevelDB for write-intensive workloads can be limited by the processing that merges data in DRAM to disk. It happens on SCM too. The logs' usages are often changed, thus they are kept in DRAM to reduce the latency of accesses to them. SCMKV can learn the logs' usages by scanning them when it recovers.

Not Persisting Key-Value Objects. Persisting data needs flushing CPUs' caches to SCM and restricting write orders. Both operations can increase the latency of writes. Furthermore, persisting key-value objects will need many flushing instructions, because their sizes are often bigger than the size of the cache line. Instead, SCMKV doesn't flush appended key-value objects. It only flushes some metadata of the hash table, and stores key-value object's checksums in SCM. When power fails, some key-value objects in the end of logs may be corruptible. SCMKV detects errors in active logs, discards them and rolls back to the latest valid key-value objects when it recovers. After SCMKV boots up, it is in the consistent status and doesn't need to check errors anymore.

Using Static Hash Table and Dynamic Chains. Many dynamic hashing schemes have been developed to index keys. These schemes allow the size of the hash table to grow and shrink gracefully according to the numbers of records. However, they cause some overheads when enlarging the size of the hash table. The size distribution of key-value objects can be predicted in the real scenario. Thus we can use a static hash table as the index of the store. To reduce the size of the statically allocated hash table, buckets of the hash table are 64-bit words. Each word contains a pointer point to a key-value object or a chain of the hash table.

3   Design and Implementation of SCMKV

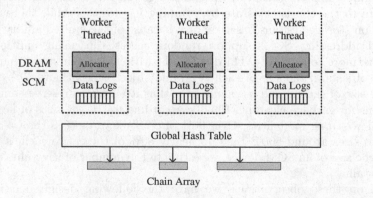

Fig. 2. The architecture of SCMKV.

3.1   Architecture

SCMKV is a persistent key-value store whose permanent data is maintained in non-volatile SCM. Figure 2 shows the architecture of SCMKV. It supports multiple threads to access key-value objects. To achieve good scalability, it uses per-thread allocators and per-thread data logs. These allocators are put on DRAM to support fast allocation. All threads share a global hash table to index key-value objects. The hash table uses dynamically allocated arrays to resolve hash collisions. Using arrays instead of lists can accelerate accesses to key-value objects by taking advantage of CPU's hardware prefetching. The source code is available on GitHub: https://github.com/page4/scmkv.

3.2   Memory Layout

Figure 3 shows the memory layout of SCMKV. The entire volume is divided into five segments. Superblock has the basic partition information and parameters of the store, which are not changeable after the store is created. Checkpoint keeps the status of the store, such as a pointer to free page list, locations of current active logs. A successful checkpoint gives a consistent status that enables the store to recover fast. The Page Information Table (PIT) contains per-page information. Each page contains a data log or some chains of the hash table. An element in the table contains information of the corresponding page, such as the number of key-value objects or chains, the size of live data and the time when the page is modified. For a free page, the element contains a pointer to next free page. The static hash table is a global hash table to locate key-value objects or its chains. Its size is not changed since the store is created. Data Area (DA) is a set of 2 MB pages. Each page is allocated and typed to be *data* or *chain*. A data page contains key-value objects, while a chain page contains chains of the hash table. A page does not store data and chains simultaneously.

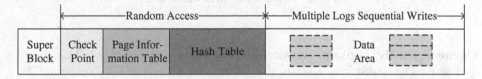

Fig. 3. SCM memory layout

3.3   Concurrent Cache-Aware Hash Table

Figure 4 shows our compact, concurrent and cache-aware hashing scheme. The numbers in the figure indicate the number of living key-value objects in a bucket, which may be smaller than the size of the chain. The bucket contains the address of a key-value object or an array. SCMKV accesses key-value objects directly when no collisions happen, and allocates dynamic arrays as chains when collisions occur. The implementation details are as follows.

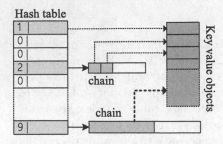

Fig. 4. Hash table structure

```
uint64_t htable_size;
struct hash_table_t {
    uint64_t has_writer:1;
    uint64_t reserved:7;
    uint64_t nr_items:8;
    uint64_t scm_addr:48;
} g_htable[htable_size];
```

Fig. 5. Layout of hash table

Buckets Management. Figure 5 shows the representation of the hash table in C/C++. It is used to give the details of Fig. 4. A bucket in the hash table is a 64-bit word. It allows multiple readers and a single writer to access the same bucket. The first field *has_writer* is used to guarantee only one writer is visiting the bucket. It is set or cleared by atomic operations. The third field *nr_items* indicates the number of key-value items located in the bucket. If *nr_items* is 1, *scm_addr* is the address of the key-value object in SCM. If *nr_items* is greater than 1, *scm_addr* is the address of a chain in SCM. Each chain contains the addresses of key-value objects.

Chains are cache aligned arrays that are dynamically allocated in the Data Area. They are multiple of cache line size. When a chain is full, SCMKV allocates a new chain whose size increases by a cache line size, copies data in the old chain to the new chain and sets *scm_addr* to the new chain.

16-bit tag	48-bit scm_addr

Fig. 6. Layout of a chian element

Cache-Friendly Lookup. An element in a chain is a 64-bit word as shown as Fig. 6. The 48-bit *scm_addr* is the address of a key-value object on SCM. The 16-bit *tag* field is a short summary of a key and can be represented as the high 16 bits of the key's hash. To keep the hash table compact, the actual keys are not stored in the hash table. When SCMKV lookups a key in a chain, it matches *tag*s, retrieves the inspected key and compares the retrieved key with the target key. *Tag* helps to avoid unnecessary retrieves and comparisons of keys. It is possible that two different keys have the same tag. However, with a 16-bit tag, the chance of a collision is only $1/2^{16} = 0.000015$. For a negative lookup operation that checks a bucket with 16 candidate elements, it makes $0.000015 * 16 = 0.00024$ pointer dereferences on average.

Consistency. SCMKV stores a key-value object (*kvobj*), the object's checksum (*kvobj_chsum*), the object's size (*obj_size*) and address of the old object with the same key (*addr_of_oldobj*). It persists *obj_size* and *addr_of_oldobj* by flushing CPUs' cache. While the object is not guaranteed to be durable. If an object is corruptible, it can be rolled back to the old object by recursively visiting *addr_of_oldobj*.

3.4 Memory Allocator

In this section, we describe the per-thread memory allocators on SCM. Each thread in SCMKV has its own memory allocators, which reduces overheads caused by synchronization primitives. SCMKV uses a multilevel memory allocation model to manage memory effectively. At the bottom of this model is the page management layer which keeps a pool of empty pages, allocates and releases pages. At the middle of this model are log allocators. The allocator requires a page from the bottom level when a new log is allocated. It will release the page to the bottom level if a page becomes empty. At the top are object allocators which allocate memory for chains or key-value objects. These object allocators require memory from the tail of logs. They can't reuse space before the tail of logs. Thus there exist many unavailable holes in the logs when key-value objects are deleted. To reuse these holes, allocators need to perform garbage collection. Garbage collection moves some living key-value objects in the evicted log to a new log, and release the page of the evicted log to the bottom level (Fig. 7).

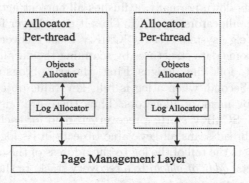

Fig. 7. SCM memory allocators

Keep Current Page Information in DRAM. For every page, there is an element in the PIT that records usages of the page. Page usages are often changed for write-intensive workloads. To reduce the number of writes to SCM, log allocators copy the element to DRAM, thus updates of page usages are kept in DRAM. When the page becomes full, the log allocator stores its usages to SCM, persists data in the log using *clwb* or *clflushopt* instructions and requires a new page from the memory pool to start a new log.

Lock-Free Updates when Allocating Memory. Due to per-thread logs, there are no multiple threads appending key-value objects to the same log. However, page usages can be modified by two threads when they want to remove key-value objects in the same log. So the updates of page usages must be atomic. SCMKV uses atomic writes or compare-and-swap (CAS) to guarantee consistency.

3.5   Garbage Collection

SCMKV uses a *Garbage Collection* thread to reclaim free memories that accumulate in the logs when key-value objects or chain arrays are deleted. After SCMKV boots up, the thread scans the PIT to learn usages of the pages, then it uses a similar cost-benefit approach as LFS [14] to select evicted logs. The evicted logs are chosen based on the amount of free space in the log and the age of the log. The age of log is estimated by the time when the log is modified. For each of the chosen logs, the garbage collection thread scans key-value objects stored in the log, copies live objects to a new log and re-insert them to the store. Then it releases the evicted logs to the memory pool, making the evicted logs' memory available for new logs.

3.6   Shutdown and Recovery

When SCMKV shuts down normally, it flushes all current active logs and some data structures (e.g. allocators) to SCM. Thus it can recover fast. In the case of unclean shutdown (e.g., system crash), SCMKV must recover to the consistent status and rebuild some data structures by scanning the data logs. The recovery process is fast due to following designs. First, the size of logs is not bigger than the size of a page. Second, when a log is full, key value objects in the log are persisted to SCM by memory allocators. Thus there are only several possible unclean logs. Third, SCMKV starts a recovery thread for each possible unclean log. The recovery thread scans all key-value objects in its log, records the first corruption object, sets the tail of the log to the address of the object, and pushes the remaining objects' *addr_of_oldobj* to a recovery stack. In the last, it rolls back all the objects in the stack.

4   Evaluation

We now describe the experimental setup for the evaluation of SCMKV. Then we present results from a detailed evaluation with several micro-benchmarks.

Experimental Setup. In our test, we use a Dell-R730 server running Linux 2.6.32. It is equipped with dual 10-core CPUs (Intel Xeon E5-2650-V3 @2.3 GHz, Ivy Bridge EP). Each CPU has 25 MB of L3 cache and each core has 10×256 KB of L2 cache. The total size of DRAM is 128 GB. We use DRAM to emulate SCM, thus some features of SCMKV can't be evaluated.

Table 1. Datasets with different key value size

Dataset	Key size	Value size	Count
Small	16 B	100 B	64 Mi
Large	128 B	512 B	8 Mi

In the evaluation, we compare SCMKV with LevelDB [9] and Masstree [13]. LevelDB relies on file systems to persist data. To test LevelDB, we reserve a continuous memory area from OS when Linux boots. An ext4 file system is created on the reserved memory. Masstree is a typical in-memory key-value store, and it has outperformed other stores as reported by [12,13]. In our evaluation, data of all these systems are stored in memory, and it will not involve any disk or network overheads.

Benchmark. We use Yahoo's YCSB [4] benchmark suite to generate read and write requests. The datasets are shown in Table 1. These datasets are generated according to two workload types: *uniform* and *skewed*. Uniform workload generates an item uniformly at random, while skewed workload generates an item according to Zipfian distribution.

4.1   Write/Read Throughput of Single Thread

Figure 8 plots the write throughput of a single thread. To show the influences of enforcing write orders, SCMKV has been run in two modes: in *scmkv-noflush* mode, it doesn't use any flush or memory barries instructions, while in *scmkv-flush* it uses *clflush* and *sfence* to enforce write orders. We don't enforce write orders in Masstree and LevelDB. The overall performance of scmkv-noflush is

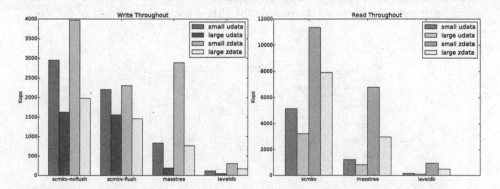

Fig. 8. Single Thread Write Throughput of Different Datasets. *udata indicates uniform workloads, and zdata refers to skewed (Zipfian distribution) workloads.*

Fig. 9. Single Thread Read Throughput of Different Datasets. *udata indicates uniform workloads, and zdata refers to skewed (Zipfian distribution) workloads.*

better than Masstree. With enforcing write orders, SCMKV suffers 40% performance reducing for small key-value objects and 20% performance reducing for large key-value objects in the skewed workloads. As expected, SCMKV has lower overheads caused by cache flushing on larger key-value objects.

In the following descriptions, we compare scmkv-flush with Masstree and LevelDB. As shown in the Fig. 8, SCMKV has 2.6x throughput in small uniform datasets and 7x throughput in large uniform datasets than Masstree. And it has 10x throughput in small uniform datasets and 30x throughput in larger uniform than LevelDB. There are similar results in large skewed datasets. However, SCMKV has smaller throughput than Masstree in the case of small skewed datasets. This is limited by overheads caused by write orders. Besides, the throughputs of skewed datasets are almost same as uniform data in scmkv-flush because SCMKV doesn't benefit from the data locality of skewed datasets. We expect the occurrence of instruction *CLWB* will improve this problem in future.

Figure 9 plots the read throughput of a single thread. Like Masstree, SCMKV returns the pointer to the *value* and the size of value when retrieving the value of a *key*. SCMKV performs better than Masstree and LevelDB in both uniform and skewed datasets due to the efficiency of our design choices. Throughputs of skewed datasets are better than uniform datasets because of the data locality of workloads.

4.2 Scalability

Figure 10 shows write throughputs of small uniform datasets with the increase in number of cores. Both SCMKV and Masstree scale well, while the throughput of LevelDB grows from 0.11Mops to 0.21Mops when we augment the number of cores from 1 core to 10 cores. SCMKV achieves 2.1Mops at 1 core and 5.4Mops at 4 cores. Due to frequency of hash collisions raising with number of cores, throughput per core becomes decreasing. SCMKV has a throughput of 6.7Mops at 10 cores.

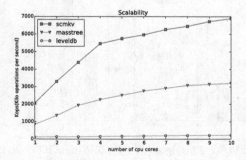

Fig. 10. Write throughput of small uniform dataset using a varying number of cores.

5   Related Work

In this section, we discuss previous studies on storage systems related to SCM and key-value systems.

Storage Class Memory Systems. Many efforts have been devoted to providing different abstractions on SCM. NV-heaps [3] and NVML [5] provide general programming interface with persistent memory and transaction mechanisms for failure recovery. NOVA [17] and PMFS [7] are file systems optimized for persistent memory. They allow for traditional file-based access to memory by POSIX file interface. PMFS uses multi-granularity atomic updates with different CPU instructions and fine-grained logging for metadata consistency and Copy on Write for data consistency.

Key-Value Systems. Key-value systems have been always been optimized for storage media. There are many systems optimized for disk, flash and DRAM. For example, LevelDB is a system based on log-structured merge trees to reduce the latency of disk by sequential writes to disk. NMVKV is a flash-aware key-value store and relies on the Flash Translation Layer (FTL) capabilities to minimal data management at the key-value store.

There are also some key-value systems optimized for Non-volatile Memory. NVMcached [16] is a key-value cache for the non-volatile memory that tries to avoid most cache flushes by using checksums to weed out corrupted data. It acts as a lookaside cache and requires re-inserted for any lost key-value objects. Echo [2] presents a persist key-value storage system that using two-level memory architecture that combining DRAM and SCM. It employs snapshot isolation to support concurrency and consistency, keeps a set of local stores on DRAM for each *worker threads* and a master store on SCM for *master threads*.

6   Conclusions

This paper presents a key-value store optimized for Storage Class Memory (SCM). It is intended to effectively manage storage class memory. It uses per-thread data structures to reduce competitions among threads. And it also reduces the number of some expensive operations such as cache flushing (e.g. unnecessary writes to SCM, explicitly cache flushing) to lower write latency. Experimental results have shown that it achieves high throughput and good scalability for both uniform and skewed datasets.

Acknowledgment. This work is supported in part by National Natural Science Foundation of China (No. 61472241, 61472254, and 61170238) and the National High Technology Research and Development Program of China (No. 2015AA015303). This work is also supported by the Program for New Century Excellent Talents in University of China, the Program for Changjiang Young Scholars in University of China, and the Program for Shanghai Top Young Talents.

References

1. Atikoglu, B., Xu, Y., Frachtenberg, E., Jiang, S., Paleczny, M.: Workload analysis of a large-scale key-value store. In: ACM SIGMETRICS Performance Evaluation Review, vol. 40, pp. 53–64. ACM (2012)
2. Bailey, K.A., Hornyack, P., Ceze, L., Gribble, S.D., Levy, H.M.: Exploring storage class memory with key value stores. In: Proceedings of the 1st Workshop on Interactions of NVM/FLASH with Operating Systems and Workloads, p. 4. ACM (2013)
3. Coburn, J., Caulfield, A.M., Akel, A., Grupp, L.M., Gupta, R.K., Jhala, R., Swanson, S.: Nv-heaps: making persistent objects fast and safe with next-generation, non-volatile memories. ACM Sigplan Not. **46**(3), 105–118 (2011)
4. Cooper, B.F., Silberstein, A., Tam, E., Ramakrishnan, R., Sears, R.: Benchmarking cloud serving systems with YCSB. In: Proceedings of the 1st ACM Symposium on Cloud Computing, pp. 143–154. ACM (2010)
5. Corporation, I.: Nvm library (2017). https://github.com/pmem/nvml
6. DeCandia, G., Hastorun, D., Jampani, M., Kakulapati, G., Lakshman, A., Pilchin, A., Sivasubramanian, S., Vosshall, P., Vogels, W.: Dynamo: amazon's highly available key-value store. ACM SIGOPS Operating Syst. Rev. **41**(6), 205–220 (2007)
7. Dulloor, S.R., Kumar, S., Keshavamurthy, A., Lantz, P., Reddy, D., Sankaran, R., Jackson, J.: System software for persistent memory. In: Proceedings of the Ninth European Conference on Computer Systems, p. 15. ACM (2014)
8. Fitzpatrick, B.: Distributed caching with hmemcached. Linux J. **2004**(124), 5 (2004)
9. Ghemawat, S., Dean, J.: Leveldb (2011). https://github.com/google/leveldb
10. Hosomi, M., Yamagishi, H., Yamamoto, T., Bessho, K., Higo, Y., Yamane, K., Yamada, H., Shoji, M., Hachino, H., Fukumoto, C., et al.: A novel nonvolatile memory with spin torque transfer magnetization switching: Spin-ram. In: IEEE International Electron Devices Meeting, IEDM Technical Digest, pp. 459–462. IEEE (2005)
11. Kawahara, A., Azuma, R., Ikeda, Y., Kawai, K., Katoh, Y., Hayakawa, Y., Tsuji, K., Yoneda, S., Himeno, A., Shimakawa, K., et al.: An 8 mb multi-layered cross-point reram macro with 443 mb/s write throughput. IEEE J. Solid-State Circ. **48**(1), 178–185 (2013)
12. Lim, H., Han, D., Andersen, D.G., Kaminsky, M.: Mica: A holistic approach to fast in-memory key-value storage. Management **15**(32), 36 (2014)
13. Mao, Y., Kohler, E., Morris, R.T.: Cache craftiness for fast multicore key-value storage. In: Proceedings of the 7th ACM European Conference on Computer Systems, pp. 183–196. ACM (2012)
14. Rosenblum, M., Ousterhout, J.K.: The design and implementation of a log-structured file system. ACM Trans. Comput. Syst. (TOCS) **10**(1), 26–52 (1992)
15. Wong, H.S.P., Raoux, S., Kim, S., Liang, J., Reifenberg, J.P., Rajendran, B., Asheghi, M., Goodson, K.E.: Phase change memory. Proc. IEEE **98**(12), 2201–2227 (2010)
16. Wu, X., Ni, F., Zhang, L., Wang, Y., Ren, Y., Hack, M., Shao, Z., Jiang, S.: Nvm-cached: An nvm-based key-value cache. In: Proceedings of the 7th ACM SIGOPS Asia-Pacific Workshop on Systems, p. 18. ACM (2016)
17. Xu, J., Swanson, S.: Nova: a log-structured file system for hybrid volatile/non-volatile main memories. In: FAST, pp. 323–338 (2016)

Adaptive Length Sliding Window-Based Network Coding for Energy Efficient Algorithm in MANETs

Baolin Sun[1](✉), Chao Gui[1], Ying Song[1], and Hua Chen[2](✉)

[1] School of Information and Engineering, Hubei University of Economics,
Wuhan 430205, China
blsun@163.com, prisong@163.com, gui_chao@126.com
[2] Department of Public Basic Course,
Wuhan Technology and Business University, Wuhan 430065, China
qiuchen_1022@163.com

Abstract. A key problem in network coding (NC) lies in the complexity and energy consumption associated with the packet decoding processes, which hinder its application in mobile ad hoc networks (MANETs). Sliding-window Network Coding is a variation of NC that is an addition to TCP/IP and improves the throughput of TCP on MANETs. In this paper, we propose an Adaptive Length Sliding Window-based Network Coding for Energy Efficient algorithm in MANETs (ALSW-NCEE). The performance of this ALSW-NCEE is studied using NS2 and evaluated in terms of the network throughput, encoding overhead, energy consumption, and energy efficiency when packet is transmitted. The simulations result shows that the ALSW-NCEE with our proposition can significantly improve the network throughput and achieves higher diversity order.

Keywords: MANET · Sliding window · Network coding · Energy efficient

1 Introduction

Due to the rapid growth of mobile devices such as laptops and smartphones, wireless data traffic has significantly increased, driving the many efforts to increase wireless bandwidth [1–5]. Recently, wide attention has focused on a novel paradigm called network coding (NC) to maximize the link utilization of a given wireless bandwidth. Energy efficient technique has been widely acknowledged as a promising diversity technique to combat wireless fading [1–5]. Two research areas are exploring this approach: energy efficient and network coding by a neighbor node.

Network coding (NC) is an area that has emerged in 2000 [3], and has since then attracted an increasing interest, as it promises to have a significant impact on both the theory and practice of networks. NC provides some benefits in terms of performance

---

This work is supported by The National Natural Science Foundation of China (No. 61572012).

X. Shi et al. (Eds.): NPC 2017, LNCS 10578, pp. 13–23, 2017.
DOI: 10.1007/978-3-319-68210-5_2

efficiency and throughput in dynamic environments such as mobile ad hoc network (MANET). Suppose a source node sends a set of data packets, grouped into what are referred to as generations, to several destination nodes. Network coding allows the intermediate nodes to combine the different data packets of the same generation.

The advantages of NC come however at the price of additional computational complexity, mainly due to the packet encoding and decoding process. In [4], Guang *et al.* study the performance of random linear network coding (RLNC) for the well-known butterfly network by analyzing some failure probabilities. Ho *et al.* [5] present a distributed RLNC algorithm for transmission and compression of information in general multisource multicast networks. The authors show that the RLNC can take advantage of redundant network capacity for improved success probability and robustness. Papanikos *et al.* [6] focus on the problem of multiple sources broadcasting in MANETs. The authors propose a connected dominating set-based algorithm that works in synergy with RLNC on the "packet generation level".

How to improve the energy efficient is an important issue for packet transmission in MANETs. This paper proposes an Adaptive Length Sliding Window-based Network Coding for Energy Efficient algorithm in MANETs (ALSW-NCEE). We apply network coding over $GF(2^q)$ on symbols rather than on packets to fully exploit the advantages of network coding including adaptive length sliding window, energy efficient. The main contribution of this work is summarized as:

(1) We present an efficient approach to construct adaptive length sliding window and network coding coefficients in a pseudo-random manner on each user. We provide a thorough description of adaptive length sliding window, network coding, and energy efficient in MANETs (ALSW-NCEE), a novel class of network codes.
(2) Second, an analytical model of ALSW-NCEE decoding complexity is derived allowing to matching the decoding computational cost to the capacity of the mobile node.
(3) The performance of the ALSW-NCEE is studied using NS2 and experimentation to assess the encoding efficiency of ALSW-NCEE enabled mobile node. The ALSW-NCEE is shown to achieve significant performance gain.

The rest of the paper is organized as follows. Section 2 discusses the some related work. Section 3 describes models of sliding encoding window model in MANETs. Some simulating results are provided in Sect. 4. Finally, the paper concludes in Sect. 5.

2 Related Works

In this section, we overview the existing literature on lower complexity NC and energy efficient for MANETs. In its best known algorithm, NC is defined over finite fields such as $GF(2^q)$, as the size of the field to ensure the node receives the packet has the very high decoding ability.

In MANET, network coding in higher finite field has been proved with solid performance improvement over binary codes. A key problem in network coding (NC) lies in the complexity and energy consumption associated with the packet decoding processes, which hinder its application in mobile environments. Energy efficiency directly affects battery life and thus is a critical design parameter for MANETs. Applying network coding for wireless applications in general has also been proposed and investigated in the more recent literature. Keller *et al*. [7] present SenseCode, a new collection protocol for sensor networks, which leverages network coding to balance energy efficiency and end-to-end packet error rate. Fiandrotti *et al*. [8] propose a band codes algorithm, a novel class of network codes specifically designed to preserve the packet degree distribution during packet encoding, recombination and decoding. Seferoglu *et al*. [9] propose a network coding aware queue management scheme (NCAQM) that is implemented at intermediate network coding nodes and bridges the gap between network coding and TCP rate control. The NCAQM scheme is grounded on the network utility maximization framework, stores coded packets at intermediate nodes, and drops packets at intermediate nodes. Hong *et al*. [10] present a cooperative relaying strategy for half-duplex multihop relay networks. The author propose a short message noisy network coding with sliding-window decoding (SNNC-SW), the SNNC-SW has a better rate-scaling, lower decoding complexity and delay. Lee *et al*. [11] focus on multiparty video conferencing via a satellite. The author proposed protocol uses the multicasting routing information and number of video frame packets to generate coded packets. The proposed protocol ensures the reliable transmission of multicasting packet for mobile users using the decoding error rate for the random linear network coding batch.

Although some network coding algorithms are proposed to improve network performance, most of these approaches do not consider mobile energy efficient scenario. In this paper, we focus primarily on the mobile packet network problem of MANETs. We take into account maximizing network throughput, consider minimizing decoding delay. By constructing the appropriate network coding structure, we can achieve the higher energy efficient.

Qin *et al*. [12] proposed an energy-saving scheme for wireless sensor networks based on network coding and duty-cycle (NCDES). The scheme determines the node's status based on the ID information which embedded in data information. When combining network coding and duty-cycle in wireless sensor networks, it will reduce transmission coding coefficients and retransmissions. Jiang *et al*. [13] proposes an energy-efficient multicast routing approach to achieve the data forwarding in the multi-hop wireless network. Analysis of the multi-hop networks energy metric and energy efficiency metric. Then the corresponding models are given network coding is used to improve network throughput. Antonopoulos *et al*. [14] propose an ANC-aided game theoretic energy-efficient layout (ANGEL) for data dissemination in wireless networks. Júnior *et al*. [15] propose a show-case that applying Network Coding to data dissemination for Wireless Sensor Networks provides benefits even for small values (CodeDrip). CodeDrip is a data dissemination protocol with network coding capability. CodeDrip utilizes network coding to improve energy efficiency, reliability, and speed of dissemination. Qu *et al*. [16] develop an efficient network coding strategy for secondary users while considering the uncertain idle durations in cognitive radio networks. The authors propose a coding parameter selection algorithm for systematic network coding by considering the complicated correlation among the receptions at different receivers. Nawaz *et al*. [17] proposes a gradient based energy efficient with network coding routing protocol (GREEN). The GREEN algorithm improves the lifetime of industrial wireless sensor network. Energy efficiency increases as more data is routed towards the sink with less number of transmissions.

3   Adaptive Length Sliding Window

We now focus to the adaptive length sliding window and the random network coding approaches. When using this approach, not all packets need to be coded together in a generation, only the code group operating in the same window.

3.1   Network Model

The network model is represented as $G = (V, E)$ where V represents the set of nodes in the network and E denotes the set of directed edges. Each link $e = (i, j) \in E$ means that node i can transmit to node j. We assume links are symmetric that if $(i, j) \in E$; $(j, i) \in E$ as well. Whether two links interfere with each other depends on the interference model adopted.

3.2   Adaptive Length Sliding Window

The conventional sliding window algorithm using a fixed window length, the computational complexity of the algorithm can increase the additional and proportional to the length of the sliding window. In order to effectively improve the performance of sliding window, we proposed an adaptive length sliding window algorithm using a network coding length. Adaptive length sliding window algorithm of the general structure and process the same as the traditional sliding window algorithm, just in the process according to the performance of adaptive window to resize the sliding window. The adaptive length sliding window of algorithm will be adaptive set the length of each sliding window, which can avoid the length of the sliding window is too big or too small.

Figure 1 illustrates the conceptual structure of the proposed adaptive length sliding window algorithm with a sliding window length of w information bits and a frame length of N information bits, assumed to be an integer multiple of w. Let us define the i-th ($1 \leq i \leq N/w$) forward recursion and the i-th backward recursion computation as the forward metric and backward recursion computation computed from the beginning of the $(i - 1)$-th sliding window to the beginning of the i-th sliding window, respectively.

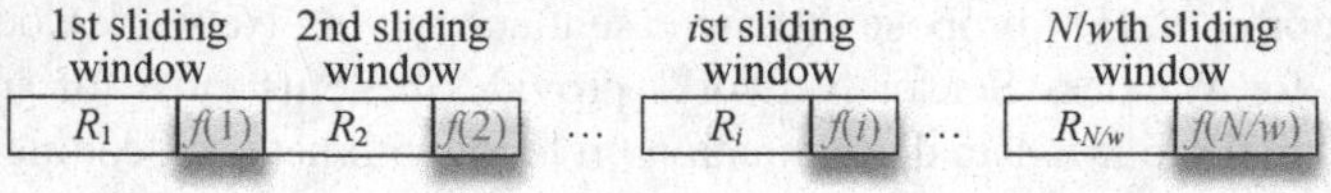

1st sliding window		2nd sliding window			ist sliding window			N/wth sliding window	
R_1	$f(1)$	R_2	$f(2)$	...	R_i	$f(i)$	...	$R_{N/w}$	$f(N/w)$

Fig. 1. Depiction of the proposed adaptive length sliding window algorithm.

In the conventional sliding window algorithm, the length of the sliding window is fixed for all encoding windows, decoding windows and all decoder iterations. However, in the proposed adaptive length sliding window algorithm, the length of the sliding window is adaptively varied for each encoding windows, decoding window and each iteration depending on the reliability information obtained from the backward recursion.

We define the following formula to aggregate the most recent received packet R_i, given the packet R_i is the i-th packet in current sliding window W_i.

$$R_i = \alpha \cdot f(i) + (1 - \alpha) \cdot R_{i-1}, \text{ and } f(i)=k \cdot i + C \tag{1}$$

$$W_i = \beta \cdot W_{i-2} + (1 - \beta) \cdot W_{i-1} \tag{2}$$

where α, $\beta(0 \leq \alpha, \beta < 1)$ is the weight assigned to the predictive sliding window value of latest received packet in window W_i. $f(i)$ is the linear regression function on packets. When the behavior of a service changes, current sliding window value R_i will be updated in a new sliding window, therefore current sliding window may be updated as the new sliding window.

3.3   Network Coding Operation

The network coding process consists of randomly combining source symbols by using coefficients randomly selected within a finite field GF(2^q). Let $x_1, x_2, ..., x_n$ denote the source packets associated with the nodes. Linear network coding allows inter-mediate nodes to combine incoming packets (symbols). Each packet contains a linear combination of the source packets, as described by a vector of coefficients with respect to the source symbols called coding vector, which is sent appended to the packet.

The coding vector can be used by network nodes to decode the data, or further encode it. Encoding can be performed recursively, namely, with already encoded packets. Consider a node that has received and stored a set (a^1, X^1), (a^2, X^2), ..., (a^m, X^m), where X^i denotes the information symbols and a^i the appended coding vector to packet. This node may generate a new encoded packet (a', X') by picking a set of coefficients $e = (e_1, e_2, ..., e_m)$ and computing the linear combination $X' = \sum_{j=1}^{m} e_j X^j$. The corresponding coding vector a' is not simply equal to e, since the coefficients are with respect to the original packets $x_1, x_2, ..., x_n$; in contrast, straightforward algebra shows that it is given by $a_i' = \sum_{j=1}^{m} e_j a_i^j$. This operation may be repeated at several nodes in the network.

The node has received m the corresponding linear combinations of the source symbols. Each node v collects the coding vectors for the packets it receives (or generates) in a decoding matrix G_v. To transmit, the node generates a linear combination whose coding vector lies in the vector space of its decoding matrix. Once a node receives linearly independent combinations, or equivalently, a basis of the n-dimensional space, it is able to decode and retrieve the information of the n sources. Decoding amounts to solving a system of linear equations with complexity bounded as $O(n^3)$.

3.4   Assigning Probabilities to Sliding Windows

Once the window boundaries have been set around each position of each of the result sets that are to be fused, the next stage in the fusion process is to assign a probability score to each position based on those positions contained in the window surrounding it.

$P(d_p, w|s)$, the probability of relevance of packet d in position p using a window size of w packets either side of p, given that it has been returned by input system s is given by

$$P(d_{p,w}|s) = \frac{\sum_{i=f}^{e} P(d_i|s)}{e - f + 1} \tag{3}$$

The use of the sliding window results in a smoother decrease in the probabilities later in the result set, when compared with using probabilities based on data available at each position alone.

4   Energy Efficiency

Focusing on the energy aspect of the problem, we have chosen the utility function so as to quantify the lifetime of the nodes. The energy efficiency (η_{EE}) is evaluated as the expected number of successfully transmitted information bits L divided by the total consumed energy E_{tot} in the MANET, i.e.,

$$\eta_{EE} = \frac{L(\text{bits})}{E_{tot}(\text{Joule})} \tag{4}$$

where L is the total amount of useful data delivered and E_{tot} denotes the total energy consumed.

In MANETs, as long as the mobile nodes are deployed in the transmission range of the transmitting nodes, they receive these packets for free even if these packets do not belong to their duties. Having analyzed the ALSW-NCEE's performance, we are able to derive a closed-form formula that describes the average energy consumption in the network

$$E_{tot} = E_{NC} + E_{min} + E_{EC} + E_{SW} \tag{5}$$

where E_{NC} represent the average energy consumption during the network coding and the initial transmission from the source node, E_{min} denotes the energy waste in a perfect scheduled cooperative phase, E_{EC} is the energy consumed during the contention phase, and E_{SW} is the sliding encoding window during the sliding energy consumption.

The energy consumed in transmitting and receiving a packet is denoted by P_T, P_R, respectively. Furthermore, the relationship between energy and power is given by $E = P \cdot t$, where the terms ε, P and t represent the energy, the power and the time, respectively. We recall that the network consists of a source node, a destination node and a set of n intermediate nodes (code node and sliding node). Therefore, considering the network topology, we have:

$$E_{NCS} = P_T \cdot T_A + (n+1) \cdot P_R \cdot T_A \tag{6}$$

where E_{NCS} represents the average energy required to transmit a NC packet during the contention phase among all the intermediate nodes. Computing the energy consumed during the sliding encoding window phase constitutes one of the most challenging parts in this analytical model. Let us start by defining that:

$$E_{NC} = E_r \cdot E_{NCS} \tag{7}$$

With coding, packets are delivered to the application in a packet-by-packet manner. For every coding packet, the receiver node needs to receive B independent coded packets in order to decode and recover the original coding packet. Let N_i denote the number of transmitted coded packets until the receiver decodes coding block i. p is the packet loss rate. The probability that the receiver receives exactly B coded packets after the n-th packet transmission by the sender for coding packet i is given by a negative binomial distribution, i.e.,

$$P\{N_i = n\} = \binom{n-1}{B-1}(1-p)^B p^{n-B}, \; n \geq B \tag{8}$$

which is the probability that B-1 packets out of the first n-1 transmissions are received successfully and the last transmission is a success too. Recall that, for the moment, we are assuming all coded packets are independent following the mechanism described earlier. Therefore, we obtain that,

$$
\begin{aligned}
P\{N_i \leq n\} &= \sum_{i=B}^{n} \binom{i-1}{B-1}(1-p)^B p^{i-B} \\
&= (1-p)^B \sum_{i=0}^{n-B} \binom{B+i-1}{B-1} p^i
\end{aligned}
\tag{9}
$$

5 Simulation Experiments

In this section, we evaluate and compare the performance of the proposed ALSW-NCEE algorithm for MANETs with SenseCode algorithm [7] and ANGEL algorithm [14]. We implemented the code by integrating the Network Simulator NS-2 [18] to perform the simulations for the MANETs with adaptive length sliding window network coding with energy efficient algorithm.

5.1 Simulation Scenario

We evaluate ALSW-NCEE in a wireless packets scenario where one source distributes a packet sequence to receiver nodes. Nodes are randomly and uniformly located over a 1000 m × 1000 m area, with a node transmission range of 250 m [19]. Node mobility follows the random waypoint model. The generation distributed by the source is called seeding position within the wireless packets stream. The results of the simulation are positive with respect to performance. The corresponding simulation parameters are summarized in Table 1.

Table 1. Simulation parameters

Number of nodes	100
Network area	1000 m × 1000 m
Transmission range	250 m
Simulation time	600 s
Transmission range	250 m
Beacon period	100 ms
Communication model	Constant Bit Rate (CBR)
Message size (b_{msg})	512 bytes/packet
E_{elec}	50 nj/bit
E_{start}	2500 nj/packet
Max sending power	100 mW
Receive power	56 mW
Examined routing proto-col	SenseCode [7], ANGEL [14]

5.2 Simulation Results

In this section, we evaluate and compare the performance of the proposed ALSW-NCEE algorithm for MANETs with SenseCode algorithm [7] and ANGEL algorithm [14].

In Fig. 2, we compare the average network throughput of ALSW-NCEE with those of SenseCode and ANGEL under node's mobility speed for three algorithms. From the Fig. 2 we can see that when the node's mobility speed increases, SenseCode and

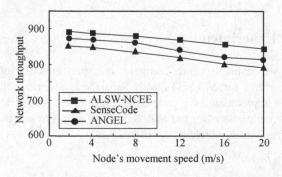

Fig. 2. Network throughput vs. Node's mobility speed (m/s).

ANGEL average network throughput is lower than that of ALSW-NCEE. Therefore we emphasize that the main aim of these algorithms is to avoid any source of energy consumption that rise due to bad wireless links, hence, ALSW-NCEE has an advantage in transmission, than consuming energy by limiting the transmitted packets, and its utilization to adaptive length sliding window network coding algorithms allows for reliable transmission and less energy due to decreased re-transmissions encountered.

In Fig. 3, we test the ALSW-NCEE performance in encoding overhead. We plot the encoding overhead versus node's mobility speed for three algorithms. The encoding overhead increases as the packets transmission increases because the node's mobility speed increases. ALSW-NCEE reduces the encoding overhead the best. Figure 3 shows the encoding overhead of ALSW-NCEE, SenseCode and ANGEL, which use the adaptive length sliding window network coding and energy efficient that minimize the encoding overhead.

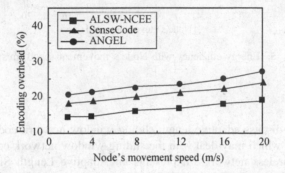

Fig. 3. Encoding overhead with Node's movement speed (m/s).

As the node's movement speed is increased, the distance between the nodes is changing, the energy consumption of the nodes increases. Observe in Fig. 4 that ALSW-NCEE significantly improves the energy consumption of the nodes, hence reducing the frequency of path update events. The energy consumption of ALSW-NCEE is lower than that of SenseCode and ANGEL, especially when the node's movement speed changes from 0 to 20.

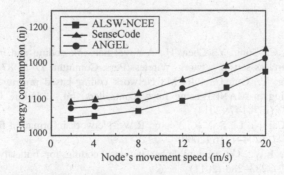

Fig. 4. Energy consumption with Node's movement speed (m/s).

Figure 5 illustrates the energy efficiency versus the node's movement speed with various traffic communication scenarios. The energy efficiency presents the network throughput by multipath receivers versus the number of network coding data packets supposed to be received. The proposed ALSW-NCEE scheme has the better energy efficiency than that of SenseCode and ANGEL algorithm.

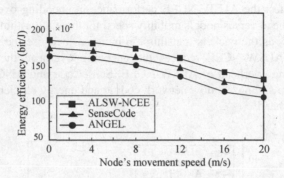

Fig. 5. Energy efficiency with Node's movement speed (m/s).

6 Conclusion

In this paper, we discuss adaptive length sliding window network coding and energy efficient problem, which may deal with the sliding window network coding model for researching in wireless networks. It presents an Adaptive Length Sliding Window-based Network Coding for Energy Efficient algorithm in MANETs (ALSW-NCEE). We provide a thorough description of adaptive length sliding window, network coding, and energy efficient in MANETs. When the destination node receives enough original and coded packets from two transmission phases, it retrieves all the packets by solving a set of linear equations. The performance of the ALSW-NCEE is studied using NS2 and experimentation to assess the network throughput, encoding overhead, energy consumption, energy efficiency of ALSW-NCEE enabled mobile node. The ALSW-NCEE is shown to achieve significant performance gain.

References

1. Sun, B.L., Gui, C., Song, Y., Chen, H.: A novel network coding and multi-path routing approach for wireless sensor network. Wireless Pers. Commun. **77**(1), 87–99 (2014)
2. Sun, B.L., Song, Y., Gui, C., Luo, M.: Network coding-based priority-packet scheduler multi-path routing in MANET using fuzzy controllers. Int. J. Future Gener. Commun. Networking **7**(2), 137–147 (2014)
3. Ahlswede, R., Cai, N., Li, S.-Y.R., Yeung, R.W.: Network information flow. IEEE Trans. Inf. Theory **46**(4), 1204–1216 (2000)
4. Guang, X., Fu, F.W.: On random linear network coding for butterfly network. Chin. J. Electron. **20**(2), 283–286 (2011)

5. Ho, T., Médard, M., Koetter, R., Karger, D.R., Effros, M., Shi, J., Leong, B.: A random linear network coding approach to multicast. IEEE Trans. Inf. Theory **52**(10), 4413–4430 (2006)
6. Papanikos, N., Papapetrou, E.: Deterministic broadcasting and random linear network coding in mobile ad hoc networks. IEEE/ACM Trans. Networking **PP**(99), 1–15 (2017)
7. Keller, L., Atsan, E., Argyraki, K., Fragouli, C.: SenseCode: network coding for reliable sensor networks. ACM Trans. Sens. Networks **9**(2), 1–20 (2013)
8. Fiandrotti, A., Bioglio, V., Grangetto, M., Gaeta, R., Magli, E.: Band codes for energy-efficient network coding with application to P2P mobile streaming. IEEE Trans. Multimedia **16**(2), 521–532 (2014)
9. Seferoglu, H., Markopoulou, A.: Network coding-aware queue management for TCP flows over coded wireless networks. IEEE/ACM Trans. Networking **22**(4), 1297–1310 (2014)
10. Hong, S.-N., Marić, I., Hui, D.: Short message noisy network coding with sliding-window decoding for half-duplex multihop relay networks. IEEE Trans. Wireless Commun. **15**(10), 6676–6689 (2016)
11. Lee, K.-H., Kim, J.-H.: Multi-way relay system with network coding in multi-spot beam satellite networks. Wireless Netw. **23**(1), 205–217 (2017)
12. Qin, T.F., Li, L.L., Yan, L., Xing, J., Meng, Y.F.: An energy-saving scheme for wireless sensor networks based on network coding and duty-cycle. J. Beijing Univ. Posts Telecommun. **37**(4), 83–87 (2014)
13. Jiang, D.D., Xu, Z.Z., Li, W.O., Chen, Z.H.: Network coding-based energy-efficient multicast routing algorithm for multi-hop wireless networks. J. Syst. Softw. **104**, 152–165 (2015)
14. Antonopoulos, A., Bastos, J., Verikoukis, C.: Analogue network coding-aided game theoretic medium access control protocol for energy-efficient data dissemination. IET Sci. Meas. Technol. **8**(6), 399–407 (2014)
15. Júnior, N.S.R., Tavares, R.C., Vieira, M.A.M., Vieira, L.F.M., Gnawali, O.: CodeDrip: Improving data dissemination for wireless sensor networks with network coding. Ad Hoc Netw. **54**, 42–52 (2017)
16. Qu, Y., Dong, C., Tang, S., Chen, C., Dai, H., Wang, H., Tian, C.: Opportunistic network coding for secondary users in cognitive radio networks. Ad Hoc Netw. **56**, 186–201 (2017)
17. Nawaz, F., Jeoti, V.: GREEN protocol: gradient based energy efficient routing with network coding capacity. Telecommun. Syst. **62**(1), 135–147 (2016)
18. The Network Simulator - NS-2. http://www.isi.edu/nsnam/ns/
19. Waxman, B.: Routing of multipoint connections. IEEE J. Sel. Areas Commun. **6**(9), 1617–1622 (1988)

A Virtual Machine Migration Algorithm Based on Group Selection in Cloud Data Center

Zhen Guo[1,3], Wenbin Yao[1,3(✉)], and Dongbin Wang[2,3]

[1] Beijing Key Laboratory of Intelligent Telecommunications
Software and Multimedia, Beijing, China
guozhen402@163.com, yaowenbin_cdc@163.com
[2] National Engineering Laboratory for Mobile Network Security, Beijing, China
[3] Beijing University of Posts and Telecommunications, Beijing 100876, China
dbwang@bupt.edu.cn

Abstract. Live migration of virtual machine (VM) is a promising technology that helps physical machines (PMs) adapt to load changes and guarantees Quality of Service (QoS) in cloud data center. Many individual-based VM migration studies ignore the association between VMs, resulting in high communication cost. Some research on multiple VMs migration migrates the VM group as a whole, which is likely to result in ineffective migration and increase the network burden. In this paper, a VM migration algorithm based on group selection (VMMAGS) is proposed, which takes into account the migration cost, communication cost, and VM heat to optimize migration performance. The appropriate VM groups are selected as migration options, and the optimal migration scheme is obtained according to the integration cost of partitions of selected VM groups. Extensive experiments show that our algorithm can effectively reduce the migration cost and communication cost, improve the system reliability compared with other related algorithms.

1 Introduction

Virtualization [1] is a rapidly evolving technology that enables flexible allocation of resources in cloud data centers [2]. VMs are created according to the amount of required resources and then run on a PM to host application to meet requirements of customers [3]. However, the application load changes constantly in the cloud computing environment, which is likely to cause SLAs violations and affect QoS. Therefore, some VMs on the overloaded PM need to be migrated, so as to ensure the stable operation of cloud data center.

In recent years, the VM migration problem has received much attention. Many individual-based VM migration studies [4] are presented to achieve optimal migration. Shrivastava [5] took the single VM as the migration object, and realized the remapping of VM individual and the PM according to the communication cost. The authors in [6, 7] proposed a multi-objective VM migration algorithm to optimize traffic between VMs, while minimizing the frequency of migration. But they ignored the overhead of the migration itself. More importantly, these individual-based migration strategies will result in higher communication cost due to the association between VMs.

X. Shi et al. (Eds.): NPC 2017, LNCS 10578, pp. 24–36, 2017.
DOI: 10.1007/978-3-319-68210-5_3

Although some studies take into account the association between VMs, such as [8], which takes the entire associated VM group as the migration object. However, such migration is likely to result in ineffective migration and increase the network burden. Sun [9] focused on the efficient online live migration of multiple correlated VMs to optimize system performance. However, the VM groups to be migrated were not obtained according to the resource states of the data center, but were given as known conditions. When VM migration is performed, the appropriate VM group should be selected as the migration object to ensure low communication cost and migration time.

An excellent migration strategy should also provide users with better service. Although the VM that is being migrated does not suspend execution during live migration, its execution may become slowed down somewhat due to the migration. Many studies [10, 11] do not take into account the operating state of the VM during the migration, so that the VM that needs to be migrated may be dealing with high-intensity tasks, which will not only result in a higher dirty page rate, but also greatly affect the response time of the PM. We use the VM heat to reflect the operating state of the VM and take it into consideration to guarantee the better service provided to users.

In this paper, a VM migration algorithm based on group selection (VMMAGS) is proposed. The association between VMs and the resource utilization of the VM are taken into account. According to the resource status of the overloaded PM and the degree of connectivity (DoC) of the remaining VMs, the algorithm selects the appropriate VM group as the migration object. The optimal migration scheme is obtained based on the integration cost of the partitions of selected VM groups.

The remainder of the paper is organized as follows. In Sect. 2, we investigate the problem of the migration of VMs and present the definition of objective functions. Section 3 describes the proposed algorithm. An empirical evaluation is presented in Sects. 4 and 5 concludes the paper.

2 Problem and Objectives Description

2.1 Problem Description

When resources of the PM are tight, migrate some VMs on the overloaded PM to ensure that the remaining VMs and the migrated VMs can both work properly. Different migration strategies will produce different migration results, and the results directly affect the performance of the data center. Figure 1 shows two different migration solutions. PM_1 is overloaded, and some VMs on it need to be migrated. In Fig. 1(a), calculate the optimal migration scheme for the single VM. First, VM_3 is migrated to PM_2 which is closer to PM_1. Next, VM_4 is selected for migration. Since PM_2 does not have enough resources to place VM_4, PM_3 is selected as its target PM. As can be seen from Fig. 1, this migration solution is likely to result in a higher communication cost between VM_3 and VM_4. In Fig. 1(b), VM_3 and VM_4 are both migrated to PM_3. This migration solution guarantees a lower communication cost. Based on the above analysis, we should take the VM group as the migration object, rather than the

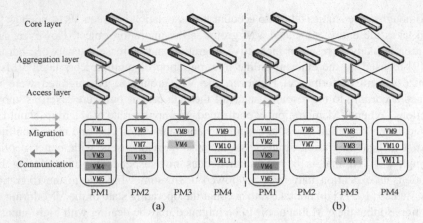

Fig. 1. Two different migration solutions.

VM individual. The work of this paper is to select the best migration VM group for overloaded PM and find the target PM for each VM in the group, so as to reduce the migration cost, communication cost and VM heat.

2.2 The VM Model

In order to cooperate with each other in handling tasks, there may be frequent communication between VMs. Therefore, we model the associated VMs as an undirected graph $G(V, E)$, in which vertices represent VMs and the edge value represents traffic between VM pairs. The attributes of VM_i include its source PM, the requirements for CPU and RAM, denoted by $(PM_{i,src}, vc_i, vm_i)$. Without loss of generality, it is assumed that VMs on the same PM are connected and that VMs on different PMs may also be associated. So the VM model is shown in Fig. 2.

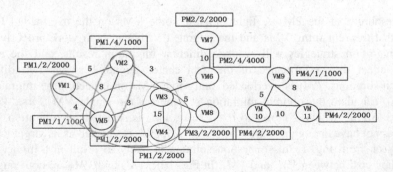

Fig. 2. The VM model.

2.3 Objective Functions Definition

The focus of the paper is to reduce the migration cost, communication cost and the VM heat during the migration process, so we first quantify these objective functions.

Migration Cost. We use the pre-copy strategy to migrate a VM. In the process of live migration, the dirty pages are transferred from the source PM to the target PM through continuous iterations. The longer the migration time, the more resources it occupied, and the greater the impact on network link communication. Therefore, we use the total migration time to reflect the migration cost.

Assume the pre-copy algorithm proceeds in $n_i + 1$ rounds. The amount of data transmitted and transmission time for VM_i in the k-round is $v_{i,k}$ and $T_{i,k}$ ($0 \leq k \leq n_i$), respectively. The entire memory of the VM needs to be transferred to the target PM in the 0-round, so $v_0 = vm_i$. $v_{i,k}(k \neq 0)$ is determined by the dirty page generated by the previous round. So $v_{i,k} = r_i T_{i,k-1}$ ($1 \leq k \leq n_i$), where r_i is page dirty rate, and $T_{i,k} = v_{i,k}/B_i = (vm_i/B_i) \cdot (r_i/B_i)^k$. Therefore, the total time T_i is calculated as:

$$T_i = \sum_{k=0}^{n_i} T_{i,k} = \frac{vm_i}{B_i} \cdot \frac{1 - \left(\frac{r_i}{B_i}\right)^{n_i+1}}{1 - \frac{r_i}{B_i}}. \tag{1}$$

n_i is calculated according to the memory threshold vm_{th}. The iteration is stopped when the threshold is reached. So we can obtain:

$$n_i = \left\lceil \log_{\frac{r_i}{B_i}}\left(\frac{vm_{th}}{vm_i}\right) \right\rceil. \tag{2}$$

The downtime of VM_i in the migration process is represented as $T_{down\_i} = T_{d\_i} + T_{resume\_i}$. T_{d_i} is the time of transferring the remaining dirty pages, and T_{resume_i} denotes the time spent on resuming the VM on the target PM. Therefore, the migration cost of VM_i is calculated as:

$$Cost\_mig(VM_i) = \frac{vm_i}{B_i} \cdot \frac{1 - \left(\frac{r_i}{B_i}\right)^{n_i+1}}{1 - \frac{r_i}{B_i}} + T_{down\_i}. \tag{3}$$

Communication Cost. The communication cost is mainly related to the distance and traffic between the migrated VM and other VMs. The communication cost of VM_i is represented by (4).

$$Cost\_com(VM_i) = \sum_{j \neq i} D\left(PM_{i,target}, PM_{j,src}\right) \cdot f\left(VM_i, VM_j\right). \tag{4}$$

VM Heat. The VM heat represents the strength of the VM to handle tasks. We use the resource utilization of the VM to reflect its heat. The resource utilization of the VM varies with the dynamic application load. When it is necessary to migrate VMs for an overloaded PM, some VMs may be dealing with high-intensity tasks, and their resource utilization is likely to be high. The calculation of the VM heat depends not only on the resource utilization at the migration moment, but also on historical data. Higher historical utilization represents that the VM is generally dealing with a lot of tasks, and it is also likely that the tasks will be intense in the future. Therefore, we use (7) to calculate the VM heat of the VM group.

$$H(VM_i) = \big(H(CPU)_i + H(RAM)_i\big)/2. \tag{5}$$

$$H(CPU)_i = \lambda \cdot AVG\left(\sum_{j \in T} U\_CPU_j\right) + (1-\lambda) \cdot U\_CPU_t, H(RAM)_i$$

$$= \lambda \cdot AVG\left(\sum_{j \in T} U\_RAM_j\right) + (1-\lambda) \cdot U\_RAM_t. \tag{6}$$

$$H(VMgroup) = AVG\left(\sum_{VM_i \in VMgroup} H(VM_i)\right). \tag{7}$$

In (6), U_CPU_j and U_RAM_j represent CPU utilization and RAM utilization at time j. t represents the migration moment. T is the total duration of historical data. We use the average of the utilization within T before t as the VM's historical resource utilization. Historical data is obtained by sampling. A sampling was conducted at each Δt interval during the T. The data at t should be given greater weight, so that we can calculate the VM heat more accurately. So we set $\lambda = 0.3$. In the experiments, we set T to one hour, and Δt is set to 30 s.

3   Algorithm

3.1   VM Group Selection

In order to avoid frequent migration, it is necessary to set the resource safe range (SR). When the resource occupied after the migration is in the SR, it represents the end of the migration on this PM. First, we will select all appropriate VM groups as migration options. The selected VM groups should include all possible scenarios to prevent the loss of the best solution, and the size of each group can't be large. So, traverse the VM associated graph on the overloaded PM, select all VM groups that make the occupied resources of the PM after the migration are in the SR and the DoC of the remaining VMs reaches a certain value. There can be a single VM or multiple VMs in the selected VM group. The 2 to 9 lines of Algorithm 1 show the selection of VM groups.

A binary string *Binary_set* with the same length as the number of VMs on PM_k reflects the selected state of the VM. 1 indicates that the VM is selected, 0 is the opposite. *checkAvailable*() is used to determine whether the occupied resources of the

---

Algorithm 1. VMMAGS

1. Get $G_k(V_k, E_k)$ on PM_k from $G(V, E)$;
2. **for** *Binary_set* in *all_set*
3.   *subG, remG is* the adjacency table of selected VMs, remaining VMs;
4.   **if** (*checkAvailable* (G_k, *low, high, PM_i_CPU, PM_i_RAM*) &&
           checkConnectNum (G_k, *remG*, θ))
5.   All selected VMs *make up VMgroup$_i$*;
6. $< Cost\_norm\_VMgroup_i, VM_{mig}, PM_{dist} >=$ CCMS (*VMgroup$_i$, subG, PMList*);
7. **end for**;
8. **if** no VM group meets the conditions
9.   Make each VM on PM_k as the selected VM group and calculate its
           $<Cost\_norm\_VMgroup_i, VM_{mig}, PM_{dist} >$;
10. *min = min* (*Cost_norm_VMgroup*);
11. Calculate σ of all *Cost_norm_VMgroup*;
12. Get *VMgroupList* with *Cost_norm* in [*min, min+ σ*];
13. Calculate $H(VMgroup_j)$ of *VMgroup$_j$* in *VMgroupList*;
14. Get *min* (*Cost_ integrated*);·
15. **return** VM migration scheme $< VM_{mig}, PM_{dist} >$;

PM after the migration are within the SR. $\theta(0 \leq \theta \leq 1)$ represents the value of the DoC that needs to be reached. *checkConnectNum*() is used to check whether the number of connected VMs has reached θ times the total number of remaining VMs. If both conditions are satisfied, the VM group consisting of the selected VMs is used for the next step. If no VM group meets the conditions, make each VM on PM_k as the selected VM group. Optional VM groups on PM_1 in the VM model are circled in Fig. 2. The total resource of PM_1 is (16-core, 16000M). The SR is [0.5, 0.6], and θ is 0.5.

3.2 Objective Functions Integration

It is difficult to find the best migration scheme to meet these three goals. But if we integrate the three goals, the difficulty will be significantly reduced.

We define the *Cost_mig* and *Cost_com* weighted sum as the total cost. The simple weighted summation is susceptible to the larger value, so *Cost_mig* and *Cost_com* need to be normalized to eliminate the difference in magnitude. For VM_i on PM_k, we use the max-min method to normalize its cost.

$$Cost\_mig\_norm(VM_i) = \frac{Cost\_mig(VM_i) - \min(Cost\_mig)}{\max(Cost\_mig) - \min(Cost\_mig)}, \max(Cost\_mig)$$

$$= \frac{\max(vm)}{\min(B)} \cdot \frac{1 - \left(\frac{\max(r)}{\min(B)}\right)^{n+1}}{1 - \frac{\max(r)}{\min(B)}}. \tag{8}$$

$$Cost\_com\_norm(VM_i) = \frac{Cost\_com(VM_i) - \min(Cost\_com)}{\max(Cost\_com) - \min(Cost\_com)}, \max(Cost\_com)$$
$$= \max(degree)\max(D) \cdot \max(f). \tag{9}$$

$Cost\_mig$ is normalized by (8) to obtain $Cost\_mig\_norm$. $\max(vm)$, $\max(B)$ and $\max(r)$ represent the maximum RAM of the VM on PM_k, the maximum bandwidth of the data center and the maximum dirty page rate. $Cost\_com$ is normalized in the same way, using (9) to obtain $Cost\_com\_norm$. $\max(D)$ represents the maximum distance between PMs. $\max(f)$ represents the maximum traffic between VMs on PM_k. $\max(degree)$ represents the maximum degree of VMs on PM_k. The calculation method of min is opposite to that of max.

$Cost\_norm$ is calculated using (10), where $\alpha + \beta = 1$, and we will determine their values through experiments.

$$Cost\_norm(VM_i) = \alpha \cdot Cost\_mig\_norm(VM_i) + \beta \cdot Cost\_com\_norm(VM_i). \tag{10}$$

Next we will integrate $Cost\_norm$ and the VM heat. The implementation of various migration schemes will result in different $Cost\_norm$. The cost of many schemes may have only a small difference, but the heat of VM groups in these schemes may be quite different. It is unreasonable to sacrifice the service of VMs in exchange for the small $Cost\_norm$ difference. The 10 to 14 lines of Algorithm 1 show the specific steps to get the best migration scheme. σ represents the standard deviation of all VM groups and the integration cost $Cost\_integrated$ is calculated as:

$$Cost\_integrated(VMgroup_j) = \gamma \cdot Cost\_norm(VMgroup_j) + (1 - \gamma) \cdot H(VMgroup_j). \tag{11}$$

γ controls the weight of $Cost\_norm$, $\gamma \in [0, 1]$. Calculate the minimum value of $Cost\_integrated$, and the corresponding migration scheme is the best solution.

3.3   VM Migration Algorithm

In this section, we use the greedy strategy to determine the optimal migration scheme based on selected VM groups.

For the selected VM group, we can't guarantee that the cost of migrating them to the same target PM is less than the cost of individual migration. Moreover, a VM group has multiple partitions. All partitions of $VMgroup_2(VM_3, VM_4, VM_5)$ on PM_1 in Fig. 2 are as follows: $partition_1 = \{\{VM_3\}, \{VM_4\}, \{VM_5\}\}$, $partition_2 = \{\{VM_3, VM_4\}, \{VM_5\}\}$ $partition_3 = \{\{VM_3, VM_5\}, \{VM_4\}\}$, $partition_4 = \{\{VM_4, VM_5\}, \{VM_3\}\}$, $partition_5 = \{\{VM_3, VM_4, VM_5\}\}$.

Therefore, we should calculate all partitions of the VM group to get the best solution. Multiple VM collections will be generated in one partition. In order to guarantee a lower communication cost, it is necessary to require that the VMs in the same collection are connected, and they are migrated to the same PM. It means that $partition_4$ does not meet the condition. Algorithm 2 gives the specific steps to calculate the $Cost\_norm$ value and the migration scheme of $VMgroup_i$. $availableResource()$ is used to determine whether the resource exceeds the upper limit of the SR after the PM adds the migrated VM. *checkConnected()* is used to determine whether the VMs in the collections are connected. It should be noted that the placement conditions of the collection need to meet the resource requirements of all VMs in the collection. Calculate the minimum value of *Cost_norm* for all partitions as the *Cost_norm* value of this VM group.

Algorithm 2. CCMS (Calculate Cost and Migration Scheme)

Input: *VMgroup$_i$* , *subG*, *PMList*

Output: <*Cost_norm_ VMgroup$_i$*, *VM$_{mig}$* , *PM$_{dist}$* >

1.   **for** *partition$_k$* of *VMgroup$_i$*
2.   **for**(*PM$_j$* in *PMList*)
3.   **if** (*availableResource* (*partition$_k$*, *PM$_j$*) && *checkConnected* (*partition$_k$*, *subG*))
4.   Get the minimum *Cost_ norm* and its < *VM$_{mig}$* , *PM$_{dist}$* >;
5.   **end for;**
6.   **end for;**
7.   **return** <*Cost_norm_ VMgroup$_i$*, *VM$_{mig}$* , *PM$_{dist}$* >;

The complete VM migration algorithm based on group selection (VMMAGS) is shown in Algorithm 1. For *VMgroup$_i$* that satisfies the selection conditions, CCMS is used to calculate its <*Cost_norm_ VMgroup$_i$*, *VM$_{mig}$*, *PM$_{dist}$*> . After obtaining *Cost_norm* of all groups, calculate their *Cost_integrated* according to the integration method mentioned in Sect. 3.2. Finally, we get the minimum value of *Cost_integrated* and the best VM migration scheme.

4   Experiments and Results

4.1   Experimental Setup

We use CloudSim [12] to carry out experimental tests in this section to verity the performance of VMMAGS. The performance of VMMAGS is evaluated by comparing with the algorithm AppAware [5] and TAVMS [8] in terms of migration cost, communication cost and response time. AppAware takes the single VM as the migration object, and uses the greedy strategy to find the migration scheme with the minimum communication cost. TAVMS solves the problem of multiple VMs migration and migrates the VM group as a whole. However, we find that the objectives of them are different from ours. For achieving fair comparison, we modify these two algorithms by replacing the objectives of them with *Cost_norm* defined in this paper.

In Fat-tree topology [13], the parameter *k* defines the data center size. We use three common structures in real cloud data centers for experiments. Structure1: *k* = 12, there are 432 PMs and 156 switches; Structure2: *k* = 14, there are 686 PMs and 210 switches; Structure3: *k* = 16, there are 1024 PMs and 272 switches. The link capacities in Fat-tree are set ranging from 1 GBps to 10 GBps. The distance between PMs is computed as shown in [14]. In addition, we model four instances of PMs with different capacity in the simulations, as shown in Table 1. Each PM belongs to one of the four instances, with each instance having probability 1/4. Each VM has CPU requirement of 1, 2, 4 or 8 cores and memory requirement of 1 to 16 GB, which is generated randomly from discrete uniformly distributions. We use FCFS algorithm for VM placement. Each VM runs a web-application with variable workload to generate different resource utilization, thus reflecting the different heat of the VM. The traffic between VMs is set according to what is suggested in [15]. If there is flow between VMs, a Gaussian distribution is used to generate the transmission rate. The mean is 10 MBps. The standard deviation is 1 MBps, and the probability is 0.75. In our experiments, the page dirty rate is set to 100 MBps. vm_{th} is set to 100 MB, which is a reasonable compromise based on other parameters, and T_{resume_i} is set to 20 ms.

Table 1. Configuration information of PMs.

Configuration	CPU cores	RAM (GB)	MIPS
PM Instance 1	16	32	3000
PM Instance 2	16	16	2800
PM Instance 3	8	16	2500
PM Instance 4	4	8	2100

4.2   Parameters Analysis

VMMAGS involves some parameters, and different parameter settings will directly affect results. So we first experimentally analyze the best value of different parameters.

Two important parameters that affect VM group selection are the SR [*low, high*] and the DoC of the remaining VMs θ. Besides, these two parameters directly affect the total migration cost and communication cost of the data center. In order to control the number of VMs that need to be migrated, we set the minimum value of *low* to 0.5. We compare the total migration cost of the different SRs and the communication cost corresponding to different θ values in Structure3 with 2400 VMs to get their best values. The results are shown in Figs. 3 and 4.

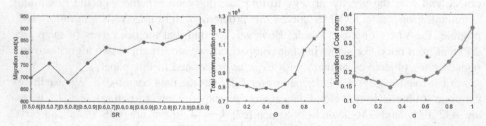

Fig. 3. The total migration cost of different SRs in Structure3

Fig. 4. The total communication cost of different θ in Structure3.

Fig. 5. The fluctuation of *Cost_norm* under different α.

It can be seen from Fig. 3, when *high* becomes larger, the migration cost increases. With the expansion of the SR, that is, the gap between *high* and *low* becomes larger, the migration cost decreases. This is because with the expansion of the SR, the optional VM groups increased, so easier to get the best migration scheme. When the SR is [0.5, 0.8], the migration cost is minimal, so we set SR to [0.5, 0.8].

In Fig. 4, when θ changes from 0 to 0.3, the communication cost is gradually reduced. This is because when the required DoC is low, it is likely to cause the selected VM group is not the best choice, producing more communication cost than migrating a single VM. When θ is in [0.3, 0.5], the corresponding communication cost is minimal and changes little. Then as θ becomes larger, the communication cost increases significantly. Taking into account the stability of the algorithm and the calculation time, we finally set θ to 0.4.

The calculation of *Cost_norm* involves the weight parameter α. A better weight parameter can guarantee the stability of the algorithm, so the effect on the system performance is reduced to the minimum. For all overloaded PMs in Structure1 with 800 VMs, we experimentally compared the average fluctuation of *Cost_norm* under different α settings. The fluctuation is the difference between the maximum and the minimum values of *Cost_norm*. As shown in Fig. 5, the performance of the algorithm will fluctuate with the change of α. When $\alpha = 1$, the fluctuation of *Cost_norm* reaches the maximum. When $\alpha = 0.3$, the performance of the algorithm is stable, and the value of *Cost_norm* floats in a small area. Therefore, the α value is set to 0.3 in the following experiments with considering the migration performance of the algorithm.

Next we determine the optimal value of γ in (11) to get *Cost_integrated*. We choose the overloaded PM that hosts the most VMs in Structure1 to carry out the experiment, denoted by PM_k. There are 148 selected VM groups. Figure 6 shows *Cost_norm* of all groups, *Cost_norm* in [min(*Cost_norm*), min(*Cost_norm*) + σ] and VM heat. There are four groups with *Cost_norm* in the range. We have experimentally proved that when the value of γ changes from 0.1 to 0.9, *Cost_ integrated* of group$_{95}$ in Fig. 6 is always the minimum. Without loss of generality, we set γ to 0.5 in the following experiments.

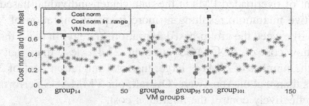

Fig. 6. *Cost_norm* of all selected VM groups on PM_k, *Cost_norm* in [min(*Cost_norm*), min (*Cost_norm*) + σ] and the VM heat of the group.

4.3 Results Analysis

Total Migration Cost. We compare the total migration cost of our proposed VMMAGS with that of the other two algorithms, with the variation of VMs in three structures. The results are shown in Fig. 7.

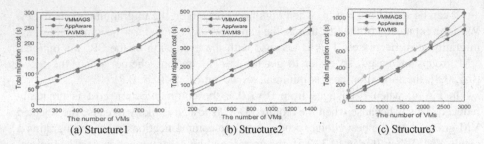

Fig. 7. The total migration cost of all VMs in three structures

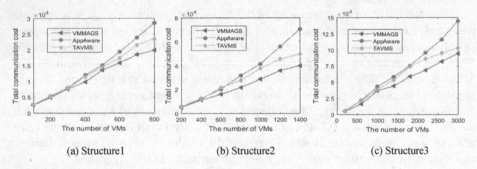

Fig. 8. The total communication cost of all VMs in three structures

It can be seen from Fig. 7, our VMMAGS and AppAware performance is relatively similar, and TAVMS is the worst. That is because TAVMS migrates the entire VM group, resulting in a larger memory migration. When the number of VMs is small, the migration cost of AppAware is lower. But we find a rule from the results, that is, when the number of VMs in the data center increased to a certain extent, the migration cost of AppAware exceeds VMMAGS, even more than TAVMS. This is because when there is a large amount of overloaded PMs in the data center, individual-based migration is prone to ineffective migration, resulting in more frequent migration of VMs, and the migration cost will exceed the group-based migration strategy. In these three structures, the total migration cost of VMMAGS is about 27.4% less than that of TAVMS. Besides, when the number of VMs is large, the total migration cost of VMMAGS is about 18.8% less than that of AppAware. Overall, our VMMAGS performance is more stable, and can effectively control the migration cost.

Total Communication Cost. The communication cost is another important metric to evaluate the performance of VM migration. So we compare the total communication cost of the three algorithms with the variation of VMs in three structures. In Fig. 8, we can observe that our VMMAGS consumes less communication cost than other algorithms in all cases. With the increase of the number of VMs, the total communication cost of VMMAGS increases almost linearly, but the cost of AppAware increases significantly. That is because as VMs become more, individual-based strategy can't get the optimal solution, resulting in the associated VMs migrated to different PMs, so that the increase of the communication cost. When there are enough VMs in the data center, the total communication cost of VMMAGS is about 14.5% less than that of TAVMS, about 36.2% less than that of AppAware.

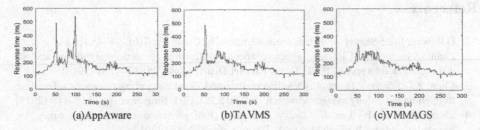

|(a)AppAware|(b)TAVMS|(c)VMMAGS|

Fig. 9. The response time of the PM in Structure1.

Response Time. The VM heat directly affects the system response time, so we observe the changes in the response time of a PM using different algorithms in Structure1. Figure 9 depicts the results. When t = 50 s, the response time surged, indicating that the PM resources were tight. At this point, a migration occurred. As we can see from Fig. 9(a), the PM carried out two migrations, and the response time fluctuated significantly. In Fig. 9(b), the response time had been significantly reduced with TAVMS for migration. But the response time fluctuated greatly during migration. While using VMMAGS, the response time was relatively stable, and could be maintained within 300 ms. These results show that VMMAGS can effectively guarantee the system service.

5 Conclusions and Future Work

In this paper, we propose a multi-object VM migration algorithm named VMMAGS, which takes into account the migration cost, communication cost and VM heat to optimize the performance of the data center. According to the SR and the DoC of the remaining VMs, the VM groups that satisfy the conditions are obtained as migration options. Get the optimal migration scheme based on the integration cost of all partitions of selected groups. We assess VMMAGS performance using simulation and compare it with AppAware and TAVMS. Experimental results show that the total migration cost of VMMAGS is about 27.4% less than that of TAVMS, and the total communication cost of VMMAGS is about 36.2% less than that of AppAware. Besides, our algorithm can better control the response time. In the future, we consider the efficient migration of VMs across data centers.

Acknowledgments. This work was partly supported by the NSFC-Guangdong Joint Found (U1501254) and the Co-construction Program with the Beijing Municipal Commission of Education and the Ministry of Science and Technology of China (2012BAH45B01) and National key research and development program (2016YFB0800302) the Director's Project

Fund of Key Laboratory of Trustworthy Distributed Computing and Service (BUPT), Ministry of Education (Grant No. 2017ZR01) and the Fundamental Research Funds for the Central Universities (BUPT2011RCZJ16, 2014ZD03-03) and China Information Security Special Fund (NDRC).

References

1. Goldberg, R.P.: Survey of virtual machine research. Computer **7**(6), 34–45 (1974)
2. Zhan, Z.H., et al.: Cloudde: a heterogeneous differential evolution algorithm and its distributed cloud version. IEEE Trans. Parallel Distrib. Syst. **28**, 704–716 (2016)
3. Chen, Z.G., Zhan, Z.H., et al.: Deadline constrained cloud computing resources scheduling through an ant colony system approach. In: 2015 ICCCRI, Singapore, pp. 112–119 (2015)
4. Zhang, J., Ren, F., Lin, C.: Delay guaranteed live migration of virtual machines. In: Proceedings of the IEEE INFOCOM, Toronto, pp. 574–582 (2014)
5. Shrivastava, V., Zerfos, P., Lee, K.W., et al.: Application-aware virtual machine migration in data centers. In: Proceedings of the IEEE INFOCOM, Shanghai, pp. 66–70 (2011)
6. Huang, D., Gao, Y., Song, F., et al.: Multi-objective virtual machine migration in virtualized data center environments. In: 2013 IEEE ICC, pp. 3699–3704. IEEE (2013)
7. Zhang, X., Shae, Z.Y., Zheng, S., et al.: Virtual machine migration in an over-committed cloud. In: 2012 IEEE NOMS, Hawaii, pp. 196–203 (2012)
8. da Silva, R.A.C., da Fonseca, N.L.S.: Energy-aware migration of groups of virtual machines in distributed data centers. In: 2016 IEEE GLOBECOM, Washington, pp. 1–6 (2016)
9. Sun, G., Liao, D., Zhao, D., et al.: Live migration for multiple correlated virtual machines in cloud-based data centers. IEEE Trans. Serv. Comput. (2015)
10. Tao, F., Li, C., Liao, T.W., et al.: BGM-BLA: a new algorithm for dynamic migration of virtual machines in cloud computing. IEEE Trans. Serv. Comput. **9**(6), 910–925 (2016)
11. Yao, X., Wang, H., Gao, C., et al.: VM migration planning in software-defined data center networks. In: 2016 IEEE HPCC, Sydney, pp. 765–772 (2016)
12. Calheiros, R.N., Ranjan, R., Beloglazov, A., et al.: CloudSim: a toolkit for modeling and simulation of cloud computing environments and evaluation of resource provisioning algorithms. Softw. Pract. Exp. **41**(1), 23–50 (2011)
13. Li, Y., Wang, H., Dong, J., et al.: Application utility-based bandwidth allocation scheme for data center networks. In: PDCAT, Beijing, pp. 268–273 (2012)
14. Meng, X., et al.: Improving the scalability of data center networks with traffic-aware virtual machine placement. In: Proceedings of the IEEE INFOCOM, San Diego, pp. 1–9 (2010)
15. Biran, O., Corradi, A., Fanelli, M., et al.: A stable network-aware vm placement for cloud systems. In: 2012 IEEE CCGrid, Ottawa, pp. 498–506 (2012)

Two-Stage Job Scheduling Model Based on Revenues and Resources

Yuliang Shi[1](✉), Dong Liu[2], Jing Hu[1], and Jianlin Zhang[1]

[1] School of Computer Science and Technology, Shandong University,
Shunhua Road 1500, High-tech Development Zone, Jinan, Shandong, China
shiyuliang@sdu.edu.cn, hujing_1125@163.com,
dareway_zjl@126.com
[2] Marketing Department, State Grid Chongqing Electric Power Company
Marketing Department, Zhongshan Three Road 21,
Yuzhong District, Chongqing, China
LD8803@163.com

Abstract. In the big data platform, multiple users share the resources of the platform. For platform providers, it is a problem to be solved urgently that how to multi-user jobs are scheduled efficiently to take full advantage of the resources of the platform, get the maximum revenue and meet the SLA requirements of the users. We research the project of job scheduling for MapReduce framework further. The paper proposes a two-stage job scheduling model based on revenues and resources. In the model, we design a scheduling algorithm of the maximum revenue (SMR) based on the latest start time of the jobs. The SMR algorithm ensures that the jobs which have larger revenues can be completed before the deadlines of the jobs, and then providers can gain the largest total revenue. Under the premise of ensuring the maximum revenue, a sequence adjustment scheduling algorithm based on the maximum resource utilization of the platform (SAS) is developed to improve the resource utilization of the platform. Experimental results show that the two-stage job scheduling model proposed in this paper not only realizes the maximum revenue of the provider, but also improves the resource utilization of the platform and the comprehensive performance of the platform. What is more, the model has great practicability and reliability.

Keywords: Big data · Job scheduling · Revenue · Resource utilization

1 Introduction

In recent years, with the vigorous development of cloud computing and Internet technology, the data show an explosive growth mode to make big data quietly come. Traditional data processing technology and tools are unable to meet the requirements of data processing in the new era, so the big data platform emerges at a historic moment. The big data platform supports a variety of computing frameworks that can serve multiple users simultaneously. However, it is an urgent problem for platform service providers that the mixed jobs of multiple users are reasonably scheduled so as to meet the requirements of resources utilization, the SLA of users and the maximum revenue.

X. Shi et al. (Eds.): NPC 2017, LNCS 10578, pp. 37–48, 2017.
DOI: 10.1007/978-3-319-68210-5_4

At present, many researchers have studied the problem of job scheduling in big data platform and put forward a lot of solutions. A resource configuration optimization model based on deadline estimation for the Pig job is proposed [1]. The model eliminates the non-deterministic problem when Pig program executes jobs concurrently. However, the model does not consider the revenue of the platform. In [2, 3], researchers study the job scheduling project on basis of MapReduce framework. While taking into account deadline constraints and resource allocation, they do not consider the revenues of the platform and resource utilization. The proposed scheduling algorithms [4, 5] focus on the job deadlines. Although these algorithms are not suitable for our study, they provide a great guide. Liu et al. [6] propose a priority scheduling algorithm to divide the computing capacity of each node into a front-end virtual machine layer and a background virtual machine layer. The algorithm balances the workload of the platform, makes full use of the CPU resources, improves the execution efficiency of the job and shortens the response time of the job. However, it still does not consider the revenue of the platform. Koutsandria et al. [7] first investigate the problem of efficient resource allocation strategies for time-varying traffic, and propose a new algorithm, MinDelay, which aims at achieving the minimum service delay while taking into account the revenue of the providers.

To sum up, the above researches have been studied deeply in different constraints and different backgrounds for the job scheduling project and a series of achievements have been made. However, the methods in these achievements do not solve the problems of our study. We propose a two-stage job scheduling model based on revenues and resources in MapReduce framework and the main contributions of this paper are summarized:

- We design a scheduling algorithm of the maximum revenue (SMR) based on the latest start time of the jobs. According to the deadlines of the jobs and the revenue rate, SMR pre-allocates the resources of the platform to the jobs and adjusts the allocation result to make the provider gain the maximum revenue.
- According to SMR, we propose a sequence adjustment scheduling algorithm based on the maximum resource utilization of the platform (SAS). The job sequence on basis of the maximum revenue is adjusted to realize the maximum resource utilization under the premise of the maximum revenue.

The rest of the paper is organized as follows. In Sect. 2, we discuss the related work of job scheduling. Section 3 presents relevant definitions and the design of two-stage job scheduling model. The model is described detailedly in Sect. 4. In Sect. 5, the experimental results of the scheduling model are given and analyzed. Section 6 concludes the paper.

2   Related Work

Job scheduling in the big data platform is crucial to the optimization of the platform performance. In order to improve the efficiency of the job execution and optimize the performance of the platform, the researches [8–10] propose data placement strategy and job scheduling algorithm based on the minimum data transmission time to reduce the data transmission time and improve the efficiency of the job execution. However, the revenue is not considered in the algorithms. The key factors affecting the availability requirement of the parallel task and the guarantee of the resource availability are analyzed, and a parallel task scheduling algorithm based on usability perception is proposed [11]. Although the methods [12–14] optimize the performance of the platform, they do not take into account the revenues of the platform. These researches [15–17] optimize the performance of the platform by reasonably scheduling jobs, but the revenue and the resource utilization are not considered. In order to improve the utilization of the network and reduce the completion time of the job, a job-aware priority scheduling algorithm is proposed by monitoring the application layer [18]. The algorithm not only achieves network load balancing, but also improves the execution efficiency of the job. Kumar et al. [19] propose a scheduling algorithm based on perceptual and heterogeneous cluster to improve the resource utilization, whereas they do not consider the revenues.

In [20], job scheduling is studied from the perspective of resource allocation, and a flexible resource allocation algorithm is proposed to enable the job to be completed and consume the minimum computing resources before the deadline. The algorithm provides a fine guide for the resource scheduling. An intelligent job scheduling and workload balancing mechanism is proposed to realize the application performance with the least resources [21]. The framework does not guarantee the maximum resource utilization. The research [22] solves the issue of the maximum revenue, but there are some limitations. The method does not take into account the situation of parallel execution for multiple jobs. However, these methods do not take into account the maximum revenue and the maximum resource utilization at the same time. Therefore, this paper considers the constraints of the deadline, the maximum revenue and the maximum resource utilization and proposes a two-stage job scheduling model. The model not only meets the requirements of the deadlines, but guarantees to maximize the revenue and the resource utilization.

3   Two-Stage Job Scheduling Model

3.1   Basic Definitions

In order to facilitate the description of the job scheduling model, we give some basic definitions and formulas in this section.

Definition 1. *Total Number of Computing Resources (TR): the number of all Containers in the platform.*

The big data platform that one master node and N_{dn} workers. Each node is configured with c cores and m GB RAM. Each Container is configured with c_c cores and m_c GB RAM. The total number of resources of the platform:

$$TR = min(c/c_c, m/m_c) \times N_{dn}. \tag{1}$$

Where $min(c/c_1, m/m_1)$ is the maximum number of Containers for each node.

Definition 2. *A Set of Submitted Jobs: when the jobs are submitted by multiple users signing the SLAs with the provider to the big data platform, a set of submitted jobs is generated. It is expressed as $J = \{j_1, j_2, \ldots, j_n\}$, where n is the number of the submitted jobs.*

We focus on the job scheduling in the isomorphic cluster, so we set identical nodes that have identical hardware configuration and performance. What is more, in this paper, we do not consider data skew so that we think the running time of every map task or reduce task is same by default. We pay attention to the execution time, required resources, the deadline and the revenue for each job. Any job j is expressed as $j = (ms, rs, mt, rt, dl, rf(t))$. Where ms is the number of map tasks, rs is the number of reduce tasks, mt is the average execution time of map tasks, rt is the average execution time of reduce tasks, dl is the deadline of the job and $rf(t)$ is the revenue function of the job. The revenue function is following:

$$rf(t) = \begin{cases} a, & t \leq j.dl \\ b, & t > j.dl \end{cases}. \tag{2}$$

Where a is the revenue gained for the provider when the job is completed before the deadline and when the job is not completed on time, b is positive value as the revenue that is less than a. If b is negative value, the provider compensates the user for the loss.

Definition 3. *The Total Revenue Function: the job j_i has $j_i.dl$ and $j_i.rf(t)$. The actual completion time of j_i, $j_i.end$, may be more than $j_i.dl$ or less than $j_i.dl$. For all jobs, the total revenue function is following:*

$$R = \sum_{i=1}^{n} j_i.rf(j_i.end). \tag{3}$$

3.2 Scheduling Model Design

In this section, we design the architecture of job scheduling model. In the first part of Fig. 1, the processing of job scheduling is divided into two stages. The first stage is a scheduling algorithm of pre-allocation resources based on the latest start time and maximum revenue. The second stage is a sequence adjustment scheduling algorithm based on the maximum resource utilization of the platform. In the first stage, the submitted jobs generate a set of jobs awaiting to be scheduled. Then, the jobs are scheduled firstly by pre-allocating the resources of the platform based on the latest start time and maximum revenue. The result of the first stage is that a primary sequence of scheduled jobs is got by SMR. In the second stage, the primary sequence is adjusted by SAS according to the remaining resources. The final result of the model is that generating a job execution sequence to make the provider gains the maximum revenue and improve the resource utilization. In the second part, the job scheduler launches scheduled jobs based on the optimal start time of the jobs. The resource scheduler allocates resources to launched jobs and the jobs gain resources from different nodes.

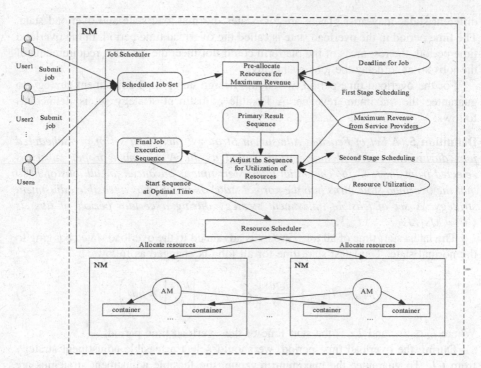

Fig. 1. The architecture of two-stage job scheduling model

4 Model Implementation

4.1 SMR Algorithm

In the section, it is showed that the implementation of SMR algorithm and the definition of equations needed in the SMR algorithm.

Definition 4. *Initial Latest Start Time $j_i.T_{ols}$: the job is just completed at the deadline when the resources are not competed by other jobs. If the deadline of j_i is $j_i.dl$, the initial latest start time is following:*

$$j_i.T_{ols} = j_i.dl - \left(\left\lceil \frac{j_i.ms}{M} \right\rceil \times J_i.mt + \left\lceil \frac{j_i.rs}{M} \right\rceil \times j_i.rt \right). \tag{4}$$

Where M is the available resources of the platform. $J_i.ms/M$ is the execution rounds of map tasks and $J_i.rs/M$ is the execution rounds of reduce tasks.

The job j_i is launched before $J_i.T_{ols}$ to ensure the job completed before the deadline of the job when there is no resource contention. The job j_i is not completed before $j_i.dl$ when j_i is launched at $J_i.T_{ols}$. Therefore, we should adjust the latest start time for jobs competing resources. To determine the time period for resource contention, we should pre-allocate the resources to all jobs based on the initial latest start time of the jobs. The total computing resources are counted at statistics time period. At different time period, different states may arise. There are two states, normal load state and overload state. The time period in the overload state is called the overload time period. In the overload time period, the resources of the platform could not meet the resource requirements of the jobs so as to delay the jobs eventually.

For the overload time period, we should design an optimal adjustment strategy to guarantee the maximum revenue. A feasible adjustment strategy set is defined as follows:

Definition 5. *A Set of Feasible Adjustment Strategy: there is a set of pre-scheduled jobs during the overload time period, called as Ju. A minimum proper subset is selected from Ju, Js ⊆ Ju. The initial latest start time is advanced for all jobs of Js so that the overload state turns into the normal state. Js is called as a feasible adjustment strategy. A set of feasible adjustment strategy during a certain period of time is* $CL = \{Js_1, Js_2, \ldots, Js_m\}$.

The latest start time of all jobs, in Js_i, is advanced to the overload state changing to the normal state. The latest start time for all jobs is changed as follows:

$$j_i.T_{ls} = T_{cs} - \left(\left\lceil \frac{j_i.ms}{M} \right\rceil \times J_i.mt + \left\lceil \frac{j_i.rs}{M} \right\rceil \times j_i.rt \right). \tag{5}$$

Where $j_i \in Js_i$, and T_{cs} is the start time of the overload time period.

During the overload time period, we should select a feasible adjustment strategy from *CL*. To guarantee the maximum revenue, the feasible adjustment strategies are evaluated for the revenues. Main factors of the evaluation are following two aspects, the Evaluation of the revenue (*Sp*) and adjustment cost.

$$Sp = |a - b|. \tag{6}$$

Taking into account the two factors, the paper presents an evaluation function of the adjustment strategy based on the goal of the maximum revenue. The adjustment strategy of the minimum score is the optimal adjustment strategy. The evaluation function is following:

$$Js_i.pf = \frac{\sum\limits_{m \in Js_t} j_m.Sp}{\sum\limits_{m \in Ju} j_m.Sp} \times lastsize. \tag{7}$$

Where $\sum_{m \in Js_t} j_m.Sp$ is the sum of the revenue valuation for all jobs in the adjustment strategy $\sum_{m \in J_u} j_m.Sp$ is the sum of the revenue valuation for pre-scheduled jobs during the overload time period and *latesize* is the ratio of the remaining resources of the current time period and the total resources of the platform.

The SMR algorithm is outlined in Algorithm 1. The initial latest start time is calculated for each job and the resources are pre-allocated to submitted jobs according the initial latest start time (lines 1–3). The resources are counted for every time period based on the result of pre-allocation, which is called as *P_R* (line 4). If the overload time period is existing, the initial latest start time are adjusted for all jobs during the overload time period (lines 5–21). The last overload time period is selected (line 6) and the set of pre-scheduled jobs is got during the overload time period (line 7). The adjustment strategies are evaluated by the evaluation function and the optimal adjustment strategy is selected (lines 8–13). The latest start time of the jobs in the adjustment strategy are adjusted and P_R is updated (lines 14–20). Looping through lines 6-20 until there is no overload time period in P_R.

Algorithm 1. SMR algorithm

    Input: $J=\{j_1, j_2, ..., j_n\}$
    Output: P_R //Resource preemption results
  1.   **for** each job $j_i \in J$ **do**
  2. $j_r.T_{ols}=j_r.dl-(\lceil(j_r.ms)/M\rceil\times j_r.mt+\lceil(j_r.rs)/M\rceil\times j_r.rt)$;
  3.   Preempted resource for j_i at $j_r.T_{ols}$;
  4. $P\_R=\{(P_1, R_1), (P_2, R_2), ..., (P_\rho, R_i)\}$; //Calculate resources required at each period
  5.   **while** $\exists (P_i, R_i) \in P\_R, R_i > TR$ **do**
  6.   Select the last $(P_n, R_n) \in P\_R, R_n > TR$;
  7. Ju is equal to the jobs executed at P_n;
  8.   Get $CL= \{Js_1, Js_2, ..., Js_m\}$; $ZYCL= Js_1$;
  9. $Js_1.pf=(\sum_m \in_{Js1} j_m.Sp)/(\sum_m \in_{Ju} j_m.Sp) \times lastsize$; $maxPf=Js_1.pf$;
 10.   **for** each $Js_n \in CL$ **do**
 11. $Js_n.pf=(\sum_m \in_{Jsn} j_m.Sp)/(\sum_m \in_{Ju} j_m.Sp) \times lastsize$;
 12.   **if** $Js_n.pf > maxPf$ **then**
 13. $maxPf=Js_n.pf$; $ZYCL= Js_n$;
 14.   **for** each $j_i \in ZXCL$ **do**
 15. $j_r.T_{ls} = T_{cs}-(\lceil(j_r.ms)/M\rceil\times j_r.mt+\lceil(j_r.rs)/M\rceil\times j_r.rt)$;
 16.   **if** $j_r.T_{ls} > 0$ **then**
 17.   Preempted resource for j_i at $j_r.T_{ls}$;
 18.   **else**
 19.   Abandon j;
 20.   Update P_R;
 21. **return** P_R;

4.2 SAS Algorithm

In the section, we should consider the pre-allocation of resources based on the SMR algorithm to ensure the jobs completed on time. To maximize the resource utilization of the platform, we evaluate the utilization of the computing resources using the rate of waste resources (W_{rr}). W_{rr} is the ratio between the non-reusable resources W_r after scheduling jobs and the sum of the currently used computing resources A_r. The smaller the waste resource rate, the larger the resource utilization of the platform currently. W_{rr} is following:

$$W_{rr} = \frac{W_r}{A_r} \tag{8}$$

The SAS algorithm is presented in Algorithm 2. A set of jobs E_j is found to be executed at T time and the required resources of E_j do not conflict with pre-allocated resources (lines 2–8). If E_j is not null, the job is selected that makes the waste resource rate minimize and the optimal start time of the job is T (lines 10–16). If E_j is null, T is set to the start time of the next time period in P_R (line 18). Looping through lines 3–20 until every job has an optimal start time.

Algorithm 2. SAS algorithm

Input: $J = \{j_1, j_2, \cdots, j_n\}$, P_R
Output: *ResultSet* //An execution sequence of jobs contains start time of each job
1.   **while** $J=null$ **do**
2. $E_j=null$;
3.   **for each** $j_i \in J$ **do**
4. $N\_P\_R=P\_R.remove(j_i)$;
5. $N\_P\_R=N\_P\_R.add(j_i, T)$;
6.   **if** $\forall (P_i, R_i) \in N\_P\_R$, $R_i \leq TS$ **then**
7.   Compute j_i, W_{rr};
8. $E_j.add(j_i)$;
9.   **if** $E_j=null$ **then**
10.   Sort jobs in E_j;
11.   Get the job j_l with the least W_{rr};
12.   **if** j_l has advanced resources **then**
13. $P\_R=P\_R.remove(j_l)$;
14.   *ResultSet.add(j_l, T)*;
15.   *J.remove(j_l)*;
16. $P\_R=P\_R.add(j_l, T)$;
17.   **else**
18. T is equal to the start time of next period in P_R;
19. **return** *ResultSet*;

After the second adjustment scheduling, we adjust the initial scheduling sequence to reset the start time for each job. As the result of the second adjustment and scheduling, the resource utilization of the platform becomes larger and the actual start time and the completion time of the job are advanced. Many of the jobs discarded due to insufficient resources in the SMR algorithm have opportunity to be executed newly. Therefore, the revenue for the provider may get greater.

5   Performance Evaluation

5.1   Experiment Setup

Platform Configuration. We experiment with the proposed algorithm in a big data platform based on MapReduce computing framework. The platform contains one master node and 20 workers that have identical configuration. The configuration information of the node is CPU 8 cores, 8 GB RAM, 1 TB hard disk, Red Hat

Enterprise Linux 6.5, and Hadoop 2.7.1. Each Container is configured with 1 core and 2 GB RAM so that each node has 4 Containers and the platform has 80 Containers.

Performance Indicators. In order to verify the effectiveness of the scheduling algorithm proposed in this paper, two - phase scheduling algorithm (TPS) is compared with FIFO and EDF Scheduler in the effect of different performances. We evaluate the algorithm using three indicators, the platform resource utilization (*PRU*), the job completion rate (*JCR*) and the total revenue (*PR*). The three indicators are as follows:

$$PRU = \frac{\sum_{j=1}^{k} RE\_j_i}{TR}. \tag{9}$$

Where RE_j_i is the occupied resources of the job i executed in the platform.

$$JCR = \frac{n}{N}. \tag{10}$$

Where n is the number of the jobs completed before the deadlines and N is the number of all jobs submitted by users.

$$PR = \sum_{j=i}^{n} a_j - \sum_{i=1}^{m} b_i. \tag{11}$$

Where a_j is the revenue when j is completed before the deadline, b_i is the compensation to users when the completion time of i is more than the deadline of i and m is the number of jobs completed after the deadline ($b_i < 0$).

5.2 Experiment Results

In Fig. 2, the resource utilization rate is not affected by the job set size in three algorithms. The resource utilization of TPS is the highest in the three algorithms and the resource utilization of EDF is slightly lower than that of TPS. The resource utilization of FIFO is the lowest. As shown in Fig. 3, due to the limited computing capacity, the job completion rates are reduced in three algorithms when the job set size

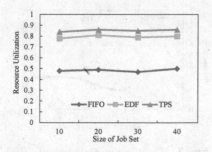

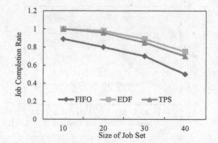

Fig. 2. The effect of job set size on *PRU*   **Fig. 3.** The effect of job set size on *JCR*

increases. Because EDF and TPS consider the deadlines and TPS also takes into account the revenues, EDF has a higher completion rate than TPS. FIFO only considers the revenues so the algorithm has the lowest completion rate.

From Fig. 4, the revenues show a tendency to increase first and then decrease when the size of the job set increases for three algorithms. However, when the number of jobs exceeds the computing capacity of the platform, the number of jobs completed on time is reduced so that the total revenue declines. From Fig. 5, it can be seen that the wastage rates of the three algorithms are roughly same and decrease with the increase of the number of computing resources. However, the resource utilization of EDF and TPS increase with the increase of the number of computing resources and the TPS rise is more than that of EDF.

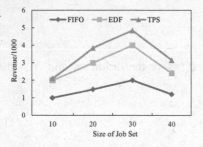

Fig. 4. The effect of job set size on *PR*   **Fig. 5.** The effect of resources on *PRU*

Figures 6 and 7 show the effect of the number of computing resources on job completion rate and the total revenue. It can be seen from the figures that with the increase of the number of computing resources, the completion rates and the total revenues are increased by TPS and EDF and the revenue of TPS is much larger than that of EDF. The job completion rate and the total revenue increase with the increase of resources in FIFO when the resources of the platform are less. However, because the jobs are executed serially to waste a large amount of resources, the job completion rate and the revenue do not increase with the increase of the resources and are stabilized at a fixed value when the resources of the platform are larger than the average job input size.

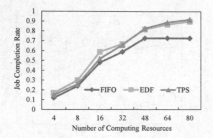

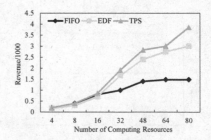

Fig. 6. The effect of job set size on *JCR*   **Fig. 7.** The effect of resources on *PR*

6   Conclusion

The big data platform could serve multiple users at the same time. When users sub-mitted jobs to the big data platform, jobs were reasonably scheduled not only to meet the requirements of users, but also improve the performance of the platform. Therefore, the two-stage job scheduling model was proposed for the jobs with the deadline constraints. In the model, the SMR algorithm calculated and adjusted the latest start time for every jobs based on the deadlines and the revenues of the jobs, which pre-allocated resources to jobs according to the result of adjustment to guarantee the jobs with the larger revenues to be completed before the deadlines. Under the premise of ensuring the maximum revenue, the SAS algorithm was developed to improve the resource utilization of the platform. Experimental results showed that the two-stage job scheduling model not only realized the maximum revenue of the provider, but improved the resource utilization of the platform. Moreover, the comprehensive per-formance of the platform was promoted.

Acknowledgments. The research work is supported by the TaiShan Industrial Experts Pro-gramme of Shandong Province No. tscy20150305, and the Key Research \& Development Program of Shandong Province No. 2016GGX101008, 2016ZDJS01A09.

References

1. Zhang, Z., Cherkasova, L., Verma, A., Loo, B.T.: Optimizing completion time and resource provisioning of pig programs. In: IEEEACM International Symposium on Cluster, Cloud and Grid Computing, pp. 811–816 (2012)
2. Khan, M., Jin, Y., Li, M., Xiang, Y., Jiang, C.J.: Hadoop performance modeling for job estimation and resource provisioning. Parallel Distrib. Syst. 27(2), 441–454 (2016)
3. Verma, A., Cherkasova, L., Campbell, R.H.: ARIA: automatic resource inference and allocation for mapreduce environments. In: International Conference on Autonomic Computing, pp. 235–244 (2011)
4. Cheng, D., Rao, J., Jiang, C., Zhou, X.: Resource and deadline-aware job scheduling in dynamic hadoop clusters. In: Parallel and Distributed Processing Symposium, pp. 956–965 (2015)
5. Li, S., Hu, S., Wang, S., Su, L., Abdelzaher, T., Gupta, I., Pace, R.: WOHA: deadline-aware map-reduce workflow scheduling framework over hadoop clusters. In: Distributed Computing Systems, pp. 93–103 (2014)
6. Liu, X., Wang, C., Zhou, B.B., Chen, J., Yang, T., Zomaya, A.Y.: Priority-based consolidation of parallel workloads in the cloud. Parallel Distrib. Syst. 24(9), 1874–1883 (2013)
7. Koutsandria, G., Skevakis, E., Sayegh, A.A.: Can everybody be happy in the cloud? Delay, profit and energy-efficient scheduling for cloud services. J. Parallel Distrib. Comput. 96, 202–217 (2016)
8. Clinkenbeard, T., Nica, A.: Job Scheduling with minimizing data communication costs. In: ACM International Conference on Management of Data, pp. 2071–2072 (2015)
9. Wang, Q., Li, X., Wang, J.: A data placement and task scheduling algorithm in cloud computing. J. Comput. Res. Dev. 51(11), 2416–2426 (2014)

10. Sun, M., Zhuang, H., Li, C., Lu, K.: Scheduling algorithm based on prefetching in mapreduce clusters. Appl. Soft Comput. **38**(C), 1109–1118 (2016)
11. Cao, J., Zeng, G., Niu, J., Xu, J.: Availability-aware scheduling method for parallel task in cloud environment. J. Comput. Res. Dev. **50**(7), 1563–1572 (2013)
12. Zheng, X., Xiang, M., Zhang, D., Liu, Q.: An adaptive tasks scheduling method based on the ability of node in hadoop cluster. J. Comput. Res. Dev. **51**(3), 618–626 (2014)
13. Li, Z., Chen, S., Yang, B., Li, R.: Multi-objective memetic algorithm for task scheduling on heterogeneous cloud. Chin. J. Comput. **39**(2), 377–390 (2016)
14. Lee, M.C., Lin, J.C., Yahyapour, R.: Hybrid job-driven scheduling for virtual mapreduce clusters. Parallel Distrib. Syst. **27**(6), 1687–1699 (2016)
15. Wang, X., Shen, D., Bai, M., Nie, T., Kou, Y., Yu, G.: Sames: deadline-constraint scheduling in mapreduce. Front. Comput. Sci. **9**(1), 128–141 (2015)
16. Wang, Y., Shi, W.: Budget-driven scheduling algorithms for batches of mapreduce jobs in heterogeneous clouds. Cloud Comput. **2**(3), 306–319 (2014)
17. Song, Y., Sun, Y., Shi, W.: A two-tiered on-demand resource allocation mechanism for VM-based data centers. Serv. Comput. **6**(1), 116–129 (2013)
18. Liu, W., Wang, Z., Shen, Y.: Job-aware network scheduling for hadoop cluster. KSII Trans. Internet Inf. Syst. **11**(1), 237–252 (2017)
19. Kumar, K.A., Konishetty, V.K., Voruganti, K., Rao, G.V.P.: Cash: context aware scheduler for hadoop. In: International Conference on Advances in Computing, Communications and Informatics, pp. 52–61 (2012)
20. Mao, M., Humphrey, M.: Auto-scaling to minimize cost and meet application deadlines in cloud workflows. In: High PERFORMANCE Computing, Networking, Storage and Analysis, pp. 1–12 (2011)
21. Gasior, J., Seredynski, F.: Metaheuristic approaches to multiobjective job scheduling in cloud computing systems. In: IEEE International Conference on Cloud Computing Technology and Science, pp. 222–229 (2016)
22. Wang, X., Shen, D., Yu, G., Bai, M., Nie, T., Kou, Y.: Resource on maximum benefit problem in a mapreduce cluster. Chin. J. Comput. **38**(1), 109–121 (2015)

TCon: A Transparent Congestion Control Deployment Platform for Optimizing WAN Transfers

Yuxiang Zhang[1], Lin Cui[1,4(✉)], Fung Po Tso[2], Quanlong Guan[1], and Weijia Jia[3]

[1] Department of Computer Science, Jinan University,
Guangzhou, People's Republic of China
{tcuilin,gql}@jnu.edu.cn, samuelzyx0924@gmail.com
[2] Department of Computer Science, Loughborough University, Loughborough, UK
p.tso@lboro.ac.uk
[3] Department of Computer Science and Engineering, SJTU,
Shanghai, People's Republic of China
jia-wj@cs.sjtu.edu.cn
[4] Guangdong Key Laboratory of Big Data Analysis and Processing, Guangzhou,
People's Republic of China

Abstract. Nowadays, many web services (e.g., cloud storage) are deployed inside datacenters and may trigger transfers to clients through WAN. TCP congestion control is a vital component for improving the performance (e.g., latency) of these services. Considering complex networking environment, the default congestion control algorithms on servers may not always be the most efficient, and new advanced algorithms will be proposed. However, adjusting congestion control algorithm usually requires modification of TCP stacks of servers, which is difficult if not impossible, especially considering different operating systems and configurations on servers. In this paper, we propose *TCon*, a light-weight, flexible and scalable platform that allows administrators (or operators) to deploy any appropriate congestion control algorithms transparently without making any changes to TCP stacks of servers. We have implemented *TCon* in Open vSwitch (OVS) and conducted extensive test-bed experiments by transparently deploying BBR congestion control algorithm over *TCon*. Test-bed results show that the BBR over *TCon* works effectively and the performance stays close to its native implementation on servers, reducing latency by 12.76% on average.

Keywords: Congestion control · BBR · Transparent

1 Introduction

Recent years, many web applications have moved into cloud datacenters to take advantage of the economy of scale. Since bandwidth remains relatively cheap,

© IFIP International Federation for Information Processing 2017
Published by Springer International Publishing AG 2017. All Rights Reserved
X. Shi et al. (Eds.): NPC 2017, LNCS 10578, pp. 49–61, 2017.
DOI: 10.1007/978-3-319-68210-5_5

web latency is now the main impediment to improving service quality. Moreover, it is well known that web latency inversely correlates with revenue and profit. For instance, Amazon estimates that every 100ms increase in latency cuts profits by 1% [7]. Reducing latency, especially the latency between datacenter and clients through WAN environment, is of primary importance for providers.

In response, administrators adopt network appliances to reduce network latency. For example, TCP proxies and WAN optimizers are used for such optimization [5,9]. However, when facing dramatically increasing traffic, they would degrade performance [5]. Furthermore, the split-connection approach used in TCP proxy would break a TCP connection into several sub-connections, destroying TCP end-to-end semantics. Applications may receive an ACK for the data which are actually still in transmitting, potentially violate the sequential processing order [3,6]. On the other hand, WAN optimizers perform compression on data which may add additional latency and require additional decompression appliances in ISPs for decompressing data from optimizers [3].

In addition to using network appliances, enhancement of TCP congestion control is considered to reduce latency, since most web services use TCP. Many TCP congestion control algorithms have been proposed, e.g., Reno [8], CUBIC [10] and recent BBR [4]. These proposals perform very well in their target scenarios while have performance limitations when working under different circumstance. And the degradation of performance caused by in-appropriate congestion control algorithms can lead to loss and increased latency. Furthermore, cloud datacenters have many web servers[1] which have different operating systems and configurations, e.g., Linux or Windows with different kernel versions and congestion control algorithms. Considering such diversity and large number of web servers in cloud datacenters, adjusting congestion control algorithms (e.g., deploying new advanced algorithms) is a daunting, if not impossible, task. Hence, a question arise in our mind: *Can we find a way to transparently deploy advanced congestion control without modifying TCP stacks of web servers?*

In this paper, we present *TCon*, a Transparent Congestion control deployment platform without requiring changing TCP stack of servers. *TCon* can implement target TCP congestion control within Open vSwitch (OVS) to reduce the latency of WAN transfers. At a high-level (as illustrated in Fig. 1), *TCon* monitors packets of a flow through OVS and modifies packets to reconstruct important TCP parameters for congestion control (e.g., *cwnd*). *TCon* runs congestion control specified by administrators and then forces intended congestion window by modifying the receive window (*rwnd*) on incoming ACKs.

The main contributions of this paper are as follows:

1. We designed a transparent platform *TCon*, which allows network administrators (or operators) deploying new advanced congestion control algorithms without modifying TCP stacks of servers.

---

[1] Those web servers can be either physical servers or VMs in cloud datacenters. For consistency, we use "web server" to refer both cases.

2. A prototype of *TCon* is implemented based on OVS. *TCon* is light-weight, containing only about 100 lines of code. BBR congestion control algorithm is implemented on *TCon* as an example, using around 900 lines of code.
3. Extensive test-bed experiments are conducted, including WAN connections from both Shanghai and Oregon. Experiment results show that *TCon* works effectively, reducing latency by 12.76% on average.

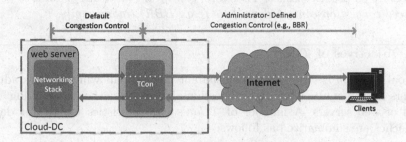

Fig. 1. High-level illustration of TCon.

2 Motivations and Objectives

2.1 Motivations

Latency is important for web service which is closely linked to revenue and profit [7]. Large latency degrades service performance, resulting in worsening customer experience and hence revenue loss. In light of this, it is always in service providers' interest to minimize the latency.

Many service providers use network functions such as TCP proxies and WAN optimizers to improve the latency performance [5,9]. TCP proxy can quickly prefetch packets from servers at a high rate, then send them to the destination using several sub-connections. While WAN optimizer performs compression and caching operation on data for shaping network traffic. However, the scalability of these network functions is a great challenge. When there is a burst of requests for service, the performance of such network functions can be easily saturated due to the insufficient processing capacity. Moreover, TCP proxy goes against TCP end-to-end semantics. For instance, a barrier-based application may believe that all its packets were ACKed, and advance to the next phase, while they were not actually received, potentially causing errors in the application [3,6]. Furthermore, WAN optimizer adopts compression to speed up transfers but this may add additional latency on service and require ISPs to offer co-operating decompression appliances [3].

On the other hand, TCP congestion control algorithm is known to significantly impact network performance. As a result, TCP congestion control has been widely studied and many schemes have been proposed to improve performance [4,8,10]. These schemes perform well in their own target scenarios while get limiting performance in other circumstance. However, service providers usually deploy a diverse of web servers which may run on different versions of operating systems (e.g., Linux and Windows) and be configured with different congestion control algorithms. Adjusting TCP stacks of such large amount of web servers is a daunting task, if not impossible. Furthermore, in multi-tenants cloud datacenters, network operators may be prohibit from upgrading TCP stacks of web servers for security issues. Therefore, *significant motivations exist to deploy advanced congestion control algorithms (e.g., BBR) transparently.*

2.2   Objectives of *TCon*

The goal of *TCon* is to provide a transparent platform allowing network administrators to deploy new advanced congestion algorithms without modifying TCP stacks of web servers. A number of *TCon*'s characteristics led to our design approaches are summarized as follows:

1. **Transparency.** *TCon* allows network administrators or operators to enforce advanced congestion control algorithms without touching TCP stacks of servers. Deployment and operations of *TCon* should be transparent to both web servers and clients. This is important in untrusted public cloud environments or simply in cases where servers cannot be updated due to a dependence on a specific OS or library [13].
2. **Flexibility.** *TCon* allows different congestion control algorithms to be applied on a per-flow basis. This is useful because each congestion control algorithm has its own deficiency and suitable scenarios. Allowing adjusting congestion control algorithms on a per-flow basis can enhance flexibility and performance.
3. **Light-weight.** While the entire TCP stack may seem complicated and prone to high overhead, the congestion control aspect of TCP is relatively lightweight and simple to implement. Indeed, the prototype implementation of *TCon* on OVS has around 100 lines of code for basic functionalities. And the BBR algorithm over *TCon* contains about 900 lines of code.

2.3   BBR Congestion Control

Recently, BBR is proposed in [4], which adopts a novel control window computation algorithm based on bandwidth delay product (BDP). In BBR, sender needs to continuously estimate the bottleneck bandwidth (BtlBw) and round-trip propagation time (RTprop) and let the total data in flight be equal to the BDP (= BtlBw × RTprop). By adjusting the *cwnd* (otherwise the sending rate) based on BDP, BBR guarantees that the bottleneck can run at 100% utilization and preventing bottleneck starvation but not overfilling. Therefore, BBR can keep low latency since its *cwnd* is not based on loss but network capacity. Meanwhile, loss and RTT fluctuations are not rare in WAN. However, loss is not considered as congestion signals in BBR, which uses RTprop as the metric of network capacity to get rid of RTT fluctuations caused by queuing delay [4].

Because of those reasons above, BBR is suitable for most WAN environment. As a case study, we will deploy BBR over *TCon* to demonstrate its effectiveness.

3   Design and Implementation

This section provides an overview of *TCon*'s design details. For simplicity, we use BBR as an example for explanation. Other congestion control algorithms can also be easily implemented on *TCon* similarly.

3.1   Obtaining Congestion Control State

Since *TCon* is implemented in the *datapath* of the OVS (illustrate in Sect. 3.3), all traffic can be monitored. We now demonstrate how congestion control state (e.g., RTprop and BtlBw) can be inferred on packet level.

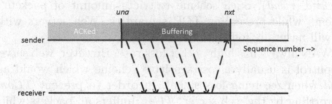

Fig. 2. Variables for TCP sequence number space.

Figure 2 provides a visual of TCP sequence number space. The *una* is the first packet's sequence number which has been sent, but not yet ACKed. The *nxt* is the sequence number of the next packet to be sent (but *TCon* hasn't received it yet). Packets between *una* and *nxt* are inflight. Variable *una* is simple to update: each ACK contains an acknowledgement number (*acknum*), and *una* is updated when *acknum* > *una*. When a packet is received from web servers, *nxt* is updated if its sequence number is larger than or equal to current value of *nxt*.

Measuring RTprop is relatively simple. The arriving timestamps of each packet is recorded. When ACK arrives, RTT is obtained by computing the difference between ACK and corresponding arriving timestamps. The minimal RTT in a short period is regarded as RTprop [4]. BtlBw can be estimated by monitoring the delivery rate. The *delivered* variable is the delivery size between conjoint ACK which can be measured by counting being acknowledged packets' size. Then delivery rate can be inferred as dividing *delivered* by the difference between conjoint ACK's arriving timestamps. BtlBw is the maximal delivery rate in a short period [4]. Detecting packet loss is also relatively simple. If *acknum* ≤ *una*, the a local *dupack* counter is updated. When *dupack* counts to 3, it means a packet loss happened [12].

3.2   Enforcing Congestion Control

The basic parameters of BBR, e.g., BtlBw and RTprop, can be tracked as described in Sect. 3.1 for each connection. Then the sending rate is computed by multiplying BtlBw and RTprop, which is translated into window size later, i.e., *cwnd*. Our implementation closely tracks the Linux source code of BBR and more details can be found in [4].

Moreover, there must be a mechanism to ensure a web server's TCP flow adheres to the window size determined in the *TCon*. Luckily, TCP provides built-in functionality that can be reprovisioned for *TCon*. Specifically, TCP's flow control allows a receiver to advertise the amount of data that it is willing to process via a receive window (*rwnd*) [12]. Ensuring a web server's flow adheres to *rwnd* is relatively simple. The *TCon* computes a new congestion window *cwnd* every time an ACK is received, which provides an upper bound on the number of bytes the web server's flow is now able to send. If it is smaller than the packets' original *rwnd*, *TCon* overwrites *rwnd* with its computed *cwnd*, i.e., *rwnd*=min(*cwnd*, *rwnd*). Such scheme restricts amount of packets sent from server to clients while preserving TCP semantics. Web servers with unalterd TCP stacks will naturally follow the standard.

Besides, WAN always has high packet loss rate. However, web server's default congestion control is usually a loss sensitive scheme which would aggressively reduces *cwnd* when receiving loss signal. In order to prevent *TCon*'s sending rate from throttling by the web server, *TCon* buffers all packets which restricts the size of buffering size less than the computed window size and retransmit the loss rather than web server does it. Meanwhile, *TCon* handles all congestion signals (e.g., ECN feedback and three duplicated ACKs), preventing them from reaching to web servers, which would reduce *cwnd* of web servers.

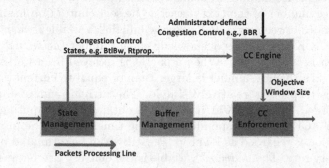

Fig. 3. The architecture of *TCon*.

3.3   Implementation

We have implemented *TCon* on Open vSwitch (OVS) v2.6.0 [1]. About 100 lines of code are used to implement *TCon*'s basic functions, e.g., obtaining congestion control states and managing buffer. Another 900 lines of code are for the implementation of BBR on *TCon*. Flows are hashed on a 5-tuple (IP addresses, ports and protocol) to obtain a flow's state which is used to maintain the congestion control state mentioned in Sect. 3.1. SYN packets are used to create flow entries, and FIN packets are used to remove flows entries. Other TCP packets, such as data and ACKs, trigger updates to flow entries. Since there are many more table lookup operations (to update flow state), Read-Copy-Update (RCU) hash tables are used to enable efficient lookups. Additionally, individual *spinlocks* are used on each flow entry in order to allow for multiple flow entries to be updated simultaneously. Furthermore, *skb_clone()* is used for packet buffering to prevent deep-copy of data.

Finally, the overall architecture of *TCon* is shown in Fig. 3. A web server generates a packet that is pushed down the network stack to OVS. The packet is intercepted in *ovs_dp_process_packet()*, where packet's flow entry is obtained by *StateManagement*. Sequence number state is updated and the sending timestamps are recorded. Then these packets are buffered by *BufferManagement* and sent to clients. When ACKs eventually from clients reach *TCon*, *CCEngine* module uses the congestion control states offered by *StateManagement* to compute a new congestion window. Then *CCEnforcement* module modifies *rwnd* if needed and recomputes the checksum before pushing the packet to the network.

3.4 Deployment Locations of *TCon*

Since *TCon* is implemented on OVS, it can be easily deployed in three possible locations in cloud datacenter:

- *VMs*: Deploying *TCon* in VMs allows network administrators to setup new *TCon* servers or release old ones dynamically for load-balancing. However, such scheme requires routers/switches redirecting desired traffic to *TCon* servers, which is not difficult specially for SDN-enabled environment.
- *Hypervisors*: As OVS is compatible with most hypervisors, *TCon* can also be deployed in hypervisors of physical servers. Such scheme allows *TCon* to be easily scaled with number of servers in datacenters. It also minimizes the latency between *TCon* and web servers, i.e., VMs. Furthermore, no route redirection is required in this case. However, the flexibility and scalability are limited considering migrations of VMs or situation that VMs on a server are heavy loaded.
- *Routers/Switches*: *TCon* can also be deployed with OVS on routers/switches in datacenters. Routers/switches can inherently monitoring all incoming traffic, making *TCon* can easily enforce congestion control without route redirection. However, traffic sent through a router/switch is determined by the routing algorithm of datacenters, and it is difficult to perform load balancing. And heavy traffic may also overwhelm capacity of routers/switches.

Each deployment choice is suitable for different requirements and scenarios. In our current implementation, *TCon* is deployed on VMs in datacenter. In practice, combination of these three deployment choices above can be considered.

Table 1. Servers information in the experiment

Machine	Location	CPU	Memory	Bandwidth	OS version
Web1	Guangzhou	Intel(R) Xeon(R) CPU E5-2670 v3 @ 2.30 GHz	4 GB	1 Gbps	Ubuntu 16.04 + Apache 2.0
Web2	Guangzhou	Intel(R) Xeon(R) CPU E5-2670 v3 @ 2.30 GHz	4 GB	1 Gbps	Ubuntu 16.04 + Apache 2.0
TCon	Guangzhou	Intel(R) Xeon(R) CPU E5-2670 v3 @ 2.30 GHz	4 GB	1 Gbps	Ubuntu 16.04 + OVS2.6.0
LAN	Guangzhou	Intel i7-4790 @ 3.6 GHz	16 GB	1 Gbps	Ubuntu 16.04
WAN-Shanghai	Shanghai	Intel(R) Xeon(R) CPU E5-2699A v4 @ 2.40 GHz	1 GB	5 Mbps	Ubuntu 16.04
WAN-Oregon	Oregon	Intel(R) Xeon(R) CPU E5-2686 v3 @ 2.30 GHz	1 GB	5 Mbps	Ubuntu 16.04

4 Evaluation

4.1 Experiment Setup

We have deployed three VMs (*TCon* and two web servers, see Table 1) in the campus datacenter (located in Jinan University, Guangzhou China), which contains over 400 web servers (VMs) running on 293 physical servers. The bandwidth of the datacenter to the Internet is about 20 Gbps, shared by all servers in the datacenter. And the data rate of NIC on each physical server is 1Gbps, shared by all VMs on the server.

The BBR congestion control algorithm is implement over *TCon*. The baseline scheme, CUBIC, is Linux's default congestion control, which runs on top of an unmodified web server (Web1). In the meantime, we also updated Web2 to Linux kernel 4.10 and configured its TCP stack to be BBR. Thus, three different congestion control configurations are considered. (a) *TCon with BBR*: clients connect to Web1 through *TCon*, which enforces BBR to the connection transparently. (b) *CUBIC (Direct)*: clients connect to Web1 directly and the effective congestion control algorithm is CUBIC. (c) *BBR (Direct)*: clients connect to Web2 directly and the effective congestion control algorithm is BBR.

To obtain an in-depth understanding of *TCon*, we designed a variety of benchmarks for performing comprehensive controlled experiments. And these benchmarks involve diverse clients locations and network environments. So, we setup another three servers as clients. One is located in the campus LAN (Guangzhou China). Another two are located in Shanghai China (WAN-Shanghai) and Oregon USA (WAN-Oregon) respectively, connecting to the campus datacenter

Table 2. Different type and size of file in Web server

Size	Type
1.7 MB	common pdf file (.pdf)
10 MB	common mp3 file (.mp3)
101 MB	common video file (.mp4)
562 MB	Mininet 2.2.2 image on Ubuntu 14.04 LTS - 64 bit (.zip)
630 MB	openSUSE-13.2-NET-i586 (.iso)

through the Internet. These clients experienced different RTT and packet drop rate when connecting to web servers. See Table 1 for all servers.

The metrics used are: transfer completion time (measured by CURL) and CPU usage (measured by *top*). We uploaded several files, sized from 1 MB to 630 MB (see Table 2), to quantify transfer completion time (TCT) for different size files. For each environment, we conducted experiments of all kind of files transferring for about 48 hours. Specifically, we focus on the transfer of 10 MB and 630 MB files which represent small file and large file respectively.

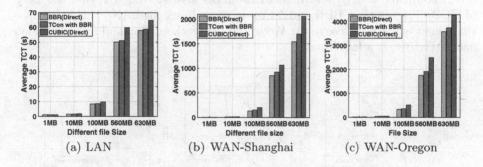

(a) LAN   (b) WAN-Shanghai   (c) WAN-Oregon

Fig. 4. The average transfer completion time in different environment.

4.2 Latency Performance

First we evaluated the average transfer completion time (TCT) of different files in different environment. Figure 4 shows the results. Among all machines, BBR has the best performance while CUBIC is the worst. And *TCon* is better than CUBIC, staying close to BBR.

In LAN, the average TCTs for small files of BBR, *TCon* and CUBIC are 1.586 s, 1.653 s and 1.7003 s respectively. Compared to CUBIC, BBR and *TCon* can reduce average TCT by 7.21% and 2.86%. In the meantime, for large files, the average TCTs of BBR, *TCon* and CUBIC are 58.0184 s, 58.6933 s and 64.8174 s respectively. Taking CUBIC as the baseline, BBR and *TCon* can get 11.72% and 10.43% improvement respectively. Then, we have a look at the performance of these three schemes in WAN-Shanghai. For small files, the average TCTs of BBR,

TCon and CUBIC are 8.3658 s, 8.8109 s and 10.0857 s respectively. Compared to CUBIC, BBR and *TCon* can reduce average TCT by 20.56% and 14.47%. For large files, the average TCTs of BBR, *TCon* and CUBIC are 1540.685s, 1696.7482 s and 2062.9752 s respectively. Taking CUBIC as the baseline, BBR and *TCon* can get 33.90% and 21.58% improvement. Last, we evaluate the performance in WAN-Oregon. For small file, the average TCTs of BBR, *TCon* and CUBIC is 35.722 s, 38.831 s and 43.519 s respectively. For large files, the average TCT of *TCon* and CUBIC are 3581.961 s, 3744.717 s and 4276.137 s respectively. *TCon* reduces TCT by 12.07% and 14.19% for small files and large files when compared to CUBIC while BBR reduces TCT by 21.83% and 19.38%.

Figure 5 shows the overall performance CDF for transferring small files. Specially, BBR and *TCon* can reduce 99.9^{th} percentile TCT by 11.24% and 9.69% when compared to CUBIC in LAN. Most transfers can finish their transfers within 1.67 s,1.7 s and 1.85 s for BBR, *TCon* and CUBIC respectively. In WAN-Shanghai, BBR and *TCon* reduce 99.9^{th} percentile TCT by 34.89% and 19.04% respectively compared to CUBIC. Most transfers can complete their transfers within 10 s, 11 s and 14 s for BBR, *TCon* and CUBIC respectively. In WAN-Oregon, most file can finish transfer within 41 s, 44 s and 46 s under BBR, *TCon* and CUBIC respectively. Moreover, *TCon* reduces 99.9^{th} percentile TCT by 4.77% compared to CUBIC while BBR reduces 8.48%. We found that the TCT of CUBIC is less than BBR and *TCon* in some cases for LAN. This is because that client of LAN is close to the Web1 and few packets drop and retransmission occur (CUBIC is a loss based).

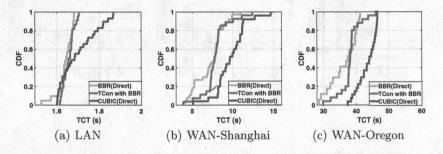

(a) LAN   (b) WAN-Shanghai   (c) WAN-Oregon

Fig. 5. The CDF of transfer completion time for small file (10 MB).

For large file, Fig. 6a shows the CDF of TCT in various environment. In LAN environment, BBR and *TCon* reduce 99.9^{th} percentile TCT by 16.87% and 10.71% respectively. Most transfers can finish within 59 s, 64 s and 69 s for BBR, *TCon* and CUBIC respectively. In WAN-Shanghai, BBR and *TCon* reduce 99.9^{th} percentile TCT by 25.99% and 24.93% respectively. Most transfers can finish within 1750 s, 1780 s and 2200 s for BBR, *TCon* and CUBIC respectively. Last, in WAN-Oregon, BBR and *TCon* reduce 99.9^{th} percentile TCT by 5.21% and 4.77% compared to CUBIC. And most TCTs are less than 4000 s, 4300 s and 4400 s for BBR, *TCon* and CUBIC respectively.

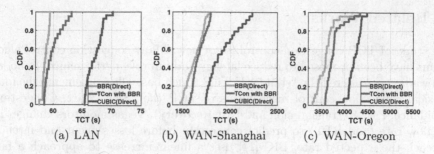

Fig. 6. The CDF of transfer completion time for large file (630 MB).

4.3   Overhead of TCon

Also, we have evaluated the overhead of our *TCon*. The buffer size of *TCon* is measured by triggering large file transfers from LAN, WAN-Shanghai and WAN-Oregon. Figure 7a depicts the CDF of the number of buffering packets in these three conditions. Results show that, most of time, *TCon* buffers around 20, 40, 105 packets for a LAN, WAN-Shanghai and WAN-Oregon transfers respectively. For a TCP connection, client would respond acknowledge segment as they receive the data from server and generate ACK segment in a short time. So, the number of inflight packets is relatively small.

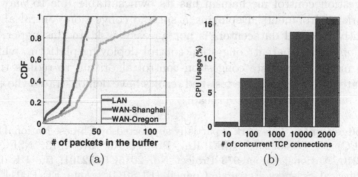

Fig. 7. *TCon* overhead: (a) CDF of the number of buffering packets and (b) CPU usage of under different scale of concurrent TCP connections.

CPU overhead of *TCon* is measured by simulating concurrent connections. Multiple simultaneous TCP flows are started from LAN server to the Web1 via *TCon* by using Web Bench [2]. Figure 7b shows the CPU overhead of *TCon* (the CPU usage of OVS process) and in the worst case with 20000 TCP connections, the maximum CPU usage of *TCon* is about 15%.

5   Related Works

The study of TCP congestion control is not new. Many congestion control algorithms have been proposed to reduce latency and improve performance. Reno [8] is nowadays considered the "standard" TCP which basically implements the four classical congestion control mechanisms of TCP (i.e., Slow Start, Congestion Avoidance, Fast Retransmission and Fast Recovery). Vegas monitors changes in the flow rate (and RTT) to predict congestion before losses occur and intends to reach the expected rate. BIC [14] uses a linear increase to approach a fair window size, and a binary search to improve RTT fairness. While CUBIC [10], which is an improvement of BIC, uses a cubic function to simplify the congestion window computation. BBR, which is proposed in [4], modifies *cwnd* according to the product of propagation time and bottleneck bandwidth.

Rather than proposing a new congestion control algorithm, our work investigates if congestion control can be implemented in a overlay manner. AC/DC [11] and vCC [6] are frontiers which converts default congestion control into operator-defined datacenter TCP congestion control. However, these two schemes target in intra-DC network environment and lack effective approaches to raise sending rate. In WAN, we need a more aggressive mechanism to handle packet loss.

6   Conclusions

Each congestion control mechanism has its own suitable role to play in various network environments. Deploying a specific congestion control algorithms transparently in cloud datacenters is not an easy task. In this paper, we presented *TCon*, a transparent congestion control deploying platform, which aims to enforce more appropriate congestion control algorithm to reduce the WAN transfers latency. Our extensive test-bed results have demonstrated the effectiveness of *TCon* with affordable overhead.

Acknowledgements. This work is partially supported by Chinese National Research Fund (NSFC) No. 61402200; NSFC Key Project No. 61532013; NSFC Project No. 61602210; National China 973 Project No. 2015CB352401; the UK Engineering and Physical Sciences Research Council (EPSRC) grants EP/P004407/1 and EP/P004024/1; Shanghai Scientific Innovation Act of STCSM No.15JC1402400 and 985 Project of SJTU with No. WF220103001; the Science and Technology Planning Project of Guangdong Province, China (2014A040401027, 2015A030401043), the Fundamental Research Funds for the Central Universities (21617409, 21617408); the Opening Project of Guangdong Province Key Laboratory of Big Data Analysis and Processing (2017009).

References

1. Open vSwitch. http://openvswitch.org/
2. Web Bench 1.5. http://home.tiscali.cz/~cz210552/webbench.html

3. Briscoe, B., Brunstrom, A., Petlund, A., Hayes, D., Ros, D., Tsang, J., Gjessing, S., Fairhurst, G., Griwodz, C., Welzl, M.: Reducing internet latency: a survey of techniques and their merits. IEEE Commun. Surv. Tutorials **18**(3), 2149–2196 (2014)
4. Cardwell, N., Cheng, Y., Gunn, C.S., Yeganeh, S.H., Jacobson, V.: BBR: congestion-based congestion control. Queue **60**(2), 58–66 (2017)
5. Chen, X., Zhai, H., Wang, J., Fang, Y.: A survey on improving TCP performance over wireless networks. In: Cardei, M., Cardei, I., Du, D.Z. (eds.) Resource Management in Wireless Networking. Network Theory and Applications, vol. 16, pp. 657–695. Springer, Boston (2005)
6. Cronkite-Ratcliff, B., Bergman, A., Vargaftik, S., Ravi, M., Mckeown, N., Abraham, I., Keslassy, I.: Virtualized congestion control. ACM SIGCOMM **2016**, 230–243 (2016)
7. Flach, T., Dukkipati, N., Terzis, A., Raghavan, B., Cardwell, N., Cheng, Y., Jain, A., Hao, S., Katz-Bassett, E., Govindan, R.: Reducing web latency: the virtue of gentle aggression. In: ACM SIGCOMM Conference on SIGCOMM, pp. 159–170 (2013)
8. Floyd, S., Gurtov, A., Henderson, T.: The NewReno modification to TCP's fast recovery algorithm (2004)
9. Gill, P., Jain, N., Nagappan, N.: Understanding network failures in data centers: measurement, analysis, and implications. In: ACM SIGCOMM Computer Communication Review, vol. 41, pp. 350–361. ACM (2011)
10. Ha, S., Rhee, I., Xu, L.: CUBIC: a new TCP-friendly high-speed TCP variant. ACM SIGOPS Oper. Syst. Rev. **42**(5), 64–74 (2008)
11. He, K., Rozner, E., Agarwal, K., Gu, Y.J., Felter, W., Carter, J., Akella, A.: AC/DC TCP: virtual congestion control enforcement for datacenter networks. In: ACM SIGCOMM 2016, pp. 244–257. ACM (2016)
12. Jacobson, V., Braden, R., Borman, D.: TCP Extensions for High Performance. RFC Editor (1992)
13. Judd, G.: Attaining the promise and avoiding the pitfalls of TCP in the datacenter. In: 12th USENIX NSDI, pp. 145–157 (2015)
14. Xu, L., Harfoush, K., Rhee, I.: Binary increase congestion control (BIC) for fast long-distance networks. In: Proceeding IEEE INFOCOM, vol. 4, pp. 2514–2524 (2004)

Regional Congestion Mitigation in Lossless Datacenter Networks

Xiaoli Liu[1,2(✉)], Fan Yang[1,2], Yanan Jin[1,2], Zhan Wang[1],
Zheng Cao[1], and Ninghui Sun[1]

[1] State Key Laboratory of Computer Architecture, Institute of Computing
Technology, Chinese Academy of Sciences, Beijing, China
{liuxiaoli,yangfan,jinyanan,
wangzhan,cz,snh}@ncic.ac.cn
[2] Institute of Computer and Control Engineering, University of Chinese
Academy of Sciences, Beijing, China

Abstract. To stop harmful congestion spreading, lossless network needs much faster congestion detection and reaction than the end-to-end approach. In this paper, we propose a switch-level regional congestion mitigation mechanism (RCM) that performs traffic management just at the congestion region edge. RCM moves the end-to-end congestion control to hop-by-hop switch level to lower the congested region's load as fast as possible. Meanwhile, to handle longer congestion, RCM detours the non-congestion flows to a light-loaded available path based on regional congestion degree to avoid the congestion region. Evaluation shows that the proposed RCM mechanism can perform timely congestion control over microburst flows, and achieve >10% improvement on mice flow's FCT and throughput than DCQCN, with rarely performance reduction on elephant flows.

Keywords: Lossless datacenter network · Congestion control · Adaptive routing

1 Introduction

RDMA (e.g. iWrap [1] and RoCEv2 [2]) has been increasingly deployed in datacenters with emerging artificial intelligence (AI) applications and distributed resource pooling systems (e.g. all-flash array with NVMe over fabric). RDMA technology relies on a lossless network to guarantee reliable transmission and high transmission performance. However, in current lossless network, the lossless link-level flow control (PFC: Priority Flow Control [3]) will back pressure the traffic, spread the congestion, and eventually build a congestion tree that saturates the whole network [4]. As shown in Fig. 1, network congestion happening at an egress port will gradually form a global congestion tree (red lines) and block other flows transmitting to non-congested hosts. Such congestion tree is a unique issue in lossless network. It will become even worse in future ultra-high bandwidth network, e.g. 100 Gb/s or 400 Gb/s Ethernet, because the burst length that a switch buffer can hold is becoming shorter and shorter. Since congestion tree will cause global congestion spreading and leads to rapid degradation of the entire

© IFIP International Federation for Information Processing 2017
Published by Springer International Publishing AG 2017. All Rights Reserved
X. Shi et al. (Eds.): NPC 2017, LNCS 10578, pp. 62–74, 2017.
DOI: 10.1007/978-3-319-68210-5_6

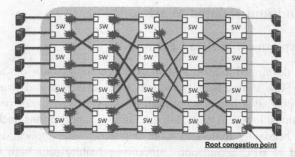

Fig. 1. Congestion spreading in lossless network (Color figure online)

network performance, it is essential to provide high efficient congestion control in the lossless network.

The key idea of mitigating congestion is to stop injecting non-admissible traffic into congested regions in time. Currently, end-to-end congestion control, such as ECN (Explicit Congestion Notification) [5] based DCTCP [6] and DCQCN [7], is main mechanism used to lower the injection rate of the source host. However, since most of congestion is caused by micro-burst traffics [8, 9], end-to-end approach may fail due to its long congestion notification latency (approaching to end-to-end round trip time). In addition, to stop congestion spreading, lossless network needs much faster congestion detection and reaction than the end-to-end approach. So, regarding the short-time congestion, we propose a regional congestion control mechanism that moves the end-to-end congestion control to hop-by-hop switch level to lower the congested region's load as fast as possible. Meanwhile, to handle longer congestion, we also propose a regional adaptive routing mechanism that detours the victim flows to avoid congestion region. Performance evaluation shows that our strategy can achieve better timeliness and fairness than the one with only end-to-end congestion control. Our key contributions are summarized as follows:

(1) **Fast Congestion Region Detection.** We check both the status of the input queue and output queue. Once an intra-switch congestion is reported, the congestion notification together with IDs (e.g. TCP/IP five tuple) of harmful flows that are contributing to congestion will be sent to neighbor switches.

(2) **Regional Congestion Control (RCC).** We perform congestion control at the edge of a congestion region. Once a switch confirms a congestion region and gets the IDs of harmful flows, it dynamically increases non-congested flows' priority to bypass the congestion flow at the output port.

(3) **Switch-level Adaptive Routing (SAR).** Once the congestion exceeds RCC's capability, the switch at the edge of congestion region will detour the victim flows to other light-loaded paths. Note that the end-to-end congestion control is still needed, the injection rate of the long-life harmful flow will be reduced by end-to-end congestion control mechanism eventually.

2 Background and Related Work

2.1 RDMA Deployment in Data Center

RDMA was first developed in HPC system to deliver high bandwidth and low latency network service [10]. It significantly reduces CPU overhead and overall latency by performing transport layer hardware offloading and OS-bypass data path between the NIC and applications. In recent years, big data analysis applications, including artificial intelligence, are becoming more and more popular. These applications can also be treated as a kind of HPC applications, since they require ultra-high computing and network performance. Therefore, more and more datacenters are trying to deploy RDMA at scale to provide better performance.

However, RDMA in HPC is deployed over lossless Layer 2 fabric (e.g. Infiniband [11]), while most data center networks are built over lossy Ethernet with the commodity switch. To enable RDMA over Ethernet, the RDMA over Converged Ethernet (RoCE and RoCEv2 [2]) was proposed. In converged Ethernet CEE standard, the link-level flow control protocol PFC was adopted. PFC [3] is a kind of point-to-point On/Off flow control that can prevent switch or NIC from buffer overflow. However, once the network congestion occurs, it will produce backpressure to its upstream switch. If the congestion lasts for long enough, such backpressure will be spread hop by hop and eventually forms congestion region.

2.2 End-to-End Congestion Control

End-to-end congestion control is current main mechanism used to lower the injection rate of the source host. TCP with ECN enabled is the classic layer 3 end-to-end congestion control mechanism, and QCN (Quantized Congestion Notification [12]) is a layer 2 end-to-end congestion control mechanism proposed for lossless network. ECN-aware switch/router sets a congestion mark in the IP header to signal impending congestion. After the receiver gets the labeled packet, it feeds back to the sender to reduce its transmission rate. Unlike ECN just using a mark bit, QCN tries to quantify the congestion degree, which keeps tracking the status of switch's output queue and calculates the quantized degree from the queue's offset between enqueuing and dequeuing rate. The QCN-aware switch detected congestion directly sends out CNMs (Congestion Notification Message) carrying the flow ID and congestion degree to the flow's source host. The source NIC handles the CNM and performs rate control.

At the host side, new transport protocols, like DCTCP [6] and DCQCN [7], were proposed to work with the ECN or QCN. In DCTCP, the host counts the fraction of ECN-marked packets (F) and adjusts the window size based on the variable F. DCQCN combines ECN's congestion notification mechanism and QCN's rate adjustment mechanism at the host. To avoid the congestion tree in the lossless data-center network, properly tuning the switch buffer's thresholds triggering ECN is rather difficult, not to mention tuning the thresholds of PFC and ECN at the same time. There are also some network measurement based end-to-end congestion control mechanisms, such as TIMELY [13].

The congestion control in network can be considered as a basic "control system" with feedback loop. As shown in Fig. 2(a), all these end-to-end mechanisms involve a long congestion notification procedure and the reaction procedure at the transport layer may take hundreds of microseconds or even milliseconds. Long congestion control loop will cause the end-to-end control fail in microburst scenarios, because the congestion may already widely spread before the end-to-end control works. Therefore, it is essential to perform timely congestion mitigation in hardware. Note that performing congestion control is not always the optimal congestion mitigating method, especially not for congestion caused by intermediate path collisions. Adaptive routing in HPC interconnection fabric [14, 15] is a candidate solution to such collision, which detours certain traffics to light-loaded path based on the switch's local port load. We borrow the idea and proposed a switch-level adaptive routing based on our congestion region detection mechanism.

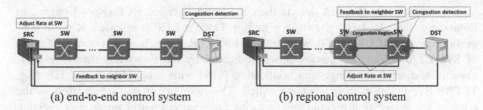

(a) end-to-end control system   (b) regional control system

Fig. 2. Network congestion control: regional control system aims to shorten the feedback loop and perform the reaction as fast as possible compared to end-to-end control system

3 Regional Congestion Mitigation Mechanism

3.1 Design Philosophy

As shown in Fig. 2(b), in our proposed RCM mechanism, a switch sends out its local congestion notification only to neighbors, and performs accurate congestion control locally based on the congestion condition it detects or receives. First, it will absorb the micro-burst congestion to a certain extent with certain free buffer, and then start the switch-level accurate reaction, which performs pacing to harmful flows at the output port. By doing this, the switch at the congested region edge can prevent the congestion spreading as fast as possible. When the reserved buffer is almost full or the switch gets neighbor's congestion notification again, it will try to detour non-harmful flows especially new flows to lightly loaded path.

Figure 3(a) illustrates the system architecture of our proposed RCM. As shown in Fig. 3(a), the congestion region is to isolate congestion within a harmless region that starts from the root congestion point and includes switches that the harmful congestion flows have passed by. The switch in Fig. 3(b) monitors the potential harmful flows that are most likely to cause congestion, and plays the role of both congestion detect and reaction point. The switch architecture includes CRD (Congestion Region Detection) module for fast congestion region detection, RCC (Regional Congestion Control) module for regional congestion control to micro-burst flows, SAR (Switch-level

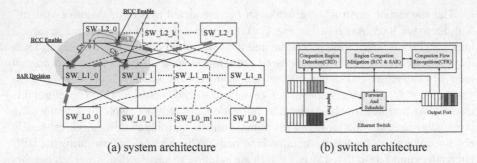

(a) system architecture   (b) switch architecture

Fig. 3. Architecture of Regional Congestion Mitigation (Color figure online)

Adaptive Routing) module for re-routing flows suffering intermediate path collision, and CFR (Congestion Flow Recognition) module for congestion flow Recognition.

The switch port that first detects the congestion is called RCP (Root Congestion Point), e.g. the SW_L2_0 shown in Fig. 3(a). Once a RCP is reported, it starts congestion control (RCC) to the flows recognized by CFR. Then, the input port0 and port1 of SW_L2_0 holding congestion flows (indicated by red flow) will detect the congestion, and send out congestion notification (CN) with congestion flows' IDs (e.g. TCP/IP five tuple) to their neighbor switch. The neighbor switch labels itself as the edge of the congestion region, and performs congestion control only on congestion flows indicated by the remote congestion notification it received, without interfering with victim flows. Correspondingly, the neighbor switch may also detect its local congestion condition and further send congestion notification with IDs to its neighbor switches. With such fine-grained hop-by-hop congestion control and congestion notification, the congestion will be back-pressured along the way as harmful flows passed by, and a harmless congestion region is formed, as the SW_L2_0, SW_L1_0 and SW_L1_1 formed the region in Fig. 3(a).

Based on RCC, traffics from congestion flows will be absorbed to a certain extent, but it may still generate back-pressure to the source node and cause congestion spreading. To provide more burst-absorption capability and achieve better load balancing, switches within the congestion region can perform adaptive routing to non-congestion flows or new flows. As the blue flow shown in Fig. 3(a), switch SW_L1_0 in the congestion region will detour it to other light-loaded paths based on the regional congestion degree.

3.2 Fast Congestion Region Detection

As shown in Fig. 3(a), the congestion region starts from the root congestion point, and includes switches that the harmful congestion flows passed through. To mark the edge of the congestion region, each switch port maintains three parameters: *congestion degree, local congestion flag and remote congestion flag*. The switch point with only the *local congestion flag* set will be marked as root congestion point and the congestion flows recognition will be conducted for following accurate congestion control. The switch point with only the *remote congestion flag* set will be marked as the edge of the congestion region, while the switch point with both *local congestion flag and remote congestion flag* set will be marked as inner congestion point inside the congestion region. The harmful congestion flow IDs at the edge and inner congestion points will be replaced by the ones getting from root congestion point.

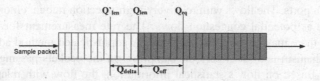

Fig. 4. Congestion detection in both input queue and output queue

Because of the link-level lossless flow control, back-pressure at the input port of switch may occur before the congestion happens at the output port. Therefore, the congestion detection is conducted on both input queue and output queue to improve the timeliness of detection, as shown in Fig. 4. Regarding each queue's congestion detection, we use similar CP algorithm introduced in QCN. The RCD module (in Fig. 3(b)) samples incoming packets with a predefined sampling interval depending on the degree of congestion. Within each sampling phase, a congestion measure F_b is computed by two factors: one is the offset of current queue length (Q_{len}) exceeding a predefined equilibrium length (Q_{eq}), represented as Q_{off}, and the other one is the differential of queue length between the instantaneous Q_{len} and the Q'_{len} when the last packet was sampled, in another word, the differential of the enqueuing and dequeuing rates, represented as Q_{delta}. Then F_b is given by the following formula:

$$F_b = Q_{off} + w_q \times Q_{delta} \tag{1}$$

$F_b > 0$ means that the queue length is exceeding the equilibrium length or the packets are accumulating, indicating a more likely congested state. Once a congestion state ($F_b > 0$) is firstly detected in an input queue, the port will set its *local congestion flag* (root congestion point) and send a feedback message containing quantified F_b to the neighbor switch. The root congestion point conducts Regional Congestion Control to the flows (harmful flows) recognized by CFR. The recognition algorithm will be introduced in Sect. 3.3.

Actually, the real F'_b sent out to the upstream neighbor will take the downstream neighbor's congestion degree F_{br} into consideration. If there is a valid congestion notification getting from the neighbor, the F'_b will be updated as:

$$F'_b \leftarrow (1 - w) \times F_b + w F_{br} \tag{2}$$

Where the parameter w depicts the weight that the received remote *congestion degree* F_{br} taken in the contribution to congestion degree.

3.3   Congestion Flows Recognition

The proposed mechanism will determine the harmful flows that are contributing to the congestion happening at the root congestion point, to make sure that congestion control only performs on harmful flows, not on victim flows.

As shown in Fig. 3(b), the congestion flow recognition is implemented by CFR at switch's output ports. The flows with relatively high injection rate in a monitor window can be treated as potential congestion flows. The rate measurement for each flow is impractical as there may be thousands of flows. A sophisticated method adopted by the proposed mechanism is to do a periodic sampling on the packets passing through the output queue. Based on flow's statistical information, the flow with relatively higher bandwidth will be sampled with higher probability.

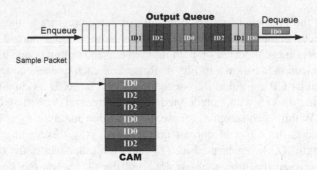

Fig. 5. Schematic diagram of CFR

Figure 5 shows the schematic diagram of CFR. For each output queue, we implement a CAM (content addressable memory) to store the IDs (here TCP/IP five-tuple) of packets which has been sampled. The CAM is written in a cyclic way, the depth of CAM decides the sampling granularity of congested flows. Statistically, the IDs of flows that contribution to the congestion are more likely to be sampled and stored in the CAM than the victim flows. Hence, we can treat the flows whose IDs are being stored in the CAM as the harmful congestion flows.

3.4   RCM: Regional Congestion Mitigation

RCC: Regional Congestion Control

To perform efficient and fair reaction to the congestion, our RCC introduces a window-based hop-by-hop congestion control. "Window" implies the amount of data can be sent during a period. The send window is running periodically, that's to say, when the window-limited data has been sent out, we can start another *window with period W*. The window is comprised of two sub-windows:

$$W = W_c + W_{nc} \tag{3}$$

Wherein, W_c is the congestion flow window, indicating the data amount of harmful congestion flows has been sent out, while W_{nc} is the *non-congestion flow window,* indicating the data amount of non-congestion flows has been sent out. The W_{nc} and W *are* estimated by the corresponding data amount sent in a time period from a given start when a congestion detected to the time when packets belong to all the congestion flow has been sent. We adjust the rate of congestion flows by controlling the W_c proportion in one window period W.

When one port detects output congestion state or receives a congestion notification message, it extracts the degree F_b from the notification message, and decreases its sending rate based on the following formula:

$$R(t) \leftarrow R(t) \times (1 - F_b \times G_d) \tag{4}$$

Where the constant G_d is chosen to satisfy $F_{bmax} * G_d = 1/2$, indicating the rate can be decreased by at most 50%. With formula (4), we can compute a new *"window"*:

$$W_c \leftarrow W_c(1 - F_b \times G_d) \tag{5}$$

$$W_{nc} \leftarrow W - W_c \tag{6}$$

Then, the switch output schedules packets from various input ports according to the *"Window"*. Once the amount of data that congestion flow has been sent reaches its window limit W_c, it cannot continue to send until the whole window W has been sent. By doing this, the congestion flow's rate can be decreased fleetly and back-pressure notifications will be generated along the path that the congestion flow passed by. Once the congestion state disappears, the window-based congestion control will quit.

SAR: Switch-level Adaptive Routing

Our proposed SAR is a switch-level adaptive routing based on the local output ports' load and their corresponding regional estimated congestion degree. We assume the equivalent path information has been pre-configured in date center network.

When the switch in a congestion region (as shown in Fig. 3(a)) has received several server congestion notifications from the neighbor switch or itself is undergoing congestion, it makes adaptive routing decision for non-congested or new flows to select the next available output port with minimum *regional congestion degree*. As depicted in Formula (2), the switch port calculates *regional congestion degree* with its local congestion degree F_b and neighbors' congestion degree F_{br}. To limit the congestion spreading, the harmful congestion flows should not be detoured by SAR. SAR will check whether the flow hits in the CAM as depicted in Sect. 3.3. If the flow is not the congestion flow indicated by the CAM, it can be detour to another path to avoid the congestion region. However, if there are no more available paths, the flow not hitting in CAM still will not be detoured.

4 Evaluation

4.1 Simulation Models

We perform the packet-level network simulation based on OMNeT++ platform, with the modeling of PFC link-level flow control, the proposed RCM mechanism, ECMP routing and DCQCN. We choose the {12-port, 3-layer} fat tree topology with 432 hosts. Each link is configured to 100 Gb/s. The switch is input-and-output queuing architecture, with virtual input queues (VOQ) at the input port and one output queue (OQ) at the output port. Each queue in the switch is 100 KB in size. The parameters of DCQCN are configured with the default values used for Mellanox 100 G adapter [17].

4.2 Performance with Micro-Benchmarks

Incast with Burst Flow: we begin with the experiment with Incast communication patterns that are common in datacenters, and evaluate the RCM's timeliness and efficiency. We use four hosts generating flows (IncastFlow) to the same destination host at the beginning of the simulation. And a micro-burst flow (BurstFlow) to the same destination is injected into the network at the time 150 μs and lasts for 20 μs. The four flows (IncastFlow in Fig. 6) are injected into the last switch from the same port, while the micro-burst flow (BurstFlow in Fig. 6) is injected from another port.

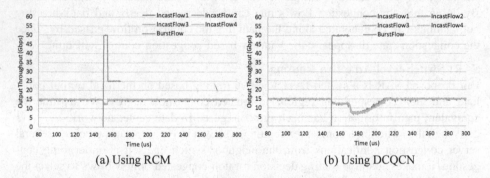

(a) Using RCM   (b) Using DCQCN

Fig. 6. Throughput of flows at the last switch's output port

Figure 6 shows each flow's instant throughput at the last switch's output port. The plots confirm that RCM can absorb the micro-burst flows with rarely impacting the rate of background flows (IncastFlow). As shown in Fig. 6(a), because of the fair scheduling, the micro-burst flow first takes 50 Gb/s, the half bandwidth of output port. Meanwhile, each IncastFlow decreases to about 12.5 Gb/s. Once the congestion is detected, the RCM reduces the micro-burst flow's rate to 25 Gb/s sharply at the switch and the throughput of four IncastFlows recovers to their maximum bandwidth quickly. While in DCQCN, as shown in Fig. 6(b), the throughput of micro-burst flow maintains at 50Gbps all the time. This is because even the micro-burst flow has already finished, the ECN congestion notifications are still on the way to source hosts. What is worse, the four IncastFlows are also tagged with ECN marks, which causes unnecessary rate control at the host.

Incast with Victim Flow: We now focus on the RCM's fairness. Considering Fig. 7(a), four hosts (*S1–S4*) send data to the same destination (*D0*). In addition, a "victim flow" from source *Sv* is sent to destination *Dv*. ECMP maps flows from *S1–S4* equally to SW_L1_0 and SW_L1_5, while victim flow from *Sv* is mapped to SW_L1_0. All hosts use the same priority. As *D0* is the bottleneck of *S1–S4* Incast, it back-pressures its incoming links with PFC pause frame, limiting 50 Gbps for each upstream port. This in turn leads to all the switches that Incast flows passed by to pause their incoming links. And eventually, SW_L0_0 is forced to pause the source hosts (*S1–S4*). Ideally, each Incast flow will get 25 Gbps throughput and *Sv* gets 50 Gbps throughput. However, we find that *Sv* only gets about 25 Gbps because of HOL blocking issue. As shown in Fig. 7(b), RCM can achieve fairness, since the victim flow can get a fair share nearly 50 Gbps throughput.

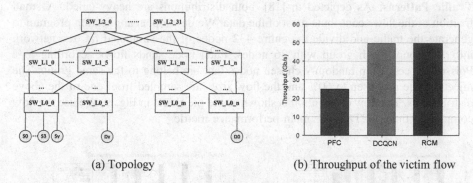

(a) Topology   (b) Throughput of the victim flow

Fig. 7. Fairness of RCM

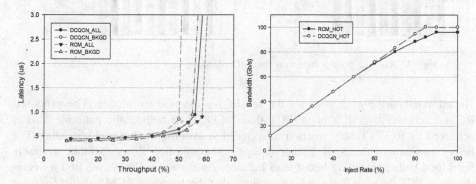

Fig. 8. Throughput and latency under hot-spot traffic pattern

Hot-spot Traffic Pattern: We now focus on its network performance with hot-spot traffic pattern. In this experiment, each host node sends its 85% traffic to uniform-randomly chosen destination node, as background flows, and the left 15% traffic is sent to the specified 12.5% nodes of the network, as hot flows. Such pattern coincides with traffic characteristics of data centers [6, 8, 16]. Figure 8 shows the throughput and latency of the background, hot and all flows respectively. As shown in Fig. 8(a), the background flows in RCM get 12.2% higher bandwidth than DCQCN, because of its accurate congestion control on hot flows and adaptive routing for background flows. Although the hot flows get a little lower performance shown in Fig. 8(b), the overall network performance of RCM still are still better than DCQCN, as there are a large proportion of background flows.

4.3   Performance with Application Traffic Patterns

This section will show experiments with realistic workloads based on two empirically observed traffic patterns in deployed datacenters [18]. The first distribution is derived from packet traces represents a large enterprise workload. The second distribution is from a large cluster running data mining jobs.

Traffic Patterns: As depicted in [18], both distributions are heavy-tailed: A small fraction of the flows contribute most of the data. We develop an application program to generate the traffic and divide the entire 432 nodes of the simulated fat tree network into 12 groups, each group with 36 nodes. Each node sends flows according to a Poisson process from randomly chosen nodes that are belong to the same group. The injection rate is chosen to 60% and the flow sizes are sampled from one of the above distributions. The flow distribution is shown as the pie charts in Fig. 9. We use the flow completion time (FCT) as the main performance metric.

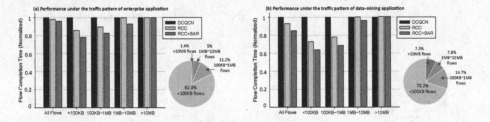

Fig. 9. Average flow completion time of enterprise and date-mining workloads

Result Analysis: Figure 9 shows the results for the two workloads. The proposed RCM has lower overall average FCT than DCQCN in both traffic patterns. This is achieved by RCC's timely reaction to congestion avoiding its harmful spreading. For heavy congestion, the SAR further detour non-congestion flows to other available light-load paths, providing better load balance. As shown in Fig. 9, we find a degradation in FCT for mice flows, which confirms that the proposed RCM benefits for mice flows (<1 MB), while it has little impact on the elephant flow (>10 MB). Figure 9(b) shows better performance promotion for data-mining workload than enterprise workload as shown in Fig. 9(a). This is because data-mining workload is more "heavily congested" than the enterprise workload. In addition, data-mining workload has more elephant flows than enterprise workload. So, there are more path collisions happen and the RCM with SAR can achieve better performance promotion for data-mining workload from the load balancing perspective.

5 Conclusion

We propose a regional congestion mitigation solution in the lossless datacenter network, which identifies the congestion region and performs traffic management just at the congestion region edge. With the timely traffic management, our solution can achieve >10% improvement over DCQCN, regarding both mice flow's FCT and throughput. However, the impact of switch's micro-architecture has not been fully considered yet. As the preliminary phase, we have not performed in-depth study on the performance impact of reserved buffer size and the ratio of out-of-order packets introduced by SAR. All these will be remained as our future work.

References

1. RDMA Consortium. iWARP protocol specification. http://www.rdmaconsortium.org/
2. Infiniband Trade Association. RoCEv2, September 2014. https://cw.infinibandta.org/document/dl/7781
3. IEEE 802.802.1Qbb - Priority-based Flow Control (2011). http://www.ieee802.org/1/pages/802.1bb.html
4. Guo, C., Wu, H., Deng, Z., Soni, G., Ye, J., Padhye, J., Lipshteyn, M.: RDMA over commodity ethernet at scale. In: Proceedings of the 2016 ACM SIGCOMM Conference, pp. 202–215 (2016)
5. IETF.org. RFC 3168: The Addition of Explicit Congestion Notification (ECN) to IP (2001). https://www.ietf.org/rfc/rfc3168.txt
6. Alizadeh, M., Greenberg, A., Maltz, D., Padhye, J., Patel, P., Prabhakar, B., Sengupta, S., Sridharan, M.: Data center TCP (DCTCP). In: Proceedings of the 2010 ACM SIGCOMM Conference (2010)
7. Zhu, Y., Eran, H., Firestone, D., Guo, C., Lipshteyn, M., Liron, Y., Padhye, J., Raindel, S., Yahia, M.H., Zhang, M.: Congestion control for large-scale RDMA deployments. In: Proceedings of the 2015 ACM SIGCOMM Conference, pp. 523–536 (2015)
8. Benson, T., Akella, A., Maltz, D.A.: Network traffic characteristics of data centers in the wild. In: Proceedings of the 10th ACM SIGCOMM Conference on Internet Measurement, pp. 267–280 (2010)
9. Kapoor, R., Snoeren, A.C., Voelker, G.M., Porter, G.: A study of NIC burst behavior at microsecond timescales. In: Proceedings of the Ninth ACM Conference on Emerging Networking Experiments and Technologies (2013)
10. Woodall, T.S., Shipman, G.M., Bosilca, G., Maccabe, A.B.: High performance RDMA protocols in HPC. In: 13th European PVM/MPI User's Group Meeting (2006)
11. Infiniband Trade Association. The InfiniBand™ Architecture [Online]
12. IEEE. 802.11Qau. Congestion notification (2010)
13. Mittal, R., Lam, V.T., Dukkipati, N., Blem, E., Wassel, H., Ghobadi, M., Vahdat, A., Wang, Y., Wetherall, D., Zats, D.: TIMELY: RTT-based congestion control for the datacenter. In: Proceedings of the 2015 ACM SIGCOMM Conference (2015)

14. Petrini, F., Feng, W.-C., Hoisie, A., Coll, S., Frachtenberg, E.: The Quadrics Network (QsNet): high-performance clustering technology. In: Proceedings of the 9th IEEE Hot Interconnects, Palo Alto, California, August 2001, pp. 125–130 (2001)
15. Ran, A., Sela, O.: Intel Omni-Path architecture technology overview. In: 21st Annual Symposium on High-Performance Interconnects (2013)
16. Benson, T., Anand, A., Akella, A.: Understanding data center traffic characteristics. In: Proceedings of the 1st ACM Workshop on Research on Enterprise Networking, pp. 65–72 (2009)
17. DC-QCN Parameters. https://community.mellanox.com/docs/DOC-2790
18. Speeding Applications in Data Center Networks. http://miercom.com/pdf/reports/20160210.pdf

A Fast and Accurate Way for API Network Construction Based on Semantic Similarity and Community Detection

Xi Yang and Jian Cao[(⊠)]

Department of Computer Science and Engineering,
Shanghai Jiao Tong University, Shanghai 200240, China
{ciciyang,cao-jian}@sjtu.edu.cn

Abstract. With the rapid growth of the number and diversity of web APIs on the Internet, it has become more and more difficult for developers to look for their desired APIs and build their own mashups. Therefore, web service recommendation and automatic mashup construction becomes a demanding technique. Most of the researches focus on the service recommendation part but neglect the construction of the mushups. In this paper, we will propose a new technique to fast and accurately build a API network based on the API's input and output information. Once the API network is built, each pair of the connected APIs can be seen as generating a promising mushup. Therefore, the developers are freed from the exhausting search phase. Experiments using over 500 real API information gathered from the Internet has shown that the proposed approach is effective and performs well.

Keywords: Web API · Mashup construction · API network

1 Introduction

With the development of Web 2.0 and related technologies, more and more service providers publish their resources on the Internet, usually in the form of web service APIs [8]. As a result, mashup technology, which aims for software developers to use multiple individual existing APIs as components to create value-added composite services [9] becomes a promising software development method in service-oriented environment [11]. To meet the developers' demand, several online mashup and web service repositories like ProgrammableWeb are established. For example, on ProgrammableWeb, there are altogether 17422 different APIs and 7881 mushups. These APIs and mushups are either manually collected by the website from different API providers or uploaded by the user. This manual work requires a lot of time for collecting and daily maintenance.

As a result of the rapid growth of the number and diversity of web APIs, it is a difficult task for developers to construct their own mashups. If a user want to search for some suitable APIs and construct a mushup with a new

© IFIP International Federation for Information Processing 2017
Published by Springer International Publishing AG 2017. All Rights Reserved
X. Shi et al. (Eds.): NPC 2017, LNCS 10578, pp. 75–86, 2017.
DOI: 10.1007/978-3-319-68210-5_7

functionality, he or she will need to do the next steps: first to select a few APIs from a variety of APIs based on the user's demand and the APIs' functionality. In this phase, normally a bunch of similar APIs will meet the requirement. Then the user must look into each API's documentation and figure out if the APIs can actually cooperate with each other and decide on how the data flows between each 2 individual APIs, meaning whose output can be the input of another. The whole process is so time consuming and cumbersome.

To address the above problem, some researchers adopt service recommendation techniques for service discovery to release manpower and contribute to a fast mashup construction. The main method includes semantic-based, Qos-based and network-based recommendation. The semantic-based way mainly focus on using the Natural Language Processing(NLP) tools for information retrieval. Latent dirichlet allocation (LDA) [5] and the later tagging augmented LDA (TA-LDA) model [2] are proposed to calculate the semantic similarity between the query and the API content. This method requires the WSDL document of the service, which is often uneasy to obtain nowadays with the privilege of RESTful services. Qos-based approach centers on the nonfunctional properties of web services and helps the user find suitable services among functionally equivalent services. Algorithms such as Collaborative Filtering [12] are employed. Similar as the semantic approach, Qos information is not always available. Another way is to use network analysis in service recommendation. Service usage patterns [10] and user behaviour patterns [4] are investigated to understand the correlation among the services and between the users and the services. The network-based approach does not take the users' functionality demand into account and therefore cannot return the user with useful service content information.

Even though the existing approaches show improvements in service recommendation, most of the methods concern about searching for the suitable APIs based on the user's query and ignore the subsequent steps. After the user's query, these methods return a bunch of unorganized APIs and don't show the user how exactly the mashup is constructed. The users still need to search for the documentation for each API and manually construct the mashup.

An ideal way to overcome the existing problem is to maintain an API network. Mashups can be seen as the connected APIs. These connections not only describe the matchable information, but also can indicate the direction of the data flow from one API's output to another's input. Therefore we proposed a fast and accurate way to build this API network based on the existing RESTful APIs' information and provide the user about the data flow information inside the mashup. Once the user has decide on which APIs to use, we can return if these APIs and actually work as a mushup and how it works. Or if a new web service API is published, we can quickly determine which existing services can construct a mushup with the new one.

Our rationale is that if 2 separate web service APIs can construct a mashup, there must be a data flow between these 2 APIs. One of the API's returned value can be used as the other's input data. We call it a pair of APIs that match with each other and can be components in the same mashup. Most of the service providers also publish the API references on their websites, containing the descriptions for the API input and output information.

Based on the above facts of APIs in the same mashup and the availability of the API information, we propose a new way by calculating the semantic similarity of the input and output description to determine if the 2 APIs match with each other to automatically construct a mashup. Also, to avoid doing the match work for each pair of input and output, we adopt the algorithm of community detection and cluster the APIs into several groups. Thus for the newly incoming APIs, we can simply compare them with the group centers instead of all the existing APIs. In this way, the computation for the matching is greatly reduced and the calculating process is accelerated.

2 Background

2.1 Motivation Example

Suppose the developer would like to build a new mashup which can recommend the tourist a complete travel route including where to visit, where to stay, where to eat, how to travel between 2 different locations and show all these information on a map. The developer may need to search separately for the key words like "map", "travel", "hotel" and so on. If user search for each of the key words listed above on ProgrammableWeb, the server will search in its 17440 APIs and return 1075/542/159 results separately for these 3 queries. Of course, among all these results, most of them are irrelevant and can not cooperate with each other to build the desired mashup. Such single query can not tell the developer whether these APIs can be used together. It is challenging for the developer to check for each API and decide which to chose and how to use them.

But if we already constructed an API network and have the information about the possible matchable APIs, knowing about how the data transfers inside these APIs, we can return the developer with a well-organized flow chart as shown in Fig. 1. This chart contains several APIs and illustrates the usage of the APIS. The example in Fig. 1 shows that the output of API a and API b can be the input of API c. The developer only need to choose from a small number of candidates and then start on building the new mushup.

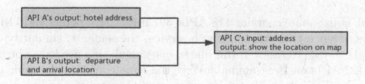

Fig. 1. An example of the API flow chart.

2.2 Requirements and Challenges

By looking into the APIs listed on ProgrammableWeb, we can find out that by June 2017, there are 17440 services collected. For each web service, there are on average more than 30 APIs provided. For each API, the number of input parameters and the output ranges from several to several tens. Take the web service FourSquare as an example, one of the API description is shown in Fig. 2. There is a API name containing the keywords to describe the functionality, a short API description, an url showing the API endpoint, a table of general information about the API, a table of input parameters and a table of output parameters. Coming along with all the input and output parameters, short descriptions are also provided. In our approach, we focus on the parameter descriptions since these descriptions give the semantic meaning of the parameters. If one input description and one output description from 2 separate APIs are talking about the same thing, which means the descriptions are semantically similar, we can conclude that these 2 APIs match with each other and can make up a mashup.

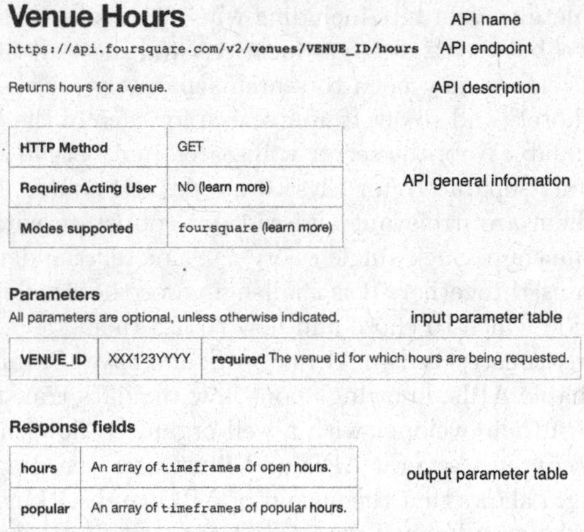

Fig. 2. Fousquare API example

In total, FourSquare contains 118 APIs, 397 input parameters and 110 output parameters. Even within this single web service, the semantic similarity calculation will take 397×110 times. If this one to one calculation needed to be done for all the 17422 APIs on ProgrammableWeb, the time consumed is unimaginable. Also, it is unrealistic to do the one to one matching every time when a new API emerges. Therefore, how to do the match calculation fast and accurate enough becomes a demand.

Therefore, we identify the major requirements for the mashup detection:

- **Comprehensive API combination detection.** The detection is based on the semantic similarity of the input and output. An good similarity calculation helps improving the accuracy for building the API network by finding as much matched pairs of input and output as possible and exclude the others.
- **Fast calculation.** With the rapid growth of the number of APIs, similarity calculation for each pair of input and output is unrealistic. Instead of the one to one comparison, a good pre-processing phase to narrow down will be helpful to greatly accelerate the calculation.

3 Method Overview

To meet the above requirements, we proposed an approach to fast and accurately build the API network. The whole process contains 2 main parts as shown in Fig. 3:

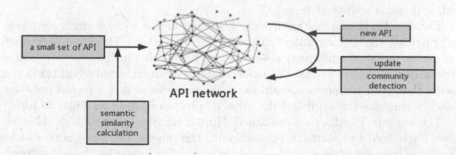

Fig. 3. Framework

Beginning with a small amount of APIs, we calculated the semantic similarity for each pair of input description and output description. This NLP technique is the first main part described in Sect. 3.1. After this calculation, all the semantically similar input and output will be connected. The results generated an undirected graph as shown in Fig. 3. The nodes are sentences indicating all the input descriptions/output descriptions and the edges meaning that the linked nodes have similar semantics.

The second main part is based on this undirected graph. Here we adopted the community detection algorithm which is already widely used in social network. By using the community detection on this graph, all the nodes will be divided into several groups with every node within the same group sharing the same semantics.

The whole construction of the API network is done in an incremental way. Every time we want to add a new API input/output into this network, in other words, find the matchable APIs for the new one, we can simply calculate semantic similarity of the new one with the center of each community. The community center should represent the whole community and extract as much common information as possible. It's defined as the most frequent words of all the nodes within the group. If the center of a group is semantically similar to the new one, we consider all the nodes in this group is possible to build mashups with the new API. So we can continue to check each node in this community. Otherwise, if one center of a group dose not mach the new one, the whole nodes in the group will be regarded as impossible to match new one and skipped. In this way, the calculation is greatly reduced. Every time a new node is added, the community detection algorithm will run again and reorganize the network.

In the following part, we will go through the details of semantic similarity calculation and community detection:

3.1 Semantic Similarity

The semantic similarity algorithm is based on WordNet [3,7] and corpus statistics [6]. WordNet is a large lexical database of English. All nouns, verbs, adjectives and adverbs are grouped into sets of cognitive synonyms unordered sets (synsets), each expressing a distinct concept.

The detail is shown in Algorithm 1. The basic idea is to vectorize 2 sentences and calculate the cosine similarity between these 2 vectors. The way to vectorize the sentence is shown in function **Vectorize**. Each value in the vector indicates the corresponding word similarity calculated in the function **wordSimilarity**. 1 means that both sentences contain exact the same word and 0 means only one sentence contains the word and the other don't even contain a similar word.

The words in WordNet are constructed hierarchically on base of lexical knowledge. Each word has semantic connection to the others. The child node can be seen as a semantic subset of the ancestor node. For example, the node "boy" and "girl" might be the children nodes of node "children". The path between 2 nodes in the structure is a proxy for how similar the words are and the height of their Lowest Common Subsumer (LCS) from the root of WordNet shows how broad the concept is and less similar. Therefore, the word similarity is calculated by these 2 measurements as shown in Eq. 1 with α and β being the weighted length and height:

$$similarity = e^{-\alpha}\frac{e^{\beta} - e^{-\beta}}{e^{\beta} + e^{-\beta}} \tag{1}$$

3.2 Community Detection

The community detection part used the louvain method described in [1]. The Louvain method is a simple and easy-to-implement yet efficient method for identifying the communities in large networks. It is one of the most widely used method for detecting communities in large networks.

In this method, "modularity" is defined to describe the structure of a network, measuring the strength of the division of a network into groups. Intuitively,

Algorithm 1. Semantic Similarity

```
 1: function SEMANTICSIMILARITY(sentence1, sentence2)
 2:     w1 ← Tokenize(sentence1)        ▷ Tokenize both of the sentence into word sets
 3:     w2 ← Tokenize(sentence2)
 4:     j ← Union(w1, w2)               ▷ Get the join set of the above 2 word sets
 5:     vector1 ← Vectorize(w1, j)
 6:     vector2 ← Vectorize(w2, j)
 7:     return CosineSimilarity(vector1, vector2)
 8: end function
 9: function VECTORIZE(w, j)
10:     vec ← initialized with the length equal to size(j)
11:     i ← 0
12:     for word in j do
13:         if word in w then
14:             vec[i] ← 1                      ▷ Set the value to 1 if word is in w
15:         else
16:             sim ← findSimilarWord(word, w)    ▷ If the word is not in w, then
        calculate the similarity between word and the most similar word in w.
17:             if sim ≥ threshold then ▷ Means that there is actually a similar word
        in w.
18:                 vec[i] ← sim
19:             else                      ▷ There is no similar word in w.
20:                 vec[i] ← 0
21:             end if
22:         end if
23:         i ← i + 1
24:     end for
25:     return vec
26: end function
27: function FINDSIMILARWORD(word, w)
28:     maxValue ← MAX
29:     for element in w do
30:         maxValue ← max(maxValue, wordSimilarity(element, word))
31:     end for
32:     return maxValue
33: end function
```

high modularity means the network has dense connection between nodes within groups but sparse connections between groups. The calculation for modularity is shown in Eq. 2:

$$Q = \frac{1}{2m} \sum_{ij} (A_{ij} - \frac{k_i - k_j}{2m}) \delta(c_i, c_j) \tag{2}$$

with

- m is the number of all edges in the graph;
- A_{ij} represents the edge between node i and j;
- k_i and k_j mean the sum of edges connected to node i and j;
- δ is a delta function.
- c_i and c_j are the communities of node i and j;

Louvain method is a greedy optimization method that attempts to optimize the modularity of a division of a network. The optimization is performed in 2 steps as shown in Algorithm 2. These 2 steps are iteratively repeated until a maximum modularity is gained.

Algorithm 2. Community Detection

Require: A network N.
Ensure: A division D of the network with maximum modularity.
 1: initialization: $D \leftarrow$ assign each node in N to its own group
 2: initialization: $Q \leftarrow$ modularity(D) ▷ modularity calculates the modularity of
        division D using Eq. 2
 3: initialization: $\Delta Q \leftarrow Q$
 4: **while** $\Delta Q > 0$ **do**
 5:     **for** all node n **in** N **do**
 6:         $maxQ \leftarrow$ modularity(D)
 7:         $maxD \leftarrow D$
 8:         **for** all group g **in** neighbours of c_n **do**
 9:             $D_{new} \leftarrow$ move n into g
10:             $Q_{new} \leftarrow$ modularity(D_{new})
11:             **if** $Q_{new} > maxQ$ **then**
12:                 $D \leftarrow D_{new}$
13:                 $maxQ \leftarrow Q_{new}$
14:                 $\Delta Q \leftarrow maxQ - Q$
15:                 $Q \leftarrow Q_{new}$
16:             **end if**
17:         **end for**
18:     **end for**
19: **end while**
20: **return** D

All the input and output description data are connected based on the semantic similarity. Thus an undirected network is generated. In the following section we will show that the community detection also works well on this kind of network.

4   Experiments and Results

In out experiment, we crawled in total 580 APIs from the providers' website to see how fast and accurate when we use the method proposed above. All these

APIs belong to 24 different categories and in total have 2775 input description and 638 output description. The average length for a single description is 9.67.

4.1   Accuracy of Semantic Similarity Algorithm

To check whether the semantic similarity can denote the matchable information for the input and output pair, we applied this algorithm to every pair of input and output in our experiment dataset, in total more than 150000 pairs. The result is shown in Fig. 4.

By manually checking, we can conclude that most of the input/output pairs don't match with each other(with the similarity less than 0.4). We find out that the higher the similarity is, the more likely this pair matches with each other. It is reasonable to use this semantic similarity to construct the API network. Therefore, we need to choose a threshold to decide whether a pair of input and output matches with each other. The threshold need to meet these 2 requirements:

- Small enough to include all the matchable pairs.
- Big enough to exclude all the impossible pairs.

We manually checked each threshold candidates ranging from 0.95 to 0.40 and finally choose 0.55 as the threshold. All the pairs with similarity greater than 0.55 are matchable and will be connected together.

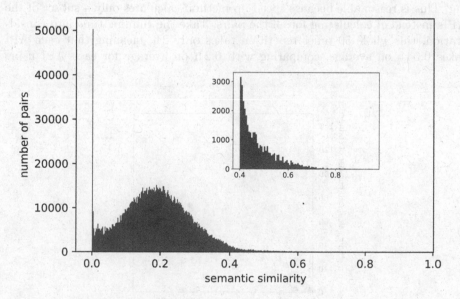

Fig. 4. The distribution of all the pairs according to their semantic similarity

4.2   Speed-Up Calculation Using Community Detection

By checking the accuracy of semantic similarity in the former experiment, we constructed the most comprehensive API network since each pair of input and output is checked and any possible pair won't be missed. But if we take the time consumption into consideration, this one-to-one approach is not practical. The total time to finish the calculation is more than 110 h. On average, every API takes about 0.2 h to finish calculating. For every input and output description, more than 600 and 2500 times of calculation is needed separately. Also, this approach will become more and more slower because new APIs show up every day and the number is growing rapidly.

To check how the speed-up way with community detection works, we will compare its running time and comprehensiveness with the one-to-one method. The network this one-to-one method build is referred as the original network.

To check the comprehensiveness, we randomly took out 1 API out of the original network. All the input, output and related connections belonging to this API are taken out. The other APIs are kept unchanged. This taken-out API will be added back into the network to build its own connections in the network using the speed-up way. The number of connections it builds will be compared with the connections in the original API network.

This experiment is repeated 50 times to get the convincing results as shown in Fig. 5. Most of the nodes are slightly blow the standard line, meaning that the speed-up method find most of the matchable pairs with a small part missing. This is reasonable because speed-up method calculates only a subset of the APIs instead of calculating for all the pairs. Take the running time into consideration, this whole 50 times repetition takes only 2 h, meaning that each API takes 0.04 h on average, comparing with 0.2 h on average for each API using

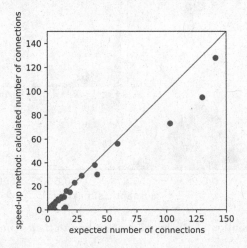

Fig. 5. Comparison for adding one API into network

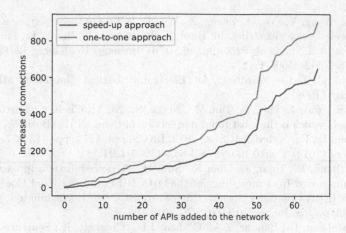

Fig. 6. Comparison for adding 67 APIs into the network

one-to-one method. This method is comprehensive enough yet with a surprisingly good time-saving capability.

We also tried taking 67 APIs out of the original network and adding back all these 67 APIs one by one to see if the incremental way still remains effective. The result is shown in Fig. 6. Even though the blue line remains lower than yellow line, it still finds around 72% connections comparing with the original network, indicating the speed-up method is practical and good enough to construct the API network. The average time it takes is 0.041 h for a single API. This approach makes it possible to find connections quickly for a newly coming API.

5   Conclusion

This paper present a new way of adopting semantic similarity and community detection for automatic generate the API network and assist mashup development in a incremental way. The experiment performed on hundreds of APIs demonstrates the effectiveness of the proposed method. It keeps a relatively good result yet reduces quite a lot of computation. This is very meaningful when a new API is released and to get the matchable information for this API without delay. Also, in this way, we can maintain an API network representing all the matchable pairs and assist the developer for mashup construction.

Acknowledgment. This work is supported by China National Science Foundation (Granted Number 61472253).

References

1. Blondel, V.D., Guillaume, J.L., Lambiotte, R., Lefebvre, E.: Fast unfolding of communities in large networks. J. Stat. Mech: Theory Exp. 2008(10), P. 10008 (2008). http://stacks.iop.org/1742-5468/2008/i=10/a=P10008

2. Chen, L., Wang, Y., Yu, Q., Zheng, Z., Wu, J.: WT-LDA: user tagging augmented lda for web service clustering. In: Basu, S., Pautasso, C., Zhang, L., Fu, X. (eds.) ICSOC 2013. LNCS, vol. 8274, pp. 162–176. Springer, Heidelberg (2013). doi:10. 1007/978-3-642-45005-1_12

3. Fellbaum, C. (ed.): WordNet: An Electronic Lexical Database. MIT Press, Cambridge (1998)

4. Huang, K., Yao, J., Fan, Y., Tan, W., Nepal, S., Ni, Y., Chen, S.: Mirror, mirror, on the web, which is the most reputable service of them all? In: Basu, S., Pautasso, C., Zhang, L., Fu, X. (eds.) ICSOC 2013. LNCS, vol. 8274, pp. 343–357. Springer, Heidelberg (2013). doi:10.1007/978-3-642-45005-1_24

5. Li, C., Zhang, R., Huai, J., Guo, X., Sun, H.: A probabilistic approach for web service discovery. In: Proceedings of the 2013 IEEE International Conference on Services. IEEE Computer Society Computing SCC 2013, Washington, pp. 49–56 (2013). http://dx.doi.org/10.1109/SCC.2013.107

6. Li, Y., McLean, D., Bandar, Z.A., O'Shea, J.D., Crockett, K.: Sentence similarity based on semantic nets and corpus statistics. IEEE Trans. Knowl. Data Eng. 18(8), 1138–1150 (2006)

7. Miller, G.A.: Wordnet: a lexical database for english. In: Proceedings of the Workshop on Human Language Technology HLT 1994. Association for Computational Linguistics, Stroudsburg, pp. 468–468 (1994). http://dx.doi.org/10.3115/1075812. 1075938

8. Papazoglou, M.P., Traverso, P., Dustdar, S., Leymann, F., Krämer, B.J.: 05462 service-oriented computing: a research roadmap. In: Cubera, F., Krämer, B.J., Papazoglou, M.P. (eds.) Service Oriented Computing (SOC). No. 05462 in Dagstuhl Seminar Proceedings, Internationales Begegnungs- und Forschungszentrum für Informatik (IBFI), Schloss Dagstuhl (2006). http://drops.dagstuhl.de/ opus/volltexte/2006/524

9. Sheth, A., Benslimane, D., Dustdar, S.: Services mashups: the new generation of web applications. IEEE Internet Comput. 12, 13–15 (2008)

10. Tan, W., Zhang, J., Foster, I.: Network analysis of scientific workflows: a gateway to reuse. Computer 43(9), 54–61 (2010)

11. Xia, B., Fan, Y., Tan, W., Huang, K., Zhang, J., Wu, C.: Category-aware api clustering and distributed recommendation for automatic mashup creation. IEEE Trans. Serv. Comput. 8(5), 674–687 (2015)

12. Zheng, Z., Ma, H., Lyu, M.R., King, I.: Qos-aware web service recommendation by collaborative filtering. IEEE Trans. Serv. Comput. 4(2), 140–152 (2011)

Improving Branch Prediction for Thread Migration on Multi-core Architectures

Tan Zhang, Chaobing Zhou, Libo Huang[⊠], Nong Xiao, and Sheng Ma

School of Computer, National University of Defense Technology,
Changsha 410073, China
{zhangtan15,zhouchaobing15,libohuang,nongxiao,masheng}@nudt.edu.cn

Abstract. Thread migration is ubiquitous in multi-core architectures. When a thread migrates to an idle core, the branch information of the branch predictor on the idle core is absent, which will lead to the branch predictor works with comparatively low prediction accuracy until the warm-up finish. During the warm-up period, the branch predictor spends quite a lot of time on recording branch information and often makes mispredictions. These are the main performance impact of thread migration. In this paper, we point out that, when a thread migrates to an idle core, the prediction accuracy can be improved by migrating branch history information from the source core to the target. Moreover, several migration strategies are introduced to fully exploit the performance of branch prediction migration. Experiment results show that, compared to the experiment baseline which doesn't migrate any branch history information, branch prediction migration reduces MPKI of the branch predictor on new core by 43.46% on average.

Keywords: Branch prediction · Thread migration · Multi-core architecture

1 Introduction

Multi-core processors which bring up large amounts of powerful computational resources, are ubiquitous today in PC and servers. To make better use of the available cores and expose parallelism, thread migration is desired in multi-core processors [1,4]. In [2], the authors point out that the most challenge work of thread migration is the migration of cache and Branch Predictor (BP). Accurate branch prediction is essential to achieving high performance for processor design. Modern processors employ increasingly complicated branch predictors to sustain instruction fetch bandwidth that is sufficient for wide out-of-order execution cores. It relies large amounts of branch history information for very high prediction accuracy. However, when a thread migrate to an idle core, branch information is absent and the predictor fails to work with high prediction accuracy, which is one of the main impact of thread migration performance. To solve

© IFIP International Federation for Information Processing 2017
Published by Springer International Publishing AG 2017. All Rights Reserved
X. Shi et al. (Eds.): NPC 2017, LNCS 10578, pp. 87–99, 2017.
DOI: 10.1007/978-3-319-68210-5_8

this problem, we migrate branch history information from the source core to the target core to accelerate the warm-up process. With the help of branch information migration, the target core doesn't have to train the branch predictor from scratch. In addition, the branch accuracy will be improved.

To Migrate branch history information more efficiently, we couldn't simply migrate the whole branch information to the idle core because migrating branch history will occupy the bus between cores and consume instruction cycles. Based on different thread length and branch information length, we should take corresponding strategies. In order to investigate the proper migration strategy in different scenarios, we introduce several simple migration strategies. There are two categories of BP migration including migrating RAM or migrating RAM&GHR (Global History Register). For the situation of migrating RAM, the migration strategies are divided into 3 classes migrating the whole RAM or a part of RAM or only the basic prediction table T0. For migrating GHR, we introduce several simple strategies to modify GHR value. The GHR does hash with PC to index the prediction table. Since the GHRs value will be updating during the migration, the branch predictor will be indexed to the wrong prediction table if we don't modify the GHR value. Based on the discussion above, finding the proper strategies for different situations is the key problem of BP migration. Some exploration work about GHR migration is shown in [3], which points out that the best solution does not transfer any global history but rather synthesizes a value in the new cores GHR. In such a way, it allows each unique thread to update and use its own branch history immediately. Compared to their work, we take migration overhead into consideration. The bus width and the RAM size is known, so we can calculate the time cost of migrating branch predictors. They assume that the BP history can be migrated in a negligible short time for short thread. In our work, we take BP migration overhead into consideration and point out that if the thread has less than 1000 instructions, migrating BP won't get performance improvement. In addition, we investigate the impact of the RAM size and the thread length.

This paper is to reduce or eliminate the cost of BP training and increase the accuracy of branch predictor for thread migration by migrating branch predictor information. With extensive simulation experiments, we find that if we only migrate RAM without GHR, instead of migrating all sub-predictors, we can reduce MPKI of the branch predictor on new core by 43.46% on average. This strategy performs steadily and is suitable for many scenarios. The remainder of this paper is organized as follows. Section 2 presents the Background of our work. Migration model is introduced in Sect. 3. Section 4 presents our experiment methodology. Performance evaluation and the discussion of migration strategies are presented in Sect. 5. Section 6 presents the related work. Finally, Sect. 7 concludes this study.

2   Background

Accurate branch prediction is essential to achieving high performance for multi-core processor design. In this work, we choose a representative branch

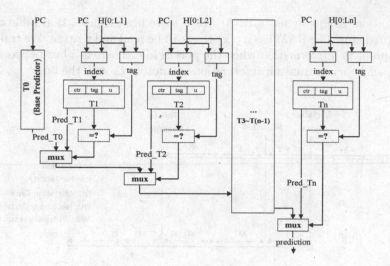

Fig. 1. TAGE Structure

predictor–TAGE to investigate the BP migration strategies. The TAGE predictor is often considered as state-of-the-art in conditional branch predictors proposed by academy. It is widespread in multi-cores because the implementation on hardware is easy.

2.1 TAGE Predictor

Structure of TAGE. As shown in Fig. 1, TAGE predictor consists of a base predictor T0 and n (T1, T2 $\cdots$ Tn) tagged predictor components. T0 is a 2-bit counter bimodal table indexed by the PC. It provides a basic prediction when other predictors are not matching. Ti ($i > 0$) is indexed by a hash result of PC and length L(i) branch history. L(i) is the number of GHR's bits we used to index Ti. And it satisfies the geometric progression, i.e. L(i) = (int) $(\alpha^{i-1} * L(1) + 0.5)$; ($i > 1$). Each tagged component contains a number of configurable entries. The design of TAGE is flexible. If the size of RAM are same, we can get different number of entries with different entry structures. Each entry is composed of ctr, tag and u. Ctr (pred, 3 or 2bit) is a saturation counter, used to indicate the direction of a branch (if $|2 * ctr + 1| \geq ([1 \ll ctrwidth] - 1)$), the prediction is strong, else the prediction is weak). Tag is used to confirm that this entry is matches the branch. The tag width of each component can be different. But in the same component, different entries have the same tag size. U (useful, 2 or 1 bit), which is an age counter, indicates whether the entry is valid.

3 Model

In this section, we present our thread migration model in multi-cores. In order to simplify the BP migration problem, we simply take dual-core architecture into consideration. Each core has a RAM which store branch prediction table of the TAGE predictor. The RAM has a port that can be read and written. We transmit branch prediction information when the port is idle. There is a bus between two cores. Each core can transmit information to another though the bus.

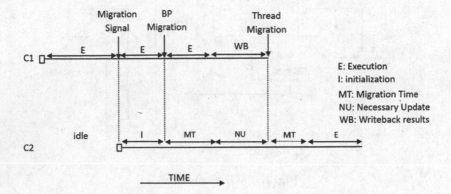

Fig. 2. Thread migration model

3.1   BP Migration Model

Our BP migration models are shown in Fig. 2. During the execution of a thread on a core (We denote as C1), there is a need for migration (e.g., load balance or temperature threshold has been reached), and it is decided that the execution should be transferred to another idle core, C2. As soon as this decision is made, a migration signal is send to the C2. When C2 is activated, it enters first the initialization phase where its resources are turned on. After initialization, the resources that a core running need is prepared. Then we are able to migrate C1's BP to C2. When the initialization finished, C2 enter the migration phase. After the C1 finish executing the remaining instructions in the pipeline, it will acquire the bus. The branch prediction migration will be interrupted and C2 enters the necessary update phase. This is the phase where state essential for correctness is updated. During this phase the architectural register state is transferred from C1 to C2, and the dirty cache blocks, in a private cache to be turned off in C1, are written in a lower level cache. When the NU phase completes, C1 becomes inactive and C2 starts to migrate the remaining branch prediction information. If the RAM on C1 has been altered during the migration, there are two cases. If the prediction table already has been migrated to C2, we keep its previous value. If the prediction table has not been migrated, we read and migrate its new value.

4   Methodology

In this section, we will describe our simulation framework, baseline, and benchmark selection.

4.1   Simulation Setup and Methodologies

We run the target benchmark on GEM5 simulator [5] and Intercept branch prediction data that conform to the CBP2014 [6] trace format specification [7]. Based on the BP simulation environment, we evaluate various BP migration strategies. To obtain simulation experiment trace, we modified the GEM5 code to print out the instructions execution information of our benchmark [6,7]. The simulation experiment trace contains 100 million instruction records. As shown in Table 1, each record contains four fields. The PC is the unique identifier for the execution instruction, known as program counter. OpType indicates the type of the instruction. The BranchTaken field records the actual branch jump information of the PC's corresponding instruction. The BranchTarget is the destination address for the jump. We configure gem5 for the arm v7 instruction set of single-core structure, the specific parameters shown in Table 2.

Table 1. Record in trace

PC	OpType	BranchTaken	BranchTarget

Table 2. System parameters setting

CPU	ARM detailed, ARM V7a, O3, 2 GHz 3-wide fetch/decode 6-wide dispatch 8-wide issue/commit 40-entry ROB; 64-entry store buffer
L1I cache	32 KB, 2-way, 2MHSRs 1-cycle latency
L1D cache	32 KB, 2-way, 6MHSRs 2-cycle latency
L2 cache	Unifined 1 MB, 16-way, 16MHSRs 12-cycle latency
Branch predictor	LSC-TAGE

Evaluation Criterion: We use MPKI (Misprediction per Kilo Instructions) as the evaluation criterion. CBP uses a trace-driven simulation. As the simulation begin, CBP gets the instruction record constantly. If the record is a conditional branch instruction, then we use branch prediction and get the prediction value. We update branch predictor with the prediction jump value, the actual jump value, the PC and the jump destination address. If the prediction jump value is inconsistent, then we record the failure times. When the trace is resolved, we calculate MPKI of the entire trace as the output.

Table 3. parameter setting of TAGE

Number of sub-predictors (N)	11
GHR length (bits)	360
Number of T0's entry (log size)	12
Entry width of T0 (bits)	2
Number of Ti's entry (log size)	8, 8, 8, 8, 7, 8, 7, 6, 6
tag width of Ti (bits)	7, 7, 7, 8, 9, 10, 10, 11, 13, 13
Entry width of Ti (tag, ctr, u)	10, 10, 10, 11, 12, 13, 13, 14, 16, 16
History length (bits)	4, 9, 13, 24, 37, 53, 91, 145, 256, 359

The Simulation of the migration process: In order to simulate the process of thread migration, we modified the CBP2014 simulation framework. Firstly, the trace runs on core 1. When the trace runs to the instruction that the thread start to migrate (we call this instruction Migration Start Point -MSP), we start to migrate branch predictor to core 2 with specified bandwidth. Core 1 continues to complete the instructions in the pipeline. When the trace runs to the instruction that the migration finish (we call this instruction Migration Over Point -MOP) on core 1, core 2 waits core 1 finish the remaining instructions and returns registers, dirty cache blocks. Then core 1 stop running trace, core 2 continues to run the remaining trace. In the basic version, we assume that IPC is 1 and the bus bandwidth between cores is 128 bits. The RAM size of TAGE branch predictor is 4 KB. The specific configuration parameters in Table 3.

5　Evaluation

In this section, we simulate various migration scenarios through a trace-driven approach to evaluate our migration strategies.

5.1　Migrate GHR and RAM

Figure 3 shows the strategies only migrate RAM. The x axis represents different programs. While the y axis means the MPKI of migration strategies divide the MPKI of our baseline. **OneCore** means the trace only runs on a single core. OneCore is the ideal situation and its MPKI should be minimum theoretically. The TAGE branch predictor consists of a basic predictor T0, a GHR and a number of tagged sub-predictors. We define **migT0** as only migrate T0. **migTi** means we migrate T0 and several sub-predictors (T1–Ti, $0 < i < n$). **migTn** represents we migrate the whole RAM (T0–Tn). **NoBPMigrate** means thread migration without migrating BP. Comparing each strategy with **NoBPMigrate**, we can get the prediction accuracy improvement of corresponding strategy. If the bar in Fig. 3 under the horizontal line, it means the corresponding migration strategy can improve the prediction accuracy. As we can see in this figure, migrating

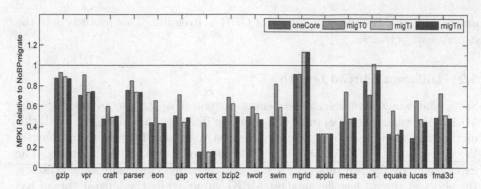

Fig. 3. Migrating RAM only

the whole RAM has the best prediction accuracy improvement. Because more branch prediction informations give predictors more reference.

Figure 4 shows the strategies which migrate RAM together with GHR. Similarly, the x axis represents different programs. While the y axis means the MPKI of migration strategies divide the MPKI of our baseline. **PreMtRAM** means we migrate GHR before migrating RAM. **AftMtRAM** means we migrate GHR after RAM Migration finish. There two strategies represent different GHR migration time strategies. Since the RAM may be updated on core 1, if we migrate GHR before migrating RAM, GHR's high bits might be not matched with RAM. So we should revise GHR's high bits. **ComPC** means we replace high bits with the first instruction's PC on core B. **ComZero** means we set high bits all 0. **AllOne** means we set GHR's every bit 1. The number of high bits depends on a counter, which records how many branch instructions have been executed during migration. Obviously, **conPC** has the best performance. Since GHR and RAM will be update during the migration, to make them match, we should modify GHR's value. But what's the correct modification strategy couldn't be point

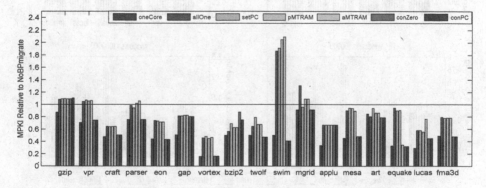

Fig. 4. Migrating RAM and GHR with different strategies

out by analysis. Because the update of GHR is irregular. This result is only the experiment outcomes.

5.2   Different Thread Length

Statistical window represents how many instructions we use to calculate the MPKI. We change this parameter to simulate different thread length. With this method, we are able to find the appropriate strategy for different thread length. We set window size to 5000, 50,000, 100,000 and 1,000,000 instructions. The experiment results are shown in Fig. 5. For the same trace and same strategy, the shortest thread has the smallest MPKI value, while the longest thread has the biggest MPKI value, which means short thread get more performance gains by migrating BP than long thread.

Based on the experiment results above, we find that short thread is more suit for BP migration. But if the thread is too short, migrating the whole RAM might cause performance loss for the large migration overhead. We assume each misprediction will cause 6 instruction cycles loss. Only migrating T0 will have 34 instruction cycles loss, and 83 instruction cycles cost for migrating T0–T4. Migrating the whole 4 KB RAM will cost 121 instruction cycles. We define the total overhead of misprediction when we do not migrate any BP information as θ. The α_i presents the overhead of i migration strategy. We define the cost of migrating BP as ε and the performance gain of migrating BP as γ. Then we have $\gamma = \theta - \alpha_i - \varepsilon$. Figure 6 shows the performance gain of short thread with different

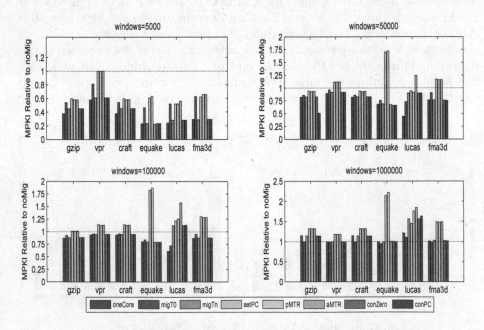

Fig. 5. Different statistical window sizes

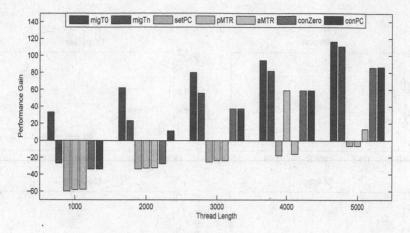

Fig. 6. Different short thread length

length when the RAM size is 4 KB. The x axis shows the thread length and the y axis shows the value of γ for different migration strategies. As we can see in the figure. If the thread is shorter than 1000 instructions, we shouldn't migrate the whole RAM. Only migrate T0 or T0–T4 has better performance. As the thread length increase, migrating the whole RAM performs better but still worse than migrating Ti. The results show that, for short thread, we migrate part of RAM is the better choice because short thread has relatively few instructions. The performance gain we get by improving prediction accuracy can't cover the cost of migrating whole RAM.

5.3 RAM Size

In order to explore the performance of BP migration under different RAM sizes, we use the DSE algorithm [8] to explore the proper TAGE parameters with RAM sizes of 8 KB, 12 KB, 16 KB, 24 KB and 32 KB. The windows size is 10,000 instructions, and the MSP is set to the 7,000,000th. Figure 7 shows the experiment results with different RAM sizes. We intuitively think that the MPKI should decrease with the increasement of RAM size for more branch information will improve the accuracy of branch prediction. But experiment results show that the RAM doesn't have any influence on MPKI since there is no law of the curves in Fig. 7. As we mentioned in Sect. 2, TAGE has a base predictor T0 and n sub-predictors (T1–Tn). Ti is indexed by a hash result of PC and length L(i) branch history. Actually, Ti indexed by short history length is much easier to be matched. Those indexed by long history length like Tn are rarely used. Although we increase the RAM size, which will increase the number of sub-predictors, the increased sub-predictors are rarely used. In addition, it will increase the overhead of migration. In order to verify our assumption. We compare MPKI of migrating T0–Tn with migrating T0–T4 and only migrating T0. As we can see in Fig. 8,

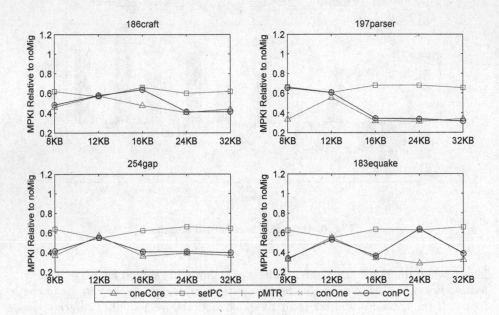

Fig. 7. Different RAM sizes

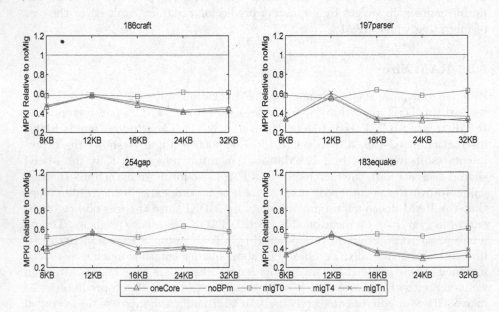

Fig. 8. Migration of T0, T0–T4 and T0–Tn

both migT4 and migTn outperform migT0. But migT4 and migTn have similar performance. So it proves that only increase RAM size is inefficient.

5.4   Discussion

Based on the experiment results, we find that migrating the whole RAM without migrating GHR is the best migration strategy. We set the statistic window size as 100,000 and the RAM size as 4 KB. For the thread on the idle core, it reduces MPKI by 43.46% averagely. For short thread, migrating the whole RAM is unadvisable. As we demonstrated in the experiments, migrating T0–T4 is the best strategy for short thread.

6   Related Work

Thread migration techniques for reducing power-density and load balance were considered in previous work [2,9–11]. [10] presents a technique which simultaneously migrates data and threads based on vectors specifying locality and resource usage. This technique improves performance on applications with distinguishable locality and imbalanced resource usage. In striving to exploit the ever-increasing availability of cores, compilers will employ techniques that create short threads to extract parallelism on multiple cores [12]. These papers try to achieve load balance or exploiting parallelism for multi-cores with thread creation or migration method. However, our purpose is to accelerate the BP training and increase prediction accuracy of Branch predictors.

Nowadays state-of-the-art predictors are derived from two categories of predictors: the neural-inspired predictors [13,14] and the TAGE-based predictors [7,15–17]. With equivalent storage budgets, the TAGE predictor that only uses global branch history generally outperforms neural global history predictors [16]. TAGE relies on prediction by partial matching and the use of geometric history lengths for branch history. [17] points out that branch prediction accuracy has relied on associating a main state-of-the-art single scheme branch predictor with specialized side predictors. It develop IUM (Immediate Update Mimicker) predictor approach for TAGE. Recent researches mainly focus on adding various small predictors in TAGE branch predictors to increase the prediction accuracy. [7,14] dedicate a small portion of their storage budget to local history components in addition to a large global history component. Such as, ITTAGE for the indirect branch prediction, COTTAGE combining TAGE and ITTAGE [15], TAGE-SC-L integrating the loop predictor and statistics corrector [7]. The purpose of these articles is to improve the performance of the TAGE branch predictor on a single core. However, this paper tries to improve branch prediction accuracy for multi-core architecture.

Previous work [3] demonstrates that significant branch predictor state is lost when control transfers across cores or contexts in a multiprocessor or multithreaded architecture. They point out that the critical loss of state lies entirely with the global branch history, as stored in the GHR. A thread migration model is given in [2]. The authors propose a training phrase which is to train BP on a new core during the thread migration. Our work's purpose is to accelerate the training phrase and increase BP's accuracy. [18] shows that more than 90% (up to 96%) of instruction cache accesses are common on cores executing a given homogeneous server workload. The authors share instruction execution information between cores using a dedicated storage. Our work is to migrate BP's local history and global history.

7   Conclusion

This paper investigates the performance implications of different BP migration strategies on multi-core Architecture. The main conclusion of our work, is that the branch prediction accuracy can be increased when a thread migrate to execute on an idle core by migrating branch prediction informations. We investigates several different migration strategies with different parameter settings. The simulation experiment results shows that we only migrate RAM can get the best performance for the most scenarios. The results also suggest that if the thread has less than 1000 instructions, we are not able to get performance gain by migrating BP because of migration overhead. In addition, if the thread is rather short, only migrating part of RAM has the best performance.

Acknowledgments. This work is supported by NSFC (No. U1435217, No. 61472435, No. 61672526 and No. 61433019).

References

1. Shim, K.S., Lis, M., Khan, O., Devadas, S.: Thread migration prediction for distributed shared caches. IEEE Comput. Architect. Lett. **13**(1), 53–56 (2014)
2. Constantinou, T., Sazeides, Y., Michaud, P., Fetis, D., Seznec, A.: Performance implications of single thread migration on a chip multi-core. ACM SIGARCH Comput. Architect. News **33**(4), 80–91 (2005)
3. Choi, B., Porter, L., Tullsen, D.M.: Accurate branch prediction for short threads. ACM SIGOPS Oper. Syst. Rev. **42**(2), 125–134 (2008)
4. Weissman, B., Gomes, B., Quittek, J., Holtkamp, M.: Efficient fine-grain thread migration with active threads. In: Parallel Processing Symposium, IPPS/SPDP 1998, vol. 17, pp. 410–414 (1998)
5. Binkert, N., Beckmann, B., Black, G., Reinhardt, S.K., Saidi, A., Basu, A., Hestness, J., Hower, D.R., Krishna, T., Sardashti, S., et al.: The gem5 simulator. ACM SIGARCH Comput. Architect. News **39**(2), 1–7 (2011)
6. CBP2014: https://www.jilp.org/cbp2014/
7. Seznec, A.: TAGE-SC-L branch predictors. JILP - Championship Branch Prediction (2014)
8. Zhou, C., Huang, L., Li, Z., Zhang, T., Dou, Q.: Design space exploration of TAGE branch predictor with ultra-small RAM. In: The 27th Edition of the ACM Great Lakes Symposium on VLSI (GLSVLSI). ACM (2017)

9. Chen, J., Shen, L., Wang, Z., Li, N., Xu, Y.: Dynamic power-performance adjustment on clustered multi-threading processors. In: 2016 IEEE International Conference on Networking, Architecture and Storage (NAS), pp. 1–2. IEEE (2016)
10. Shaw, K.A., Dally, W.J.: Migration in single chip multiprocessors. IEEE Comput. Architect. Lett. **1**(1), 12 (2002)
11. Lin, F.C.H., Keller, R.M.: The gradient model load balancing method. IEEE Trans. Softw. Eng. **SE–13**(1), 32–38 (1987)
12. Hum, H.H.J., Maquelin, O., Theobald, K.B., Tian, X., Gao, G.R., Hendren, L.J.: A study of the earth-manna multithreaded system. Int. J. Parallel Program. **24**(4), 319–348 (1996)
13. St. Amant, R., Jimenez, D.A., Burger, D.: Low-power, high-performance analog neural branch prediction. In: IEEE/ACM International Symposium on Microarchitecture, pp. 447–458 (2008)
14. Ishii, Y., Kuroyanagi, K., Sawada, T., Inaba, M., Hiraki, K.: Revisiting local history to improve the fused two-level branch predictor (2010)
15. Seznec, A., Michaud, P.: A case for (partially) tagged geometric history length branch prediction. J. Instr. Level Parallelism **8**, 1–23 (2006)
16. Seznec, A., Miguel, J.S., Albericio, J.: The inner most loop iteration counter: a new dimension in branch history. In: International Symposium on Microarchitecture, pp. 347–357 (2015)
17. Seznec, A.: A new case for the TAGE branch predictor. In: IEEE/ACM International Symposium on Microarchitecture, pp. 117–127 (2011)
18. Kaynak, C., Grot, B., Falsafi, B.: Shift: shared history instruction fetch for lean-core server processors. In: IEEE/ACM International Symposium on Microarchitecture, pp. 272–283 (2013)

Optimizing OpenCL Implementation of Deep Convolutional Neural Network on FPGA

Yuran Qiao[✉], Junzhong Shen, Dafei Huang, Qianming Yang, Mei Wen, and Chunyuan Zhang

National Key Laboratory of Parallel and Distributed Processing, College of Computer, National University of Defense Technology, Changsha, Hunan, People's Republic of China
qiaoyuran@nudt.edu.cn

Abstract. Nowadays, the rapid growth of data across the Internet has provided sufficient labeled data to train deep structured artificial neural networks. While deeper structured networks bring about significant precision gains in many applications, they also pose an urgent demand for higher computation capacity at the expense of power consumption. To this end, various FPGA based deep neural network accelerators are proposed for higher performance and lower energy consumption. However, as a dilemma, the development cycle of FPGA application is much longer than that of CPU and GPU. Although FPGA vendors such as Altera and Xilinx have released OpenCL framework to ease the programming, tuning the OpenCL codes for desirable performance on FPGAs is still challenging. In this paper, we look into the OpenCL implementation of Convolutional Neural Network (CNN) on FPGA. By analysing the execution manners of a CPU/GPU oriented verision on FPGA, we find out the causes of performance difference between FPGA and CPU/GPU and locate the performance bottlenecks. According to our analysis, we put forward a corresponding optimization method focusing on external memory transfers. We implement a prototype system on an Altera Stratix V A7 FPGA, which brings a considerable 4.76× speed up to the original version. To the best of our knowledge, this implementation outperforms most of the previous OpenCL implementations on FPGA by a large margin.

1 Introduction

Deep Convolutional Neural Networks (CNNs) bring about significant precision gains in many fields of computer vision, such as image classification, object detection and object tracing. While deeper structures produce higher accuracy, they demand more computing resource than what today's CPUs can provide. As a result, in the present situation, graphics processing units (GPUs) become the mainstream platform for implementing CNNs [1]. However, GPUs are power-hungry and inefficient in using computational resources. For example, the CNN version based on vendor recommended cuCNN lib can only achieve about 1/3

© IFIP International Federation for Information Processing 2017
Published by Springer International Publishing AG 2017. All Rights Reserved
X. Shi et al. (Eds.): NPC 2017, LNCS 10578, pp. 100–111, 2017.
DOI: 10.1007/978-3-319-68210-5_9

of the peak performance of GPU [1]. Hardware accelerators offer an alternative path towards significant boost in both performance and energy efficiency.

Usually, hardware accelerators are based on ASIC [2] or FPGA [3,4]. ASIC based accelerators provide the highest performance and energy efficiency but have to endure huge development cost. Owing to the reconfigurable nature, FPGA based accelerators are more economical considering the development expenses.

For years, FPGA developers suffer from the hard-to-use RTL (Register Transfer Level) programming languages such as VHDL and Verilog HDL. It makes programmability a major issue of FPGA. Thus, FPGA vendors begin to provide high-level synthesis (HLS) tools such as OpenCL framework [5] to enable programming FPGAs using high level languages.

Although developers can easily port codes originally designed for CPUs/GPUs to FPGAs with OpenCL framework, it is still challenging to make the OpenCL codes execute efficiently on FPGAs. The same code may exhibit different performance on different platforms due to the different architecture-related execution manners. Therefore, developers should consider the FPGA architecture when optimizing the OpenCL code.

In this paper, we make a deep investigation on how to optimize the OpenCL code on FPGA platforms. A CNN accelerator implemented in OpenCL is proposed which achieves the state of the art performance and performance density. The key contributions of our work are summarized as follows:

- We make a detailed analysis of running a CPU/GPU oriented OpenCL code of CNN on an FPGA. We explore the memory access behavior of the OpenCL FPGA implementation and point out the bottleneck of the code.
- According to the analysis result, we propose an optimized OpenCL implementation of CNN accelerator, focusing on efficient external memory access.
- We implement our design on an Altera Stratix V FPGA. A performance of 137 Gop/s is achieved using 16-bit fixed point data type. Compared with the original version, it achieves a speed up of 4.76×. To the best of our knowledge, this implementation outperforms most of the previous OpenCL based FPGA CNN accelerator.

The rest of this paper is organized as follows: Sect. 2 discusses the background of CNN and OpenCL framework for FPGA. Section 3 presents the performance analysis of the baseline code. The implementation details of our optimized design are demonstrated in Sect. 4. Section 5 provides the experiment result and Sect. 6 concludes the paper.

2 Background

2.1 Convolutional Neural Network

CNN is a trainable architecture inspired by the research findings in neuroscience. As Fig. 1 shows, a typical CNN structure consists of several feature extractor stages and a function stage. The feature extractor stages extract the input

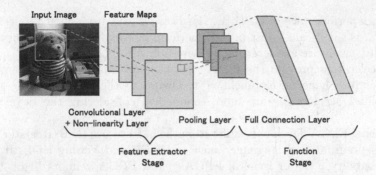

Fig. 1. A typical convolutional neural network structure

image's features and send them to the function stage. The function stage may be a classifier, a localizer or other function units customized by developers. According to the features, the function stage calculates the final result. A typical feature extractor stage consists of three layers: a convolutional layer, a non-linearity layer and a pooling layer. A function stage always consists of several full connection layers.

$$Y_r = bias + \sum_{q=0}^{Q-1} conv{<}X_q, K_{r,q}{>} \tag{1}$$

$$conv{<}X_q, K_{r,q}{>}[m][n] = \sum_{w=0}^{ks-1} \sum_{l=0}^{ks-1} K_{r,q}[w][l] * X_q[m*s+w][n*s+l] \tag{2}$$

Usually, convolutional layers generate more than 90% of the computational workload of a CNN model [6]. For a convolutional layer, Q input feature maps $X_0 \ldots X_{Q-1}$ are convolved with R*Q convolutional kernels $K_{r,q}$ (r = 0, 1 ... R − 1, q = 0, 1 ... Q − 1) to get R output feature maps $Y_0 \ldots Y_{R-1}$. Equations (1) and (2) show the procedure. *bias* is a value that is added to each pixel of Y_r. $conv{<}X_q, K_{r,q}{>}$ refers to the convolution between input feature map X_q and convolutional kernel $K_{r,q}$. *ks* is the size of the convolutional kernel and *s* denotes the stride that the convolutional window slides with each time. As the length limit, in this paper we only focus on the convolutional layers.

2.2   OpenCL Framework for FPGAs

OpenCL is an open standard for cross-platform parallel programming. As a high level synthesis (HLS) tool, the OpenCL framework for FPGA enables synthesizing designs described by a C-like language. It greatly improves the development productivity of FPGA. The OpenCL designs for CPU/GPU can also be easily ported to FPGA with little efforts. The OpenCL for FPGA liberates the developers from the burden of complicated periphery circuits design (e.g. PCIe, DDR, SerDes). The details of periphery circuits are transparent to the developers thus they can concentrate on the designing of kernel logics.

The hardware infrastructure of the OpenCL framework consists of two parts, an FPGA accelerator and a host computer. The OpenCL logic in the FPGA accelerator exists as an SoC. It consists of at least a global memory controller, a link controller to the host computer and a reconfigurable fabric. Developers use HLS tools to synthesize the OpenCL codes into kernel logics and program them to the reconfigurable fabric part. The host computer communicates with the FPGA accelerator through the host-accelerator link. As a common workflow, the host computer first offloads the data to the global memory of the FPGA accelerator. Then it starts the kernel logics to process these data. At last, the host computer gets the result back. In this paper, we use an Altera FPGA development kit to build our CNN accelerator. In particular, the global memory controller is a DDR3 controller, the link controller is a PCIe controller and the host computer is a desktop PC based on x86 architecture.

However, making the OpenCL code execute efficiently on an FPGA is not easy. It requires the awareness of many details about the OpenCL framework for FPGA.

3   Performance Analysis of the Baseline CNN OpenCL Implementation

In this section, we start with a CPU/GPU oriented OpenCL implementation of CNN provided by AMD Research [7]. We will consider it as a baseline version.

For convolutional layers, the baseline code first converts the convolutions to a matrix multiplication to utilize the efficient BLAS (Basic Linear Algebra Subprograms) library for CPU/GPU. As the computational workload of full connection layers is also matrix multiplication, this method simplifies the accelerator design.

Figure 2 shows the procedure of converting the convolutions to a matrix multiplication. Since a two-dimensional matrix is stored as an array physically, both the convolutional kernels and the output feature maps keep their data structures unchanged. Only the input feature maps need to be reorganized as the Map_matrix. Thus the computation of a convolutional layer can be divided into two parts: reorganizing the input feature maps to Map_matrix and calculating the matrix multiplication.

In the first step, there is no arithmetic operation. The main factor that determines the execution time is the memory access. As Fig. 3 shows, the baseline version divides the Map_matrix into several column vectors, each of which consists of ks^2 pixels in a convolutional window. Each work_item loads these ks^2 pixels form a input feature map and stores them back to the Map_matrix as a column vector. We can see that the memory access of each work_item to the input feature maps is in a sliding window pattern. The memory access pattern to the Map_matrix is in per-column manner.

For a DDR 3 system, the time consumption of memory access is determined by the number of memory transactions and the physical bandwidth of external memory. Each memory transaction consists of two phases: prepare phase and burst phase. The burst phase consists of several memory transmits. Assuming

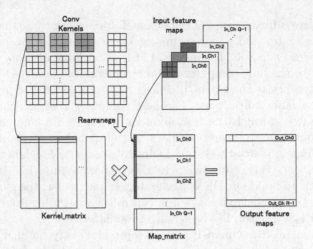

Fig. 2. The procedure of converting convolutions to matrix multiplications

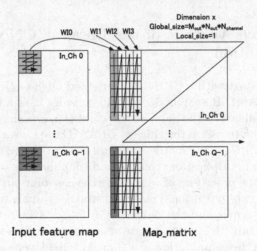

Fig. 3. The memory access pattern of the baseline version

that the kernel has M transactions and each transactions has a burst phase with N transmits ($burst\_length = N$), the time of memory access of a kernel is:

$$T_{mem} = \sum_{j=1}^{M} T_{transaction\_j} \tag{3}$$

$$T_{transaction\_j} = T_{prepare\_j} + T_{burst\_j} \tag{4}$$

$$T_{burst\_j} = \sum_{i=1}^{N} T_{transmit\_ij} \tag{5}$$

The transmits in the same burst access memory with continuous physical addresses. Moreover, if the memory access addresses are continuous, multiple transmits can be coalesced into a single wide transmit. Also, multiple bursts can be coalesced into one longer burst. By coalescing the transmits and bursts, we can reduce the proportion of prepare phase in the time of memory access and improve the utilization rate of memory bandwidth. Thus, continuous memory access is an essential factor for better performance.

From Fig. 3, we can see that for a single work_item, the length of the longest continuous memory access to the input feature maps is ks. However, this length cannot dominate $T_{transaction}$, and it is $T_{prepare}$ that will form most of the memory access time. In the output feature maps, there is no address-continuous memory access. Thus the single work_item can not make the best use of the memory bandwidth. Furthermore there are overlapped and adjacent data accesses between adjacent work_items. In a CPU/GPU platform, such data locality can be exploited by the cache hierarchy and multiple memory access can be merged. However, in a typical FPGA system, there is no ready-made cache to use. The OpenCL compiler can coalesce address continuous memory accesses from adjacent work_items automatically if the addresses are regular. To make things worse, the computation of addresses in the baseline version is very complicated, thus today's HLS tools can not recognize the data locality between adjacent work_items. For the reasons above, the memory access must be optimized.

The second step is a matrix multiplication. Most implementations of matrix multiplication in GPU/CPU use BLAS library to achieve a efficient execution. However, there is no BLAS library for FPGA using OpenCL so far. Therefore, we adopt the efficient FPGA OpenCL implementation from [8] to construct the baseline version. Such implementation has been well optimized for general-purpose matrix multiplication. However, the data precision of the baseline version is 32-bit floating point, but for CNN, it is redundant [6]. In the FPGA-specific design, low data precision may save DSP and logic resources.

4   Optimizing the OpenCL Design of CNN Accelerator on FPGA

In the last section, we discussed the baseline version and pointed out that the memory access pattern of the baseline version will cause low utilization rate of memory bandwidth. In this section, we will analyze the character of the algorithm and optimized the OpenCL implementation.

Figure 4 shows the relationship between input feature maps and Map_matrix. The coloured part of Map_matrix is corresponding to ks rows in input feature maps. Obviously, these rows are stored in external memory continuously. Compared to accessing these elements repeatedly, a better choice is to prefetch them to an on-chip buffer at first in an address continuous manner.

An optimized method is also shown in Fig. 4. Each work_group first reads a whole row of a input feature map and then write them in the format of the Map_matrix. For the prefetch part, the longest continuous memory access to the

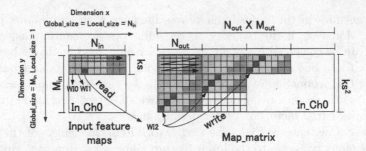

Fig. 4. The data locality in reorganizing input feature maps to map matrix and the task organization of work_items.

input feature maps in a work_group is the width of a input map (N_{in}). It is much longer than the baseline version. For the writing back part, the memory accesses between adjacent work_items are address continuous. The start addresses of the rows and the blocks can be calculated as a shared value among work_items in a same work_group. We use the local_id as the address offset so that the compiler can easily recognize the locality, thus the memory accesses in adjacent work_items can be coalesced automatically.

One pixel in the input feature maps is related to at most ks^2 elements in *Map_matrix*. Thus the efficiency of writing back dominates the memory access performance. We notice that in the optimized method above (OPT1 for short), the max length of continuous memory access to *Map_matrix* is N_{out} (the width of the output feature maps). Generally speaking, the map sizes of first several layers are large, so the burst length is large enough to make full use of the memory bandwidth. But in the last several layers, the map sizes are always small, the expense of the prepare phase becomes prominent. We can further optimize the kernel (OPT2 for short) by increasing the length of the continuous memory access.

Figure 5 shows the further optimization of the memory access. The *Map_matrix* is transposed so that the pixels in a convolutional window are address continuous. The convolutional windows with the same location in adjacent channels are also address continuous. Thus we can merge $ks^2 * Mc$ pixels into one memory transaction. Mc refers to the number of adjacent channels that can be merged. The transposed *Map_matrix* is divided to a 2-dimension grid. $Q * (M_{out}/Mc)$ work_items are used for the reorganizing task. Every work_item first loads ks rows from each of the Mc input feature maps to the on-chip buffer. In the example, the Mc is 2, the ks is 3. Then each work_item writes $ks^2 * Mc * N_{out}$ pixels into the transposed *Map_matrix*. In Fig. 5, The pixels in one dotted box are processed by one work_item $WI(y, x)$ ($x = 0, 1, ..., M_{out} - 1$. $y = 0, 1, ..., Q/Mc - 1$).

As for the input data, the total data size of OPT2 is ks times comparing to OPT1. However, the kernel performance will not degrade heavily for two reasons. Firstly, the writing back part occupies the most time of memory access.

Although we prefetch more data, the overhead is still ignorable. Secondly, the prefetch data are address continuous. The memory transactions can be coalesced. Thus the impact of the data size is not obvious.

For the output data, the maximum length of continuous memory access is $Mc * ks^2$. The total data size of OPT2 is the same as OPT1. Thus when $Mc * ks^2$ is larger than N_{out}, the kernel performance will be improved.

As the baseline version of the matrix multiplication part is already an FPGA oriented code, only minor modifications are needed to adapt it to our design. The size of matrix block of the baseline version is fixed. So we add some branch statements to enable variable matrix block size. For input data, the out-of-bounds elements are padded with zeros and written to the on-chip buffers. For the output data, before each work_item writing back its corresponding element, it will check whether the location is out-of-bounds. The out-of-bounds elements will not be written back.

The OPT2 generates Map_matrix^T, thus we need to modify the matrix multiplication kernel from $C = A * B$ to $C = A * B^T$. Each work_item can directly read the corresponding element from the transposed matrix block, but the address will not be continuous. We change the read order to the external memory to ensure the address continuous.

The baseline version adopts 32-bit floating point data format. In fact, research has proven that such high precision is redundant for the forward propagation [4,9] of CNN. We modify the optimized versions to 16-bit fixed point to increase the accelerator performance.

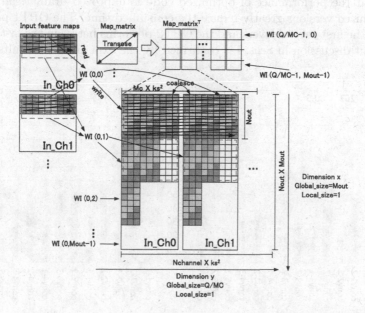

Fig. 5. A further optimizing of the memory access (OPT2)

The full connection layers can be processed by the matrix multiplication kernel independently. Although our implementation can handle matrix blocks of different sizes, using batched images can reach higher performance. In the full connection layers, for a single input image, the main computation is matrix-vector multiplication. The ratio of computation/memory access of a matrix-vector multiplication is low, because every element in parameter matrix only relates to one multiply-accumulate operation. The accelerator thus needs a high external memory bandwidth to read the parameter matrix. To achieve higher bandwidth, multiple images' full connection layers can be merged through combining a batch of matrix-vector multiplications into one matrix-matrix multiplication. Every element in parameter matrix needs to be operated with batch size elements in input matrix. The ratio of computation/memory access increases when the batch size increases.

5   System Evalution

We propose a prototype of our design in a DE5-net development board. The main chip of the board is an Altera Stratix V A7 FPGA. The work frequency of out kernel logic is 185 MHz. We implement our design using Altera OpenCL SDK 14.1. The most widely used model VGG-16 is chosen to be the benchmark.

Figure 6(a) shows the performance of reorganizing part. The vertical axis refers to the consumed time and the horizontal axis refers to different layers. Bars with three different colours represent the three different versions. The result shows that the performance of optimized code is improved dramatically. Both two optimized versions greatly reduce the consumed time. The OPT1 performs better in the first several layers and the OPT2 performs better in the last several layers. Our discussion in Sect. 4 is confirmed by the experimental results.

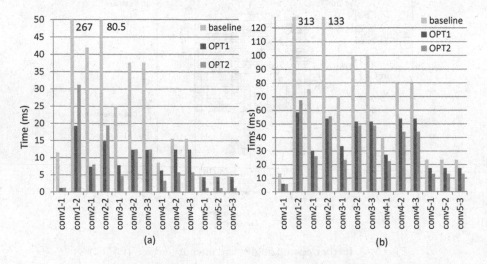

Fig. 6. Performance of the optimized versions

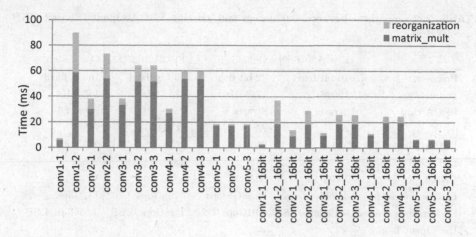

Fig. 7. Performance of different data precision

Table 1. Critical resource utilization rate in one chip

Resource	DSP	BRAM	LUT
Available	256	2560	234,720
Used	256	1456	179,850
Utilization	100%	57%	77%

Figure 6(b) shows the performance of the convolutional layers. The performance of optimized versions are still much better than the baseline version after the matrix multiplication part is added.

Figure 7 shows the performance under different data precisions, compared with the 32-bit float-point data type, the 16-bit fixed point data type nearly doubles the performance. It is because that performing a 16-bit fixed point multiply-add operation only needs 1 DSP in Altera's FPGA while performing a 32-bit floating point multiply-add operation needs 2 DSPs. Using 16-bit fixed point computation engine needs fewer DSP units and less on-chip memory resources. Compared with the baseline version, the optimized 16-bit fixed-point version has a speed up of 4.76×.

We also make a comparison between our implementation and other state-of-the-art FPGA CNN accelerators based on OpenCL. Table 1 shows the on-chip resource utilization of our implementation (OPT2). To unify the performance metric among different FPGA devices, we use performance density as the metric, the unit is Gops/DSP. As shown in Table 2, our implementation achieves the highest performance among recent works using the same device (Stratix V A7). [9] provides a throughput-optimized OpenCL implementation. To the best of our knowledge, it is the first OpenCL implementation for an entire CNN model on FPGA. However, there is still a big gap between its real performance and the peak performance of the FPGA they used. Comparing with [9], we present

Table 2. Comparison between our design and existing FPGA-OpenCL based CNN accelerators

	FPGA2016 [9]	Cnnlab [10]	FPGA2017 [11]	Our design
Precision	16-bit fixed	32-bit float	16-bit fixed	16-bit fixed
Frequency	120 MHz	171 MHz	385 MHz	185 MHz
FPGA chip	Stratix V	Stratix V	Arria 10	Stratix V
	A7	A7	GX1150	A7
DSP available	256	256	1518	256
DSP used	–	162	1378	256
CNN type	VGG-16	AlexNet	VGG-16	VGG-16
Real performance	47.5Gops	25.56GFlops	1790Gops	137Gops
Performance density	0.19Gops/DSP	0.01Gops/DSP	1.18Gops/DSP	0.53Gops/DSP
Use OpenCL only	✓	✓	✗	✓

a better memory access design and get a 2.88x speed up on the same device. [10] presents a CNN framework that using GPU and FPGA-based accelerators. They make more effort on compatibility while we focus on performance using FPGA. Compared with [10], our design has a speed up of 5.35×. [11] uses System Verilog to implement a CNN accelerator and package it into the OpenCL IP library. This work achieves a very high performance and gets better performance density than ours. However, in fact this work is an RTL design. Compared with HLS designs, the RTL design can exploit more hardware details. Thus it can get higher frequency and efficiency easily, whereas the major benefit of OpenCL design is better reusability and shorter development cycle.

6   Conclusion

In this paper, we have proposed an optimized CNN accelerator design using OpenCL FPGA. By analyzing the OpenCL implementation for CPU/GPU, we find that the bottleneck is the external memory access, because the memory system of FPGA is much different with CPU/GPU. Then we optimize the CNN design. Effort is made on the data re-arrangement and coalescing the memory accesses are applied for better usage of the external memory bandwidth. A prototype system is built. Compared with the baseline version, a performance speed-up of 4.76× is achieved. Our implementation on the Altera Stratix V device achieves a 137 Gop/s throughput under 185 MHz working frequency. This performance outperforms most of the prior work using OpenCL on FPGA.

Acknowledgement. This research is supported by the National Key Research and Development program under No. 2016YFB1000401, the National Nature Science Foundation of China under NSFC No. 61502509, 61402504, and 61272145; the National High Technology Research and Development Program of China under No. 2012AA012706; and the Research Fund for the Doctoral Program of Higher Education of China under SRFDP No. 20124307130004.

References

1. Chetlur, S., Woolley, C., Vandermersch, P., Cohen, J., Tran, J., Catanzaro, B., Shelhamer, E.: cuDNN: efficient primitives for deep learning. arXiv preprint arXiv:1410.0759 (2014)
2. Chen, Y., Luo, T., Liu, S., Zhang, S., He, L., Wang, J., Li, L., Chen, T., Xu, Z., Sun, N., et al.: DaDianNao: a machine-learning supercomputer. In: Proceedings of the 47th Annual IEEE/ACM International Symposium on Microarchitecture, pp. 609–622. IEEE Computer Society (2014)
3. Zhang, C., Li, P., Sun, G., Guan, Y., Xiao, B., Cong, J.: Optimizing FPGA-based accelerator design for deep convolutional neural networks. In: Proceedings of the 23rd ACM/SIGDA International Symposium on Field-Programmable Gate Arrays (FPGA), pp. 161–170. ACM (2015)
4. Qiu, J., Wang, J., Yao, S., Guo, K., Li, B., Zhou, E., Yu, J., Tang, T., Xu, N., Song, S., et al.: Going deeper with embedded FPGA platform for convolutional neural network. In: Proceedings of the 24th ACM/SIGDA International Symposium on Field-Programmable Gate Arrays (FPGA), pp. 26–35. ACM (2016)
5. Czajkowski, T.S., Aydonat, U., Denisenko, D., Freeman, J., Kinsner, M., Neto, D., Wong, J., Yiannacouras, P., Singh, D.P.: From OpenCL to high-performance hardware on FPGAs. In: 22nd International Conference on Field Programmable Logic and Applications (FPL), pp. 531–534. IEEE (2012)
6. Lin, D., Talathi, S., Annapureddy, S.: Fixed point quantization of deep convolutional networks. In: International Conference on Machine Learning, pp. 2849–2858 (2016)
7. Gu, J., Liu, Y., Gao, Y., Zhu, M.: OpenCL caffe: accelerating and enabling a cross platform machine learning framework. In: Proceedings of the 4th International Workshop on OpenCL, p. 8. ACM (2016)
8. Altera: Altera opencl design examples. https://www.altera.com/support/support-resources/design-examples/design-software/opencl/matrix-multiplication.html
9. Suda, N., Chandra, V., Dasika, G., Mohanty, A., Ma, Y., Vrudhula, S., Seo, J.s., Cao, Y.: Throughput-optimized OpenCL-based FPGA accelerator for large-scale convolutional neural networks. In: Proceedings of the 24th ACM/SIGDA International Symposium on Field-Programmable Gate Arrays (FPGA), pp. 16–25. ACM (2016)
10. Zhu, M., Liu, L., Wang, C., Xie, Y.: CNNLab: a novel parallel framework for neural networks using GPU and FPGA-a practical study with trade-off analysis. arXiv preprint arXiv:1606.06234 (2016)
11. Zhang, J., Li, J.: Improving the performance of OpenCL-based FPGA accelerator for convolutional neural network. In: FPGA, pp. 25–34 (2017)

ACO-inspired ICN Routing Scheme with Density-Based Spatial Clustering

Jianhui Lv[1], Xingwei Wang[2(✉)], and Min Huang[3]

[1] College of Computer Science and Engineering,
Northeastern University, Shenyang 110169, China
lvjianhui2012@163.com
[2] College of Software, Northeastern University, Shenyang, 110169, China
wangxw@mail.neu.edu.cn
[3] College of Information Science and Engineering, Northeastern University,
Shenyang 110819, China
mhuang@mail.neu.edu.cn

Abstract. This paper proposes a new Ant Colony Optimization (ACO)-inspired Information-Centric Networking (ICN) routing scheme with Density-based Spatial Clustering (DSC). At first, the content concentration model is established with network load to address interest routing; in particular, we investigate the failed situation of content retrieval. Then, the dot product method is used to compute similarity relation between two routers, which is considered as clustering reference attribute. In addition, DSC is exploited to detect core nodes which are used to cache contents during the data routing process. Finally, the proposed scheme is simulated over Mini-NDN, and the results show that it has better performance than the benchmark scheme.

1 Introduction

In recent years, Ant Colony Optimization (ACO)-inspired solutions have been proposed to address Information-Centric Networking (ICN) routing issue [1–3]. In ACO-inspired ICN solution which relies on Named Data Networking (NDN) architecture, Interest packet and Data packet are regarded as Interest ant (Iant) and Data ant (Dant) respectively. Lv et al. [3] considered user interest request and established similarity relation between two routers by the cached contents, i.e., ACO-inspired ICN Routing with Content concentration and Similarity relation (AIRCS). During the Iant routing process, similarity relation was regarded as a significant inspired factor to conduct the forwarding of Iant. This paper improves AIRCS based on Density-based Spatial Clustering (DSC), and the major contributions are summarized as follows. (i) The dot product method is used to compute similarity relation between two routers, in order to save more computation time. (ii) For the failed Iant, the corresponding updating strategy of content concentration (pheromone) is different from that of the successful Iant, and the updating process considers network load. (iii) DSC based on similarity

© IFIP International Federation for Information Processing 2017
Published by Springer International Publishing AG 2017. All Rights Reserved
X. Shi et al. (Eds.): NPC 2017, LNCS 10578, pp. 112–117, 2017.
DOI: 10.1007/978-3-319-68210-5_10

relation is used to find core routers, in order to cache the multiple content during the Dant routing process.

2 The Proposed AIRD Scheme

2.1 Content Concentration Design

The computation of content concentration regarding the edge between routers R_i and R_j (denoted by $e_{i,j}$) is the fundamental task. Let $T_{i,j}(t,I)$ denote the total content concentration over $e_{i,j}$ at time t after $I(\in \mathbb{N})$ iterations,

$$T_{i,j}(t,I) = (1 - \rho) \cdot T_{i,j}(t, I - 1) + cc_{i,j}(t,I), \tag{1}$$

where ρ is a volatilization coefficient of content concentration, $1 - \rho$ is a residual factor of content concentration, and $0 < \rho < 1$ prevents the infinite accumulation of content concentration. In addition, $cc_{i,j}(t,I)$ denotes the content concentration over $e_{i,j}$ by some of m ($\in \mathbb{N}$) Iants after the $I-th$ iteration, and it is defined as follows.

$$cc_{i,j}(t,I) = \sum_{\lambda=1}^{m} \tau_{i,j}^{\lambda}(t,I) \cdot x_{\lambda}, \tag{2}$$

where $x_{\lambda} \in \{0,1\}$. Let ia_{λ} denote arbitrary Iant, here $\lambda \in \{1, 2, \cdots, m\}$: if ia_{λ} traverses $e_{i,j}$, $x_{\lambda} = 1$; otherwise, $x_{\lambda} = 0$. In addition, $\tau_{i,j}^{\lambda}(t,I)$ denotes the content concentration over $e_{i,j}$ left by ia_{λ} after the $I-th$ iteration.

When ia_{λ} finds the content within one iteration, $\tau_{i,j}^{\lambda}(t,I)$ is defined as follows.

$$\tau_{i,j}^{\lambda}(t,I) = \frac{cos(1 - e^{-pcon_j})}{hop_j \cdot L_{\lambda} \cdot I}. \tag{3}$$

where $pcon_j$ is the times which R_j provides the content, hop_j is the hop count between interest requester and R_j, and L_{λ} is the total distance traversed by ia_{λ} within one iteration. In addition, $cos(1 - e^{-pcon_j})$ is a decreasing function regarding $pcon_j$, and its function is to reduce and balance node load with large $pcon_j$.

When ia_{λ} cannot find the content within one iteration, $\tau_{i,j}^{\lambda}(t,I)$ is defined as follows.

$$\tau_{i,j}^{\lambda}(t,I) = \gamma \cdot \frac{hop_j^{-\sigma}}{L_{\lambda}}. \tag{4}$$

Among them, σ reflects the importance of Iant to the whole network during the process of updating content concentration; γ is a regulatory factor to avoid the situation where $hop_j^{-\sigma}/L_{\lambda}$ becomes too large or small.

2.2 Similarity Relation Computation

Suppose that R_i consists of h_i types of contents and each one is regarded as a class of user interests, then

$$R_i \sim \Big(int(i)_1, int(i)_2, \cdots, int(i)_{h_i} \Big), \tag{5}$$

where $int(i)_l$ is one type of contents, $1 \leq l \leq h_i$.

Suppose that $int(i)_l$ is quantified as $int(i)'_l$ which equals to l, and that $int(i)_l$ corresponds to $N(i)_l$ content items, then

$$R_i := \Big(N(i)_1, 2 \cdot N(i)_2, \cdots, h_i \cdot N(i)_{h_i} \Big), \tag{6}$$

Assume that R_i and R_j have p same types of contents, when R_i and R_j are adjacent, then

$$r_{i,j} = \frac{1}{M} \cdot \sum_{l=1}^{max\{h_i,h_j\}} \Big(l \cdot N(i)_l \cdot l \cdot N(j)_l \Big) = \frac{l^2}{M} \sum_{l=1}^{p} N(i)_l \cdot N(j)_l, \tag{7}$$

$$M = \max_{\forall i,j} \Big\{ \sum_{l=1}^{p} N(i)_l \cdot N(j)_l \Big\}, \tag{8}$$

where $r_{i,j}$ is the similarity relation between R_i and R_j. Especially when R_i and R_j are not adjacent, $r_{i,j} = 0$.

2.3 DSC-Based Core Detection

In this paper, the DSC-based method is used to determine core routers, and similarity relation between two routers is used as clustering reference attribute. Let $N_\varepsilon(R_i)$ denote the number of routers with a neighbourhood, and it is defined as follows.

$$N_\varepsilon(R_i) = \{R_j \in \boldsymbol{D} | mr_{i,j} \geq eps\}. \tag{9}$$

Among them, $\boldsymbol{D}$ is the ε neighbourhood regarding R_i; $mr_{i,j}$ is the clustering metric between R_i and R_j; eps is a threshold.

If R_i and R_j are adjacent, $mr_{i,j} = r_{i,j}$. If R_i is connected to R_j according to k routers, denoted by $R_{c1}, R_{c2}, \cdots, R_{ck}$ respectively, we have

$$mr_{i,j} = r_{i,c1} \cdot r_{c1,c2} \cdot \cdots \cdot r_{ck,j} = r_{i,c1} \cdot r_{ck,j} \cdot \prod_{q=1}^{k-1} r_{cq,c(q+1)}, \tag{10}$$

which indicates that $mr_{i,j}$ is computed by indirect method among $k+2$ routers.

Then, the definition about core router is shown as follows.

Definition 1 (Core router): If $N_\varepsilon(R_i) \geq \xi$, R_i is a core router, where ξ is a positive constant.

2.4   Routing Decision

The routing decision consists of two parts, i.e., ACO-based Iant routing and DSC-based Dant routing. The first one is same to that in [3,4]. If the number of iterations reaches the maximum, the Iant routing is finished and the Dant routing starts, as follows.

At first, content provider generates some Dants. Let Dn denote the number of Dants, and it is defined as follows.

$$Dn = \left\lceil \frac{Sc}{2^o B} \right\rceil, \tag{11}$$

where Sc is the content size, o is a positive integer, B is the unit of byte, and the operator of ceiling guarantees that Dn is a positive integer. Dn Dants are denoted by Dant(1), Dant(2), $\cdots$, Dant(Dn).

Secondly, for one of Dn Dants, it carries the corresponding content from content provider to interest requester along the path which provides the closest content copy for interest requester. When arriving at R_i, it first checks whether R_i is a core router. If yes, two cases emerge: (i) when Content Store (CS) is not full, the carried content is cached to R_i; or (ii) when CS is full, a replacement strategy is used and then the carried content is cached to R_i. Otherwise, it checks Pending Interest Table (PIT) directly to find an appropriate interface in order to forward itself.

Finally, interest requester checks whether the generated Dn Dants have been received. If yes, their carried contents are recombined in the order of Dant(1), Dant(2), $\cdots$, Dant(Dn). Otherwise, interest requester waits until all Dants arrive.

3   Simulation Results

The proposed ACO-inspired ICN Routing scheme with DSC (AIRD) is simulated over Mini-NDN, and Deltacom topology with 97 nodes and 124 edges [4] is selected to do the performance evaluation by sending 1000 interest requests based on 100 times simulation. $\alpha = \beta = \sigma = 1$, $\eta = m = 10$, $\rho = eps = 0.5$, $\gamma = 2$, $\xi = 3$ and $o = 8$.

Figure 1 shows routing success rate for AIRCS and AIRD. We can observe that routing success rate of AIRD mainly concentrates on 96% and 97%, whilst that of AIRCS mainly concentrates on 93% and 94%. The emergence of these abnormal results is suffered from the congestion of interest requests, which causes the instability of system. Besides, the data selection has a certain randomness. From the global perspective, AIRD has higher routing success rate than AIRCS, and two reasons are as follows. (i) AIRD handles the failed Iants besides the successful Iants and conducts them to gather around the closest content copy, which increases retrieval probability. (ii) AIRD uses DSC to find core routers to cache the content during the Dant routing process, which guarantees content retrieval, especially for the similar and even same interest requests.

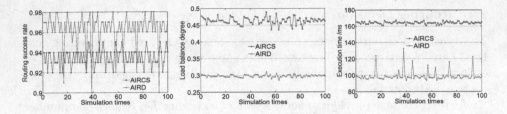

Fig. 1. Routing success rate.   **Fig. 2.** Load balance degree.   **Fig. 3.** Execution time.

Figure 2 shows load balance degree for AIRCS and AIRD. We can observe that load balance degree of AIRD is always lower than that of AIRCS, which means that AIRD is much more stable than AIRCS. Two reasons are as follows. (i) In the Iant routing stage, AIRD considers network load when updating content concentration. (ii) in the Dant routing stage, AIRD considers the fine granularity of content to divide the content into some pieces which are the uniform distribution; instead, AIRCS considers the content as an entire object, which leads to serious load in terms of some links.

Figure 3 shows execution time for AIRCS and AIRD. We can observe that execution time of AIRD is always smaller than that of AIRCS, and two reasons are as follows. (i) AIRD uses dot product method to compute similarity relation, which can save much more computation time than the using of absolute subtrahend method in AIRCS. (ii) AIRD designs and updates content concentration based on discrete model rather than continuous model, which decreases much more than AIRCS.

4   Conclusions

This paper extends and deepens the previous research on ACO-inspired ICN routing scheme, and the contributions are triple, i.e., (i) computing similarity relation based on dot product method, (ii) processing the successful packets and failed packets when the content concentration is updated and (iii) detecting core routers to cache the content during the Dant routing process. Then, the performance is evaluated, and the simulation results have shown that the proposed AIRD is more efficient and effective than the previous work.

Acknowledgments. This work is supported by National Natural Science Foundation of China (Grant No. 61572123) and National Science Foundation for Distinguished Young Scholars of China (Grant No. 71325002).

References

1. Shanbhag, S., Schwan, N., Rimac, I., Varvello, M.: SoCCeR: services over content-centric routing, In: Proceedings of ACM SIGCOMM (ICN), pp. 62–67 (2011)

2. Lv, J., Wang, X., Ren, K., Huang, M., Li, K.: ACO-inspired information-centric networking routing mechanism. Comput. Netw. **126**, 200–217 (2017)
3. Lv, J., Wang, X., Huang, M.: Ant colony optimization inspired ICN routing with content concentration and similarity relation. IEEE Comm. Lett. **21**(6), 1–4 (2017)
4. Lv, J., Wang, X., Huang, M.: ACO-inspired ICN routing mechanism with mobility support. Appl. Soft Comput. **58**, 427–440 (2017)

An Efficient Polarity Optimization Approach for Fixed Polarity Reed-Muller Logic Circuits Based on Novel Binary Differential Evolution Algorithm

Zhenxue He[1,2], Guangjun Qin[3], Limin Xiao[1,2(✉)], Fei Gu[2],
Zhisheng Huo[1,2], Li Ruan[1,2], Haitao Wang[4], Longbing Zhang[5],
Jianbin Liu[4], Shaobo Liu[4], and Xiang Wang[3]

[1] State Key Laboratory of Software Development Environment,
Beihang University, Beijing 100191, China
{hezhenxue,xiaolm}@buaa.edu.cn
[2] School of Computer Science and Engineering,
Beihang University, Beijing 100191, China
[3] School of Electronic and Information Engineering,
Beihang University, Beijing 100191, China
[4] Space Star Technology Co., Ltd, Beijing 100086, China
[5] State Key Laboratory of Computer Architecture,
Institute of Computing Technology, Chinese Academy of Sciences,
Beijing 100190, China

Abstract. The bottleneck of integrated circuit design could potentially be alleviated by using Reed-Muller (RM) logic circuits due to their remarkable superiority in power, area and testability. In this paper, we propose a Novel Binary Differential Evolution (DE) algorithm (NBDE) to solve the discrete binary-encoded combination optimization problem. Moreover, based on the NBDE, we propose an Efficient Polarity Optimization Approach (EPOA) for Fixed Polarity RM (FPRM) logic circuits, which uses the NBDE to search the best polarity under a performance constraint. To the best of our knowledge, we are the first to use DE to optimize RM circuits. The experimental results on 24 MCNC benchmark circuits show the effectiveness and superiority of EPOA.

1 Introduction

Traditional IC design based on the Boolean logic is facing serious power, area and delay challenges. Plenty of studies (e.g., [1–4]) demonstrate that compared with the circuits implemented by Boolean logic, the circuits implemented by RM logic are capable of achieving lower power and area. However, the existing polarity optimization approaches, which are based on GA or its variants, have a low convergence speed or are easily trapped into the local optimal solution [5, 6].

In this paper, we propose a binary version of the Differential Evolution (DE) algorithm according to the polarity characteristic of FPRM logic circuits, called Novel Binary Differential Evolution algorithm (NBDE), to find the optimal solution in binary

© IFIP International Federation for Information Processing 2017
Published by Springer International Publishing AG 2017. All Rights Reserved
X. Shi et al. (Eds.): NPC 2017, LNCS 10578, pp. 118–121, 2017.
DOI: 10.1007/978-3-319-68210-5_11

optimization space. Moreover, based on the NBDE, we propose an Efficient Polarity Optimization Approach (EPOA) for FPRM logic circuits, which uses the NBDE to search the best polarity.

2 An Efficient Polarity Optimization Approach for FPRM Logic Circuits

To enhance the global convergence ability, we introduce the elitism strategy to the NBDE. In addition, we propose a binary random mutation operator to increase the population diversity and improve the global searching ability.

2.1 Population Initialization

Firstly, a random number r is generated in [0,1]. Then, the j-th element of i-th individual x_{ij} is set to 1 (which represents polarity 1) if r is less than 1/2; otherwise, x_{ij} is set to 0 (which represents polarity 0).

2.2 Mutation Operator

To avoid the premature convergence and increase the population diversity, we propose a binary random mutation operator, which is represented as follows:

$$
v_{i,j} = \begin{cases} x_{i,j} + (-1)^{x_{i,j}} \cdot |x_{r2,j} - x_{r3,j}|, & rand \ge 0.5 \\ x_{best,j} + (-1)^{x_{best,j}} \cdot |x_{r2,j} - x_{r3,j}|, & rand < 0.5 \end{cases} \tag{1}
$$

where $v_{i,j}$ represents the j-th element of mutation vector v_i. $r2, r3 \in \{1, 2, \ldots, NP\}$ and $r2 \ne r3 \ne i$. x_{best} is the optimal individual in current population, and $rand$ is a random number in [0, 1].

Since the polarity of FPRM expression is taken as 0 or 1, the absolute value of difference vector is only 0 or 1 and the mutated variable is still 0-1 variable. Therefore, the mutation operator satisfies the closure. Moreover, whether one dimension variable can be mutated or not depends on the difference vector. Specifically, the $x_{i,j}$ or $x_{best,j}$ can be mutated (from 0 to 1 or from 1 to 0) when $|x_{r2,j} - x_{r3,j}| = 1$, which could increase the population diversity, improve the global searching ability and prevent the algorithm trapping into the local optimal solution. In addition, the probability of $x_{r2,j}$ is equal to $x_{r3,j}$ is increasing along with the population evolution. The $x_{i,j}$ or $x_{best,j}$ remain the same when $|x_{r2,j} - x_{r3,j}| = 0$, which could accelerate the convergence speed.

3 Experiments Results

The EPOA has been implemented in C and compiled by the GNU C complier. The results were obtained by using a PC with Intel Core i7 3.40 GHz with 4G RAM under Linux. In this paper, we set the logic minimization as the polarity optimization goal to validate the effectiveness of the EPOA.

We compared the EPOA with the GA based Polarity Optimization approach (GAPO) [7] and Whole Annealing GA based Polarity Optimization approach (WAGAPO) [8] on 24 randomly selected MCNC benchmark circuits. Moreover, we ran the GAPO, WAGAPO and EPOA 10 times on each circuit to reduce the impact of randomness on the results. The population size is set to 100, and termination criterion is that there is no improvement on the optimal solution in population over 10 iterations.

The comparison of GAPO, WAGAPO and EPOA on the average number of iterations and run time (in CPU seconds) over 10 independent run are listed in Table 1. Columns 9 and 10 denote the percentage of the number of iterations and run time saved by EPOA compared to GAPO. Columns 11 and 12 denote the percentage of the number of iterations and run time saved by EPOA compared to WAGAPO.

Table 1. Comparison of GAPO, WAGAPO and EPOA on the average number of iterations and run time

Name	Input	GAPO		WAGAPO		EPOA		Save1(%)		Save2(%)	
		iter	time(s)	iter	time(s)	iter	time(s)	iter	time(s)	iter	time(s)
b3	3	1	0.20	1	0.18	1	0.03	0.00	85.00	0.00	83.33
xor3	3	1	0.19	1	0.18	1	0.05	0.00	73.68	0.00	72.22
bw	5	6	0.96	3	0.42	1	0.06	83.33	93.75	66.67	85.71
xor5	5	8	0.82	4	0.57	1	0.05	87.50	93.90	75.00	91.23
m1	6	12	1.18	4	0.61	1	0.06	91.67	94.92	75.00	90.16
Z5xp1	7	12	1.22	5	0.63	1	0.06	91.67	95.08	80.00	90.48
lin	7	14	7.34	6	3.70	1	0.14	92.86	98.09	83.33	96.22
ex5	8	15	2.85	8	1.44	2	0.37	86.67	87.02	75.00	74.31
m3	8	14	2.21	6	1.28	3	0.55	78.57	75.11	50.00	57.03
rd84	8	22	14.92	7	5.62	4	0.62	81.82	95.84	42.86	88.97
1020	10	24	23.03	9	7.76	6	4.60	75.00	80.03	33.33	40.72
ex1010	10	20	15.78	12	6.14	7	4.81	65.00	69.52	41.67	21.66
br1	12	31	17.02	16	9.37	8	3.44	74.19	79.79	50.00	63.29
14_4color	14	55	30.08	23	15.26	10	7.05	81.82	76.56	56.52	53.80
Table 3	14	70	37.40	27	18.70	18	11.62	74.29	68.93	33.33	37.86
dk48	15	62	36.32	26	16.43	20	9.59	67.74	73.60	23.08	41.63
alcom	16	69	67.85	31	34.41	23	17.53	66.67	74.16	25.81	49.06
Table 5	17	81	84.99	52	52.90	31	22.42	61.73	73.62	40.38	57.62
src1	18	73	173.55	37	139.34	29	54.63	60.27	68.52	21.62	60.79
in2	19	84	158.64	41	127.88	33	32.26	60.71	79.66	19.51	74.77
mark1	20	127	240.91	40	195.61	30	60.75	76.38	74.78	25.00	68.94
mux	21	95	226.33	34	174.26	27	68.90	71.58	69.56	20.59	60.46
duke2	22	116	262.72	45	223.15	34	75.18	70.69	71.38	24.44	66.31
cordic	23	145	318.05	67	257.18	42	95.84	71.03	69.87	37.31	62.73

Compared with the GAPO, the greatest improvement in the number of iterations and run time, which were made by EPOA, are 92.86% and 98.09%, respectively. Moreover, compared with the WAGAPO, the greatest improvement in the number of iterations and run time, which were made by EPOA, are 83.33% and 96.22%, respectively.

4 Conclusion

In this paper, we propose a novel binary DE algorithm, called NBDE, which can solve the binary-encoded combination optimization problem. Additionally, based on the NBDE, we propose a polarity optimization approach, called EPOA, which uses the NBDE to search the best polarity of FPRM logic circuits. The experimental results over MCNC benchmark circuits show that the EPOA performs better than, or at least comparable to, the existing GA or its variants based polarity optimization approaches in terms of solution accuracy and convergence speed.

Acknowledgments. This work is supported by the National Natural Science Foundation of China (Nos. 61370059 and 61232009), Beijing Natural Science Foundation (No. 4152030), Fundamental Research Funds for the Central Universities (YWF-14-JSJXY-14), the fund of the State Key Laboratory of Computer Architecture (CARCH201507), the State Administration of Science Technology and Industry for National Defense, the major projects of high resolution earth observation system (Y20A-E03), and the fund of the State Key Laboratory of Software Development Environment (SKLSDE-2016ZX-15).

References

1. He, Z.X., Xiao, L.M., Ruan, L.: A power and area optimization approach for mixed polarity reed-muller expressions for incompletely specified boolean functions. J. Comput. Sci. Technol. **32**(2), 297–311 (2017)
2. Ma, X.J., Li, Q.Y., Zhang, J.L., Xia, Y.S.: Power optimization technique based on dual-logic diagram expression at gate level. J. Comput. Aided. Des. Comput. Graph. **29**(3), 509–518 (2017)
3. He, Z.X., Xiao, L.M., Gu, F.: An efficient and fast polarity optimization approach for mixed polarity reed-muller logic circuits. frontiers of computer science, pp. 1–15 (2017)
4. Rahaman, H., Mathew, J., Pradhan, D.K.: Secure testable s-box architecture for cryptographic hardware implementation. Comput. J. **53**(5), 581–591 (2010)
5. Wang, P.J., Wang, D.S., Jiang, Z.D.: Area and power optimization of ISFPRM circuits based on PSGA algorithm. ACTA ELECTRONICA SINICA **41**(8), 1542–1548 (2013)
6. He, Z.X., Xiao, L.M., Zhang L.B.: EMA-FPRMs: an efficient minimization algorithm for fixed polarity reed-muller expressions. In: International Conference on Field-Programmable Technology, pp. 253–256 (2016)
7. Sun, F., Wang, P.J., Yu, H.Z.: Ternary FPRM circuit area optimization based on genetic algorithm. J. Shandong Univ. (Nat.l Sci.) **48**(5), 51–56 (2013)
8. Yang, M., Almaini, A.E.A.: Optimization of mixed polarity reed-muller functions based on whole annealing genetic algorithm. J. Fudan Univ. (Nat. Sci.) **52**(3), 303–308 (2013)

Stem: A Table-Based Congestion Control Framework for Virtualized Data Center Networks

Jie Wu[1(✉)], Binzhang Fu[1], and Mingyu Chen[2]

[1] Institute of Computing Technology, Chinese Academy of Sciences, Beijing, China
jillwu1991@gmail.com
[2] University of Chinese Academy of Sciences, Beijing, China

Abstract. Congestion control is one of the biggest challenges faced by networks, and is enlarged in current data centers due to its large scale and variety of applications. Generally, different kinds of applications prefer different congestion control solutions. However, current mechanisms often exploit customized framework and require dedicated modules to realize certain functions, then deploying multiple solutions at the same time or reloading another solution when a new application is served is almost impossible. To address this problem, this paper proposes a solely table-based congestion control framework which is compatible with most of the current congestion control solutions. We implement the prototype with Open vSwitch, and the experiments results show that the proposed Stem could achieve the above claimed benefits with negligible overhead.

1 Introduction

Cloud computing has been viewed as an efficient way to provide on-demand IT capability to emerging applications, such as AI, IoT and 5G. However, the Cloud computing itself is still facing a lot of challenges. For example, traditionally VMs work in the same address space as the physical network and leads to the so-called address space problem [4]. To address these problems, the most efficient way is to exploit network virtualization.

Unfortunately, virtualized network leads to new challenges. For example, since different tenants may adopt different network stacks and configurations themselves, different reactions will be taken when congestions happen, which leads to "unfairness" in network resource utilization, especially when there are malicious tenants with specially modified network stacks. Besides that, when new network technology is found, it is hard for legacy applications to take advantage of it [2]. The last but not the least, Cloud data centers featuring multi-tenancy have to satisfy the customized requirements for network, like QoS,

This work was supported by the National Key Research and Development Program of China (13th Five-Year Plan) under Grant No. 2016YFB1000200, by National Natural Science Foundation of China (NSFC) under Grant No. 61331008, and Grant No. 61521092.

network services. Different tenants may want to do congestion control for distinct kind of traffic or distinguish congestion control laws for traffic with different preferences. These all show that there is an urgent need of the capability to specify congestion control mechanism for network operators.

The state-of-the-art solutions, such as [2,3], could solve part of the above challenges, but all failed to provide a highly extendable and unified framework to provide the Cloud vendors ability to dynamically provide tenant-specific congestion control mechanisms. To this end, this paper proposes the Stem, a solely table-based framework to implement congestion control mechanisms in virtualized data centers.

Generally, Stem takes a rate-based solution for a flexible rate-adjusting. To make the framework unified, we define a new OpenFlow action, namely EXEC_FUNC, to enable users to register their own congestion control logic. To validate the proposed solution, we build a prototype, which implements a DCTCP [1]-like congestion control solution, by exploiting the Open vSwitch. To this end, a new OpenFlow group, namely the "specific-match group", is defined to collect stateful statistics.

We summarize our contributions as follows:

1. A table-based solution is proposed for implementing flexible congestion control mechanisms for virtualized Cloud data centers;
2. A new OpenFlow action, namely the EXEC_FUNC, is defined to enable user-defined control logics with a uniform interface;
3. A new OpenFlow group, namely the specific-match group, is defined to collect stateful statistics.

2   Architecture of Stem

2.1   Overview of Stem

Stem consists of a sender-side module and a receiver-side module. Sender-side module is in charge of rate-adapting following user-specified congestion control law. The receiver-side module is responsible for recording congestion information, calculating the congestion status and setting the calculated status on feedbacks to sender. In the following, we will show how Stem could be realized in a solely table-based way. Figure 1 shows the architecture of Stem. Packets are enforced congestion indication support, ECN we use in Stem, at sender side. They will be marked Congestion Experienced(CE) when congestion is encountered in network. As packets arrive at receiver-side, congestion information is recorded in our proposed new OpenFlow group, namely *specific-match group*. Then, the congestion indications are masked to be invisible as upper VMs may not support ECN or as there shouldn't be further reaction to CE mark for those VMs who support ECN in order to achieve fairness among VMs, after which packets are sent to upper VMs. Stem gets statistics from *specific-match group*, calculates ECN mark fraction and sets that in the encapsulation header of ACK packets. When sender-side server receives ACK packets, it extracts the ECN mark fraction and send the packets to upper VMs after congestion indications get masked. Sender-side module calculates a new sending rate following tenant-specific congestion control algorithm, and enforces the new rate for Sender VM.

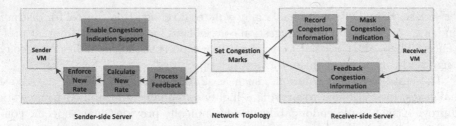

Fig. 1. Components of typical congestion control mechanism

2.2 A New Action: EXEC_FUNC

As the goal of Stem is to provide a framework of table-based congestion control, we provide a flexible and extendable way for users to add their own congestion control logic. To this end, we propose a userspace action: EXEC_FUNC(*function*), with the connotation of executing a user specified processing *function* . EXEC_FUNC action has only a parameter *function* which is simply a string. EXEC_FUNC extracts the string from OpenFlow message and developers can define their own function resolving the actual parameters of *function* to realize certain logic. We add in two functions in this use case. One is used for setting ECN mark fraction, and the other is used to do rate-limiting.

2.3 A New Group: Specific-Match Group

Stem takes a structure to group two flow entires, one for packets marked congested and the other for the rest, to collect congestion statistics and calculate the fraction of ECN-marked packets. When a packet executes the "group" action, it goes to the related "group" structure to execute actions specified in the group structure there. Basic components in a group structure are buckets. One bucket corresponds to one action(or action set). Originally, "select" group of OpenFlow has implemented a selection-method called "hash" to select a bucket. However, hash function is not flexible enough for us to implement network functions at most times. To address this problem, we add in "match" logic to implement a new selection method "specific-match". When a packet that has done a general match is directed to a "specific-match" group, it will match on the "match" part of the bucket to find the proper bucket to execute.

Now let's see how we use "specific-match" group to record congestion status. See Fig. 2, we create groups at receiver side for each sender VM to record the number of packets marked CE. There are two buckets in this group. One matches *tun_ecn*, ECN field on the outer header of tunnel. The other has no match field that it matches the rest of packets in this group. The "note" action is a kind of action that does nothing at all. We use "note" because we only want the hit statistics of these two buckets rather than executes a specific action. Obviously, if we use the hit times of the group to divide that of the bucket matches *tun_ecn*, we can get accurate ECN mark fraction at receiver side.

```
group_id=1,type=select,selection_method=specific-match,
bucket=bucket_id=1,match(tun_tos=3), actions=note:00,
bucket=bucket_id=2,actions=note:00
```

Fig. 2. Specific-match group to get ECN mark fraction

2.4   Congestion Control Algorithm

In the use case of solving "unfairness" in network resource utilization, Stem takes a DCTCP-like algorithm as an example. Particularly, the rate-decreasing part of DCTCP is kept while the increasing part is optimized by taking network congestion degree into account in the slow start phase, $rate \leftarrow 2 * rate/(1 + \alpha)$. The calculated sending $rate$ here is inversely proportional to α, congestion degree estimated for network [1]. That is, when network is more congested, Stem lowers the increase of sending rate more.

3   Evaluation

3.1   Environment Setup

We implemented a prototype in the OVS Version 2.4.0. To make the tradeoff between responsiveness and performance, we set the sampling proportion to 3000:1. Servers we use are HuaWei RH2258, with CPU of Intel(R) Xeon(R) E5645, 12 CPU cores, 2 hardware threads per core, 32G memory and all NICs are 1 Gbps. We take one server installed OVS as the switch(we call it OVS switch later) to connect servers and use TC RED for ECN marking. VMs in servers are emulated by qemu(with KVM enabled) and connected into network by Stem, or unmodified OVS as the baseline. The encapsulation protocol we take is VXLAN for the Overlay network virtualization environment.

3.2   Evaluation Results

Overhead. We run a single long iperf3 flow between a sender-side VM and a receiver-side VM, in that there isn't congestion in network. Though only rate-increasing logic is executed in this experiment, we don't think there is obvious difference in the overhead between rate-increasing and rate-decreasing logic. As there's a 50 bytes outer header for VXLAN, we set the "-M" (MSS) option of iperf3 to 1300 to not exceed MTU. The experiment result shows that Stem not only keeps the line rate of network but also gets a more stable rate. Due to the space limit, the figure is omitted.

Fairness. We apply all VMs with the same congestion control law in Sect. 2.4 to achieve fairness. We run VM1 in Server1 with network stack CUBIC and VM2 with DCTCP in Server2. We set the threshold of ECN marking for RED to 20 packets. VM1 runs an iperf flow to VM3 in Server3 and after 5 s VM2 runs an iperf flow to VM3 too. From Fig. 3, the experiment taken in an unmodified

OVS environment, we can see, DCTCP flow almost makes CUBIC bandwidth decrease to 0. Figure 4 is the result of the same experiment we take with Stem, we can see that fairness can be achieved in use of Stem.

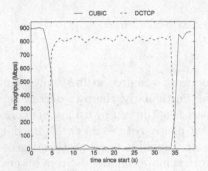

Fig. 3. DCTCP and CUBIC fairness in unmodified OVS environment

Fig. 4. DCTCP and CUBIC fairness in Stem

4 Conclusion

In this paper, we propose Stem, a table-based framework of user-defined congestion control for multi-tenant cloud computing. To achieve the goal, Stem first defines an OpenFlow action: EXEC_FUNC(*function*), which works as an interface to add new actions in more easily. After that, Stem proposes "specific-match group", which makes it possible to record the congestion status of any traffic defined by an OpenFlow entry. Stem implements a rate-based DCTCP-like algorithm in vSwitch to enforce the same congestion control law for all the VMs attached to that switch to get fairness.

References

1. Alizadeh, M., Greenberg, A., Maltz, D.A., Padhye, J., Patel, P., Prabhakar, B., Sengupta, S., Sridharan, M.: Data center tcp (dctcp). In: ACM SIGCOMM Computer Communication Review, vol. 40, pp. 63–74. ACM (2010)
2. Cronkite-Ratcliff, B., Bergman, A., Vargaftik, S., Ravi, M., McKeown, N., Abraham, I., Keslassy, I.: Virtualized Congestion Control. In: Proceedings of the 2016 Conference on ACM SIGCOMM 2016 Conference, pp. 230–243. ACM (2016)
3. He, K., Rozner, E., Agarwal, K., Gu, Y.J., Felter, W., Carter, J., Akella, A.: AC/DC TCP: virtual congestion control enforcement for datacenter networks. In: Proceedings of the 2016 Conference on ACM SIGCOMM 2016 Conference, pp. 244–257. ACM (2016)
4. Koponen, T., Amidon, K., Balland, P., Casado, M., Chanda, A., Fulton, B., Ganichev, I., Gross, J., Ingram, P., Jackson, E., et al.: Network virtualization in multi-tenant datacenters. In: 11th USENIX Symposium on Networked Systems Design and Implementation (NSDI 14), pp. 203–216 (2014)

SDAC: Porting Scientific Data to Spark RDDs

Tian Yang[1,2][(✉)], Kenjiro Taura[2], and Liu Chao[1]

[1] School of Computer Science and Engineering,
Beihang University, Beijing 100191, China
`yang@eidos.ic.i.u-tokyo.ac.jp`
[2] Graduate School of Information Science and Technology,
The University of Tokyo, Tokyo 113-0033, Japan

Abstract. Scientific data processing has exposed a range of technical problems in industrial exploration and specific-domain applications due to its huge input volume and data format diversity. While Big Data analytic frameworks such as Hadoop and Spark lack their native supports for processing increasing heterogeneous scientific data efficiently. In this paper, we introduce our work named SDAC (Scientific Data Auto Chunk) for porting various scientific data to RDDs to support parallel processing and analytics in Apache Spark framework. With the integration of auto-chunk task granularity-specify method, a better-planned theoretical pipeline can be derived to navigate data partitioning and parallel I/O. We showcase performance comparison with H5Spark within 6 benchmarks in both standalone and distributed mode. Experimental results showed SDAC module achieved an overall improvement of 2.1 times over H5Spark in standalone mode, and 1.34 times in distributed mode.

Keywords: Scientific data · Spark · RDDs · HDF5

1 Introduction

Science is increasingly becoming data-driven [1]. Nowadays, with exponentially proliferating of scientific data volume generated from scientific instruments and computer simulations, the storage capacity, processing efficiency and analytical accuracy are becoming critical challenging. To address these issues, ad-hoc frameworks such as Hadoop and Spark are taken into account. With the seamless integration of MapReduce programming paradigm, rapidly manipulating large amounts of data in parallel becomes feasible. Meanwhile a range of scientific data formats such as HDF5 (Hierarchical Data Format 5) [2] and NetCDF (The Network Common Data Format) [3] are put forward with the similar purpose of solving high volume data storage and platform-independent processing, and have been well proved for specific-domain study and analytics. However, when it comes to utilize parallel frameworks such Spark for processing scientific data, some technical defects are exposed such as lacking methods to specify semantic

© IFIP International Federation for Information Processing 2017
Published by Springer International Publishing AG 2017. All Rights Reserved
X. Shi et al. (Eds.): NPC 2017, LNCS 10578, pp. 127–130, 2017.
DOI: 10.1007/978-3-319-68210-5_13

indexing delimiters as pointed by "Scientists need a way to use intelligent indices and data organizations to subset the search" in [1].

In this paper, we introduce our module SDAC (Scientific Data Auto Chunk) to bridge the gap between scientific data and Spark RDDs. In order to be better fitted for MapReduce paradigm in Spark, we propose an auto-chunk algorithm to improve the data parallelism level by partitioning the data layout into pre-defined chunks. SDAC is available at http://github.com/TYoung1221/SDAC.

2   Methodology

2.1   Overview of SDAC

In this paper, we design and implement a module named SDAC (Scientific Data Auto Chunk) to enable various scientific data processing atop Spark framework. The architecture of SDAC module is illustrated in Fig. 1(a).

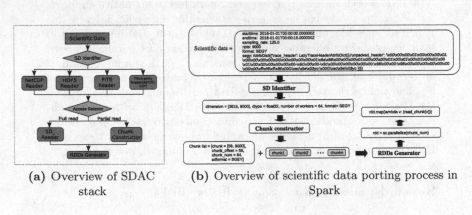

(a) Overview of SDAC stack

(b) Overview of scientific data porting process in Spark

Fig. 1. SDAC stack and porting process

In order to seamlessly integrate scientific data with Spark RDDs, we propose 3 components to implement the porting process:

1. SD Identifier: Recognize scientific data format and map with corresponding read method.
2. Access Selector: Decide data access strategy to optionally process the file entirely or to process in parallel for performance improvement.
3. RDDs Generator: Implement the bridge to port scientific data to RDDs by first parallelizing a collection of total chunk numbers from auto-chunk output. This porting process is shown in Fig. 1(b). Note that the input scientific data has 3815 rows and 9000 columns and is in SGY format.

In SDAC, we reference the Spark vanilla way of RDDs generation by parallelizing the total number of chunks from auto-chunk calculated output. Then the generated RDDs will be mapped with corresponding chunks to generate sub RDDs for distributing among workers.

2.2 Auto-Chunk Algorithm

We then propose an auto-chunk algorithm to calculate a better-planned task granularity to navigate in parallel operation. First, a dimension array to specify the chunk unit size is calculated collaboratively by total amount of input multi-dimensional array and available computer resources. Once the chunk dimension size is determined, a B-tree structure will be generated which contains chunk index and chunk offset for retrieving in parallel. The details of the auto-chunk algorithm is shown as follows:

Algorithm 1. Auto-chunk Algorithm

Precondition: n_w is number of workers in Spark, n_d is dimension of scientific data.

1: **function** auto_chunk(n_w, n_d)
2:     **if ALL** $i \in n_d$ mod $n_w \neq 0$ **then**
3:         $min_{dim} = \text{argmin}_i(\text{abs}(i - n_w))$
4:         id = dimension.index(min_{dim})
5:         **if** $min_{dim} \geq n_w$ **then**
6:             chunk[id] = int(min_{dim}/n_w)
7:         **else**
8:             chunk[id] = 1
9:         **end if**
10:    **else**
11:        $min_{dim} = \text{argmin}_i(i \text{ mod } n_w == 0)$
12:        id = dimension.index(min_{dim})
13:        chunk[id] = int(min_{dim}/n_w)
14:    **end if**
15: **end function**

---

3 Experimental Evaluation

We evaluate SDAC performance comparing with H5Spark [4] via 6 benchmarks which are evaluated on one single machine with 4 AMD Opteron(tm) Processor 6380 CPUs with 64 cores and on 8 worker nodes with a 8-core 2.10 GHz Inter E5-2620v4, 16 GB of RAM and 4 Spark executor threads in each node. And 3 datasets including 14.15 GB HDF5 and 14.37 GB NetCDF data are involved in evaluation.

Figure 2(a) shows the overall speedups relative to H5Spark in standalone mode. In which, the benchmark results of Max, Min and PKTM draw speedups between 1.8x and 4.3x, and LR, Genetic and K-means draw smaller speedups between 1.2x and 2.0x. And Fig. 2(b) draws the overall speedups over H5Spark in distributed mode. In which the benchmark result of Max, Min and PKTM draw speedups between 1.2x and 2.3x, and Genetic and K-means get relatively smaller speedups between 1.0x and 1.5x.

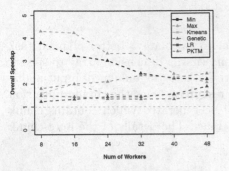 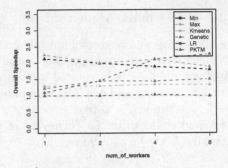

(a) The overall speedup compared with H5Spark with the number of cores ranging from 8 to 48

(b) The overall speedup compared with H5Spark with the number of workers ranging from 1 to 8

Fig. 2. Overall speedups comparison between SDAC and H5spark in standalone and distributed mode

4   Conclusion

In this paper, we propose a light-weight module named SDAC(Scientific Data Auto Chunk) atop Apache Spark framework to bridge the gap between heterogeneous scientific data to Spark RDDs. We describe our efforts in supporting scientific data formats such as HDF5, NetCDF, ADIOS, SGY and FITS. And an auto-chunk algorithm is integrated to navigate parallel I/O by offering a more meticulous strategy to determine task granularity by partitioning the input dataset into pre-defined chunks. We showcase the performance gains across 6 benchmarks compared with H5Spark in both standalone and distributed mode. As future work, we plan to exploit Spark GraphX analytics and machine learning library (MLlib) to make deeper survey of scientific data analytics.

Acknowledgments. This work was in part supported by Grant-in-Aid for Scientific Research (A) 16H01715, Japan.

References

1. Gray, J., Liu, D.T., Nieto-Santisteban, M., Szalay, A., DeWitt, D.J., Heber, G.: Scientific data management in the coming decade. ACM SIGMOD Rec. **34**(4), 34–41 (2005)
2. The hdf group, hierarchical data format version 5. http://www.hdfgroup.org/HDF5
3. Rew, R., Davis, G.: An interface for scientific data access. IEEE Comput. Graphics Appl. **10**(4), 76–82 (1990)
4. Liu, J., Racah, E., Koziol, Q., Canon, R.S.: H5spark: bridging the I/O gap between spark and scientific data formats on Hpc systems. In: Cray user group (2016)

Unified Access Layer with PostgreSQL FDW for Heterogeneous Databases

Xuefei Wang[1(✉)], Ruohang Feng[2], Wei Dong[1], Xiaoqian Zhu[1], and Wenke Wang[1]

[1] College of Computer, National University of Defense Technology, Changsha, China
{wishfay,wdong,zhu_xiaoqian,wangwenke}@nudt.edu.cn
[2] Umeng+ Company of Alibaba Group, Beijing, China
ruohang.frh@alibaba-inc.com

Abstract. Large-scale application systems usually consist of various databases for different purposes. However, the increasing use of different databases, especially NoSQL databases, makes it increasingly challenging to use and maintain such systems. In this paper, we demonstrate a framework for designing a foreign data wrapper (FDW) for external data sources. We propose a novel method to access heterogeneous databases, including SQL and NoSQL databases, by using a unified access layer. This method was applied in some real business applications of Alibaba, in which we were able to do various operations on Redis, MongoDB, HBase, and MySQL by using a simple SQL statement. In addition, the information exchange and data migration between these databases can be done by using unified SQL statements. The experiments show that our method can maintain good database performance and provide users with a lot more convenience and efficiency.

Keywords: Unified access layer · Heterogeneous databases · Foreign data wrapper

1 Introduction

In the big data era, a wide variety of non-relational NoSQL databases have been developed to meet massive data processing and analysis requirements. Different NoSQL databases are designed and built according to different feature orientations. In a practical project, in order to fully combine the advantages of using a variety of database capabilities, a large-scale system will often integrate these databases, including SQL and NoSQL, to support it [1]; this also brings some considerable challenges for deployment and maintenance. Typically, users must interact with these databases at the programming level with customized APIs. This reduces portability and requires system-specific codes. Some commercial companies have combined an SQL relational processor with a MapReduce query processor [2]. However, many of the most popular NoSQL databases, such as MongoDB and HBase, do not have SQL interfaces for their systems.

© IFIP International Federation for Information Processing 2017
Published by Springer International Publishing AG 2017. All Rights Reserved
X. Shi et al. (Eds.): NPC 2017, LNCS 10578, pp. 131–135, 2017.
DOI: 10.1007/978-3-319-68210-5_14

2   Related Work

Generally, data integration methods aim to integrate data arising from different SQL systems. However, NoSQL systems play an important role in many domains [3]. In [4], the Save Our System (SOS) was proposed, which defined a common API for Redis, MongoDB, and HBase. SOS makes it easy to access through different NoSQL databases, but it cannot handle SQL-based access well. In [5], a relational layer supporting SQL queries and joins was added on top of Amazon SimpleDB. However, this applies only to SimpleDB, and other NoSQL databases are not applicable. ISO/IEC 9075-9:2008 defined the SQL/MED, or management of external data, an extension to the SQL standard [6]. During information retrieval from heterogeneous source systems, there are three main challenges: (i) resolving the semantic heterogeneity [7] of data including resolving the structural (data model) heterogeneity of data, (ii) bridging differences in data querying syntaxes, and (iii) data integration method may decrease the performance of the system.

3   Design FDW for External Databases

Based on the SQL/MED method, we used PostgreSQL FDW as a platform to manage external data sources. As Fig. 1 shows, to design an FDW, we first need to analyze the target API set of external databases; that is, we must take care of the syntactic heterogeneity problem. Second, we need to design different SQL syntax for different data storage methods that correspond to the semantic heterogeneity problem. Finally, we need to design condition pushdown to execute a complex query without much performance loss. Following this framework, we designed and applied FDWs for HBase, MongoDB, MySQL and Redis in the business system of Alibaba. As an example, we will give a detailed overview of FDW for HBase, called HBase_FDW[1].

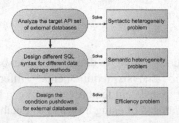   

Fig. 1. Design framework of FDW   **Fig. 2.** The process of using byte array data

Data Model and API. HBase is a sparse long-term storage, multi-dimensional, sorted mapping table [8]. The HBase API consists of: get, scan, put, and delete.

---

[1] This work can be accessed on GitHub: https://github.com/Vonng/hbase_fdw.

SQL Grammar. FDWs manage foreign data as 'relations'. We establish an abstraction for HBase according to the physical data model of HBase with the following quintuple: (rowkey family, qualifier, timestamp, value) to index a unique value. Then we set the type of these fields as byte array. For string users need to follow the encoding and decoding as Fig. 2 shows, and for other data types, they need to process data according to different serialization programs in the query statement.

Condition Pushdown. Pushdown means translating the 'where' clause in an SQL query statement to the corresponding external database API. By adding condition pushdown, we could minimize performance overheads in the system as much as possible. As Table 1 shows, we have done all the basic operations of HBase. Any complex operations can be split into a combination of these basic operations.

Table 1. Condition pushdown for HBase

Type of query	SQL statement	Original operation in HBase
Unconditional query	SELECT * FROM hbase.table	$\sigma = $ scan
Query with a rowkey	SELECT * FROM hbase.table WHERE rowkey = k	$\sigma_{key = k} = $ get(k)
Comparison	SELECT * FROM hbase.table WHERE rowkey BETWEEN k1 AND k2;	$\sigma_{k1 < key < k2} = $ scan(startRow $= k1$, stopRow $= k2$)
'in' expression	SELECT * FROM hbase.table WHERE rowkey in (k1, k2, ..., kn)	$\sigma_{key \, belongs \, to \, \{k1,k2,\cdots,kn\}} = $ getMultiple([k1, k2, ..., kn])
Regex	SELECT * FROM hbase.table WHERE name REGEXP regexp	$\sigma_{key \, \sim \, regexp} = $ scan(filter $= $ "RowFilter (='regexstring:regexp')")
List of columns	SELECT * FROM hbase.table WHERE column in (c1, c2, ..., cn)	$\sigma_{column \, belongs \, to \, \{c1,c2,\cdots,cn\}} = $ scan (column = [c1, c2, ..., cn])

4   Unified Access Layer via PostgreSQL

We carried out our research work on a business system of Alibaba, which needs to provide external queries of indicators. Each project team needs to write complex, repetitive code to handle business data queries. From project development testing to acceptance may take a group one or two months, which is very costly. So we built a unified access layer for public data, which greatly facilitated the R&D personnel who need to maintain the business logic; we called this new system EasyDB.

The architecture of EasyDB is shown in Fig. 3. Based on PostgreSQL, a unified access layer is built and makes all the other databases transparent for users. In this way, users can use SQL to operate all these databases conveniently.

In EasyDB, after a request is made by the user, it will be parsed by the controller in EasyDB. By matching different schemas, the request could be responded by the corresponding data model and DBMS. An SQL statement will be translated into the API of different databases by FDWs. By condition pushdown, all these native operations

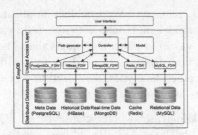

Fig. 3. Architecture of EasyDB   **Fig. 4.** A complex example in EasyDB

will be executed in external databases instead of dealing with the data fetched from external data. As Fig. 4 shows, a complex query which involves many different databases can be done by only using SQL.

5   Evaluation

In this section, we test our system in two aspects: efficiency and actual use value.

First, to evaluate the performance of the developed system, we executed runtime tests on EasyDB. Experiments were performed using a cluster with 25 nodes: each node has an Intel(R) dual-core 2.5 GHz processor, 4 GB memory, and HDD storage.

Dataset. Tests were performed on five databases, including PostgreSQL, HBase, MongoDB, Redis and MySQL. The number of data rows of each query in this test is 1,000,000.

Results. The results of the performance tests are shown in Fig. 5. **Entire running time** began when the user sent the request to the EasyDB, and the measurement ended when the operation was completed in the EasyDB. **Data retrieval time** began when the user request was sent from the unified access layer to the data source and ended when the operation was completed in the EasyDB. **Native query time** presents the running time of native database queries. The time overhead caused by unified access layer can be measured by the difference between the entire running time and data retrieval time, which only takes up 6.5% at most and 4.0% on average. In fact, for large-scale distribution heterogeneous databases, the main cost involves the round trip time (RTT), and the FDW only takes up a small part of the overhead. Thus, our method does not have much impact on the efficiency of the system, which makes the entire running time very close to data retrieval time.

Second, we conducted statistical studies on the development of multiple projects[2]. By using the unified access layer, a few weeks' work can be done in just a few days. At the same time, users can readily use various databases, even without much information about the data model or API of these databases.

---

[2] Statistical information of projects is obtained from software management system of Umeng+ of Alibaba Group.

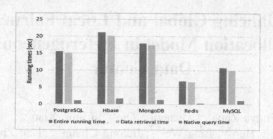

Fig. 5. Running times of queries of different databases

6   Conclusion

In this paper, based on a practical system, we designed a unified access layer for heterogeneous databases. We applied FDW technology to our production practice in order to solve practical problems, and we proposed HBase FDW to fill gaps in related fields. With only SQL, we can perform operations on all the databases in this system, and the experimental results show that the efficiency of our system is satisfactory.

Acknowledgment. The authors would like to thank the anonymous reviewers for their detailed and thoughtful feedback which improved the quality of this paper significantly. This work is funded by National Natural Science Foundation of China under Grant No. 61690203, No. 61379146 and No. 61272483.

References

1. Sellami, R., Bhiri, S., Defude, B.: Supporting multi data stores applications in cloud environments. IEEE Trans. Serv. Comput. **9**(1), 59–71 (2016)
2. Yang, H.C., Dasdan, A., Hsiao, R.L., Parker, D.S.: Map-reduce-merge: simplified relational data processing on large clusters. In: ACM SIGMOD International Conference on Management of Data, pp. 1029–1040. ACM (2007)
3. Botta, A., Donato, W.D., Persico, V.: Integration of cloud computing and internet of things. Future Gener. Comput. Syst. **56**(C), 684–700 (2016)
4. Atzeni, P., Bugiotti, F., Rossi, L.: Uniform access to non-relational database systems: the SOS platform. In: Ralyté, J., Franch, X., Brinkkemper, S., Wrycza, S. (eds.) CAiSE 2012. LNCS, vol. 7328, pp. 160–174. Springer, Heidelberg (2012). doi:10.1007/978-3-642-31095-9_11
5. Calil, A., dos Santos Mello, R.: SimpleSQL: a relational layer for SimpleDB. In: Morzy, T., Härder, T., Wrembel, R. (eds.) ADBIS 2012. LNCS, vol. 7503, pp. 99–110. Springer, Heidelberg (2012). doi:10.1007/978-3-642-33074-2_8
6. Lawrence, R.: Integration and virtualization of relational SQL and NoSQL systems including MySQL and MongoDB. In: International Conference on Computational Science and Computational Intelligence, pp. 285–290. IEEE (2014)
7. Ceruti, M.G., Kamel, M.N.: Semantic heterogeneity in database and data dictionary integration for command and control systems. In: Department of Defense Database Colloquium, p. 27 (1994)
8. George, L.: HBase - The Definitive Guide: Random Access to Your Planet-Size Data. DBLP (2011)

Balancing Global and Local Fairness Allocation Model in Heterogeneous Data Center

Bingyu Zhou[1,2], Guangjun Qin[1,2], Limin Xiao[1,2(✉)],
Zhisheng Huo[1,2], Bing Wei[1,2], Jiulong Chang[1,2], Nan Zhou[1,2],
Li Ruan[1,2], Haitao Wang[3], and Zipeng Wei[3]

[1] State Key Laboratory of Software Development Environment,
Beihang University, Beijing 100191, China
{xiaolm,zhouby}@buaa.edu.cn
[2] School of Computer Science and Engineering,
Beihang University, Beijing 100191, China
[3] Space Star Technology Co., Ltd, Beijing 100086, China

Abstract. Aiming at the problem that the bandwidth allocation method in heterogeneous data center can't take into account the global and local fairness, we propose an allocation method called GLA that satisfies fair attributes and can improve the utilization of system resources by nearly 20% when the number of clients are more than six contrasting with the existing methods. The algorithm is also protable and scalable that can adapt to most of systems.

1 Introduction

The existing methods of bandwidth allocation [6, 8] in the heterogeneous data center such as DRF, DRFH(e.g., [1–3]), BAA [4, 5] and UAF [7] have a poor performance for that the utilization only can up to 70% in the best situation and the usage of resource is unbalanced. Through contrasting the distribution result among above methods, we found the situation that the allocation in the entire data center meet the fairness but on each server is unfair or the global allocation shows unfairness and the total throughput is at a low level for applying fair allocation algorithm on each server. These methods are restricted to fair policies and the efficiency of global and local, so we must balance the allocation of global and local to enhance the utilization rate. The allocation model called *Balancing Global and Local Fairness Allocation(GLA)* we proposed in the paper can solve this problem. It includes global allocation strategy and local allocation strategy, meanwhile setting the global parameters to coordinate the consistency of the two strategies.

In the second part, we introduce the GLA model and implementation architecture. The performance evaluation results will be described in Sect. 3. In the end, we will conclude our work.

Published by Springer International Publishing AG 2017. All Rights Reserved
X. Shi et al. (Eds.): NPC 2017, LNCS 10578, pp. 136–139, 2017.
DOI: 10.1007/978-3-319-68210-5_15

2   GLA Allocation Model and Scheduling Architecture

The functions of GLA model are shown as follows:

$$\textbf{Maximize} \quad \sum_{i \in D} \left(\sum_{l=1}^{k} \left(x_{ild} \times \frac{1}{m_{il}} \right) \right) + \sum_{j \in S} \left(\sum_{l=1}^{k} \left(x_{jls} \times \frac{1}{h_{jl}} \right) \right) \tag{3.1}$$

$$\begin{cases} \sum_{l=1}^{k} \varpi_{il} = 1 \\ \sum_{l=1}^{k} (\varpi_{il} \times h_{il}) = 1 \\ i \in D(or \; i \in S) \end{cases} \tag{3.2}$$

$$\begin{cases} x_{ild} \times \left(\sum_{i \in D} + \omega \times \frac{C_{il}}{C_{il}} \times \sum_{j \in S} \frac{m_{il}}{h_{jl}} \right) \leq C_{dl} \\ x_{ild} \times \left(\sum_{i \in D} \frac{h_{il}}{m_{il}} + \omega \times \frac{C_{il}}{C_{il}} \times \sum_{j \in S} \right) \leq C_{sl} \\ \forall l \in V, \; i \in D_l, \; j \in S_l \end{cases} \tag{3.3}$$

$$\begin{cases} x_{ild} \geq \frac{C_{il}}{n}, \; x_{jls} \geq \frac{C_{il}}{n} \\ x_{ild} \geq x_{jls} \times \frac{m_{il}}{h_{jl}}, \; x_{jls} \geq x_{ild} \times \frac{h_{il}}{m_{il}} \\ \forall i \in D_l, \; j \in S_l \end{cases} \tag{3.4}$$

$$\begin{cases} \sum_{l=1}^{k} x_{ild} \geq \sum_{l=1}^{k} x_{jls} \times \frac{m_j}{h_j} \\ \sum_{l=1}^{k} x_{jls} \geq \sum_{l=1}^{k} x_{ild} \times \frac{h_i}{m_i} \\ \forall i \in D, \; j \in S \end{cases} \tag{3.5}$$

$$\begin{cases} \forall i,j \in D, \; if \; \sum_{l=1}^{k} x_{ild} \times \frac{h_i}{m_i} \geq \sum_{l=1}^{k} x_{jld} \times \frac{h_i}{m_j}, \; then \; \sum_{l=1}^{k} x_{ild} \leq \sum_{l=1}^{k} x_{jld} \\ \forall i,j \in S, \; if \; \sum_{l=1}^{k} x_{ils} \times \frac{m_i}{h_i} \geq \sum_{l=1}^{k} x_{jls} \times \frac{m_j}{h_j}, \; then \; \sum_{l=1}^{k} x_{ils} \leq \sum_{l=1}^{k} x_{jls} \end{cases} \tag{3.6}$$

The scheduling architecture of the heterogeneous data center has two layers (Fig. 1), GLA is deployed in the second layer. The first layer scheduler assigns the requests of clients to the corresponding server in terms of the original weight, the second tier calculate the bandwidth allocated to each client based on the GLA algorithm. Different form other algorithm, the global parameters produced by GLA will be send to the first layer to assist the next allocation. The algorithm obeys the principle of conservation. The throughput of allocation subjects to the limitations that are presented into progressive from local to the whole.

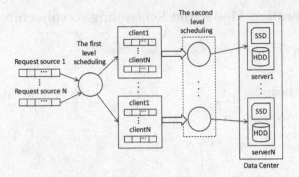

Fig. 1. The scheduling architecture of heterogeneous data center

3 Performance Evaluation

We use a parallel simulator called PFSsim and a Linux cluster test I/O performance of GLA. The cluster are configured as AMD Quad-core processor, 8 GB RAM, 1 TB Seagate 7200RPM hard drive, on which we configure three servers: $server_1(HDD : 500IOPS, SSD : 1000IOPS)$, $server_2(HDD : 1000IOPS, SSD : 2000IOPS)$, $server_3(HDD : 3000 IOPS, SSD : 500IOPS)$. The workloads we used are from Umass Trace and Microsoft Exchange server. The test will be compared between BAA and UAF.

Figure 2(a) show the allocation of UAF and GLA on each server for PFSsim. It's obviously that the local allocation of UAF does not obey fair properties. For GLA, the hit ratios on each server for clients are $h_{11} = h_{12} = h_{13} = 0.4$, $h_{21} = h_{22} = 0.96$, $h_{23} = 0.65$, $h_{31} = h_{32} = 0.9$, $h_{33} = 0.38$, the global hit ratios are $\sum_{l=1}^{3}(h_{1l} \times \varpi_{1l}) = 0.4 = h_1$, $\sum_{l=1}^{3}(h_{2l} \times \varpi_{21}) = 0.9 = h_2$, $\sum_{l=1}^{k}(h_{3l} \times \varpi_{3l}) = 0.8 = h_3$. We also get $A_{1,hdd} \geq \{A_{2,hdd}, A_{3,hdd}\}$, $A_{2,ssd} \geq A_{1,ssd}$, hence the GLA is a fair strategy. Figure 2(b) shows the throughput will increase with the number of clients arise, GLA has a best performance in the large-clients cases.

Figure 3 express the throughput of GLA are 20% high than that of UAF on Linux cluster, GLA model has practical significance.

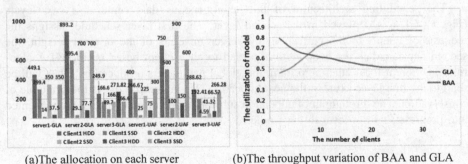

(a)The allocation on each server   (b)The throughput variation of BAA and GLA

Fig. 2. The comparison of utilization between GLA, BAA and UAF

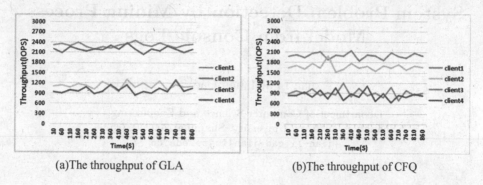

(a)The throughput of GLA   (b)The throughput of CFQ

Fig. 3. The throughput GLA and CFQ for four clients

4 Conclusion

In this paper, we focus on the problem that the existing allocation methods can't balance global and local fairness, and propose a bandwidth allocation algorithm called GLA. Through experiments, we exhibit that GLA is fairness and improve the throughput of heterogeneous data center for 19.8 % when the number of clients are more than six. GLA is more suitable for large-scale clients.

Acknowledgments. This work is supported by the National Natural Science Foundation of China under Grant No. 61370059 and No. 61232009, Beijing Natural Science Foundation under Grant No. 4152030, the fund of the State Key laboratory of Software Development Environment under Grant No. SKLSDE-2016ZX-13, the State Administration of Science Technology and Industry for National Defense, the major projects of high resolution earth observation system under Grant No. Y20A-E03.

References

1. Ghodsi, A., Zaharia, M., Hindman, B., Konwinski, A., Shenker, S., Stoica, I.: Dominant resource fairness: fair allocation of multiple resource types. In: Proceedings of 8th USENIX NSDI, Vol. 11, Berkeley (2011)
2. Dolev, D., Feitelson, D.G., Halpern, J.Y., Kupferman, R., Linial, N.: No justied complaints: on fair sharing of multiple resources. In: ITCS 2013, New York (2012)
3. Parkes, D.C., Procaccia, A.D., Shah, N.: Beyond dominant resource fairness: extensions, limitations,and indivisibilities. In: EC 2012, New York (2012)
4. Wang, H., Varman, P.: Balancing fairness and efficiency in tiered storage systems with bottleneck-aware allocation. In: Proceedings of 12th Usenix FAST, Santa Clara (2014)
5. Wang, H., Varman, P.: Brief announcement: fairness-efficiency tradeoffs in tiered storage allocation. In: SPAA 2014, Prague (2014)
6. Gutman, A., Nisan, N.: Fair allocation without trade. In: Proceedings of 11th AAMAS, Valencia (2012)
7. Huo, Z., Xiao, L. (eds.): Hybrid storage throughput allocation among multiple clients in heterogeneous data center. In: HPCC 2015, New York (2015)
8. Ito, Y., Koga, H.: A bandwidth reallocation scheme to improve fairness and link utilization in data center networks. In: Perform 2016, Sydney (2016)

System Problem Detection by Mining Process Model from Console Logs

Jian Li and Jian Cao[✉]

Department of Computer Science and Engineering,
Shanghai Jiao Tong University, Shanghai 200240, China
{jian-li,cao-jian}@sjtu.edu.cn

Abstract. Given the explosive growth of large-scale services, manually detecting problems from console logs is infeasible. In the current study, we propose a novel process mining algorithm to discover process model from console logs, and further use the obtained process model to detect anomalies. In brief, the console logs are first parsed into events, and the events from one single session are further grouped to event sequences. Then, a process model is mined from the event sequences to describe the main system behaviors. At last, we use the process model to detect anomalous log information. Experiments on Hadoop File System log dataset show that this approach can detect anomalies from log messages with high accuracy and few false positives. Compared with previously proposed automatic anomaly detection methods, our approach can provide intuitive and meaningful explanations to human operators as well as identify real problems accurately. Furthermore, the process model is easy to understand.

Keywords: Anomaly detection · Process mining · Logs · System monitoring

1 Introduction

Traditionally, operators inspect the console logs manually by searching for keywords such as "error" or "exception". But it has been shown to be infeasible due to couple of reasons. First, modern systems are large scale, and are generating huge logs everyday. Thus, it's too difficult to manually identify the real problems from tons of data. Second, the large-scale modern systems are too complex for one single developer to understand, and it makes it a great challenge for anomaly detection from huge console logs. Third, fault tolerant mechanisms are usually employed in large-scale systems. Hence, keywords like "error" or "exception" don't necessarily indicate real problems.

Recently, several automatic anomaly detection methods based on log analysis have been proposed. For example, Lin et al. [5] proposed a clustering based method to detect the abnormal log messages. Xu et al. [8] detect anomalies

X. Shi et al. (Eds.): NPC 2017, LNCS 10578, pp. 140–144, 2017.
DOI: 10.1007/978-3-319-68210-5_16

using Principal Component Analysis(PCA). Process mining [7] is a technique to distill a structured process description from a set of real executions. In this work, we proposed a bottom-up process mining method to discover the process model of the main system behaviors based on console log information. If a new log breaks certain process model, we say it is anomalous.

As the process model is intuitive with meaningful information, our approach can not only automatically detect system anomalies but also provide meaningful interpretation for problem diagnosis.

2 Process Modeling Notation

There are various process modeling notations, such as Petri Nets, Workflow Nets, BPMN and YAWL. Although they are quite different in notations, it is relatively easy to translate the process model from one notation to another. In the present work, a variant of process tree is defined to describe the models mined from log information using our algorithm.

2.1 Process Trees Variant

Definition 1 (Process Tree).

Let A be a finite set of activities. Symbol $\tau \notin A$ denotes the silent activities. $\bigoplus = \{\rightarrow, \times, \wedge_{(m,n)}, \circlearrowleft_{(m,n)}\}$ is the set of process tree operators.

- *If $a \in A \cup \{\tau\}$, then $Q = a$ is a process tree,*
- *If $Q_1, Q_2, \ldots, Q_n$ with $n > 0$ are process trees and $\oplus$ is a process tree operator, then $\oplus(Q_1, Q_2, \ldots, Q_n)$ is a process tree.*

Definition 2 (Process Tree Operators).

Let Q be a process tree over A. $L(Q)$ is the set of traces that can be generated by Q. $\Diamond(L(Q_1), L(Q_2), \ldots, L(Q_n))$ generates the set of all interleaved sequences. $L(Q)$ is defined recursively:

- *$L(Q) = \{[a]\}$ if $Q = a \in A$,*
- *$L(Q) = \{[]\}$ if $Q = \tau$,*
- *$L(Q) = \{[a_1, a_2, \ldots, a_n] | a_i \in L(Q_i), \forall i \in 1 \ldots n\}$ if $Q = \rightarrow (Q_1, Q_2, \ldots, Q_n)$,*
- *$L(Q) = \{[a_i] | a_i \in L(Q_i), \forall i \in 1 \ldots n\}$ if $Q = \times(Q_1, Q_2, \ldots, Q_n)$,*
- *$L(Q) = \Diamond(\Diamond_1(L(Q_1), L(Q_2), \ldots, L(Q_s)),$*
  $\Diamond_2(L(Q_1), L(Q_2), \ldots, L(Q_s)), \ldots,$
  $\Diamond_u(L(Q_1), L(Q_2), \ldots, L(Q_s)))$ with $u \in m, \ldots, n$ if $Q = \wedge_{(m,n)}(Q_1, Q_2, \ldots, Q_s)$,
- *$L(Q) = \{[a_{11}, a_{12}, \ldots, a_{1s}, \ldots, a_{t1}, a_{t2}, \ldots, a_{ts}] | a_{ij} \in L(\rightarrow (Q_1, Q_2, \ldots, Q_s)),$*
  $\forall j \in 1 \ldots s, \forall i \in 1 \ldots n, t \in m \ldots n\}$ if $Q = \circlearrowleft_{(m,n)}(Q_1, Q_2, \ldots, Q_s)$
- *$\wedge$ is the short form of $\wedge_{(1,1)}$, $\circlearrowleft$ is the short form of $\circlearrowleft_{(1,1)}$*

3 Proposed Approach

Our approach consists of three main steps: log parsing, process mining, and anomaly detection.

3.1   Log Parsing

Usually raw log messages are difficult to be directly processed by computers as they are unstructured. In this work, log templates are first extracted from unstructured log messages. Log messages with the same log template are grouped to the same type of event. Then the events within the same session are converted to a single sequence according to the recorded time. A sequence of events in time order is called an event trace.

3.2   Process Mining

Next, a three-phase process mining algorithm is utilized to uncover the process model which can represent main system behaviors. This approach can discover four kinds of basic control flow structures, which are sequence, choice, loop, and concurrency.

1. Discover subroutines
   A subroutine is basically a unit that contains a sequence of program instructions to perform a specific task in computer programming. Subroutines usually lead to groups of events with certain patterns in event traces. We use a statistical based method to identify the set of events that correspond to the subroutine, the structure of the events within the set, and how subroutines are called (in a roll or parallelly).
2. Discover the Main Control Flow
   In the previous step, the original events that correspond to subroutines are replaced by new combined events that represents subroutines. By taking each event in a trace as a node, and two adjoining events as two nodes connected by an edge, then each event trace is a directed acyclic graph. The directed graph was used to discover the main control flows of our target system.
3. Adjust the Model
   The process tree model mined as described above is constructed by two nodes each time iterating step by step. To make the model more concise, we do some adjust on the process tree representation of model without changing the semantic meanings in this step.

3.3   Anomaly Detection

At last, the discovered process model is applied to detect system anomalies. If an observed event sequence conforms to the process model, it will be labeled as normal. Otherwise, the ones which violate the process model are labeled as anomalies.

Our algorithm which checks whether a event trace conforms to the process tree model runs in a recursive manner. If the tree has only one node, then the conformance can be checked easily. Otherwise, we check the conformance of each subtree first, and then check whether the event trace conforms to the root node's rule. Every subtree contains a set of events. For each subtree, a sub-trace that only contains the corresponding events was extracted from the original event trace to check the conformance.

The process model mined by our approach keeps the patterns of event traces which are generated by the main system behaviors. The model depicts system execution paths in a tree structure and is easy to understand.

4   Experiments

We use HDFS log dataset [8] to evaluate the performance of our approach with the permission of the authors. HDFS dataset contains 11,175,629 log messages in total. All these log messages belong to 575,061 sessions. Among them, 16,838 sessions are manually labeled as anomalies by experts. Figure 1 shows the process model mined from HDFS logs. To evaluate the accuracy of our approach, we use three commonly used metrics: precision, recall, and f-measure.

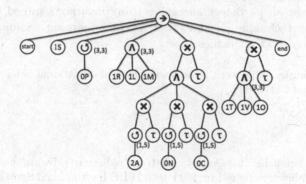

Fig. 1. Process model of HDFS logs

He et al. [4] evaluated six state-of-the-art log-based anomaly detection methods. Among these methods, Log Clustering [5], PCA [8] and Invariant Mining [6] are unsupervised methods. We repeated their experiments and got similar results. Figure 2(a) shows the results of our approach and other three unsupervised methods on HDFS data. Our approach achieved the recall of 100% while obtain high detection precision of 89%. To evaluate the stability of our method, the dataset are first split into ten subsets and we perform our method on each of them. The results are shown in Fig. 2(b). Our approach detects anomalies by constructing a model that depicts the main system behaviors. Therefore it is not sensitive to the noises in the data.

5   Related Work

Considerable research efforts have been conducted on anomaly detection. Chandola et al. [2,3] classified anomalies into three categories (point anomalies,

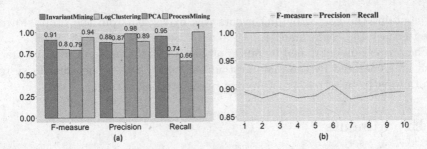

Fig. 2. Results

contextual anomalies and collective anomalies) and compared various kinds of anomaly detection techniques. Analyzing console logs for system problem detection has been an active research area. Xu et al. [8] first extract message count vectors from logs, and then detect anomalies using Principal Component Analysis(PCA). Lou et al. [6] detect anomalies using invariants mined from console logs. Clustering technique [5] and other machine learning techniques [1] have been applied to detect anomalies.

Acknowledgments. This work is supported by China National Science Foundation (Granted Number 61472253).

References

1. Alonso, J., Belanche, L., Avresky, D.R.: Predicting software anomalies using machine learning techniques. In: 2011 10th IEEE International Symposium on Network Computing and Applications (NCA), pp. 163–170. IEEE (2011)
2. Chandola, V., Banerjee, A., Kumar, V.: Anomaly detection: a survey. ACM comput. surv. (CSUR) **41**(3), 15 (2009)
3. Chandola, V., Banerjee, A., Kumar, V.: Anomaly detection for discrete sequences: a survey. IEEE Trans. Knowl. Data Eng. **24**(5), 823–839 (2012)
4. He, S., Zhu, J., He, P., Lyu, M.R.: Experience report: system log analysis for anomaly detection. In: 2016 IEEE 27th International Symposium on Software Reliability Engineering (ISSRE), pp. 207–218. IEEE (2016)
5. Lin, Q., Zhang, H., Lou, J.G., Zhang, Y., Chen, X.: Log clustering based problem identification for online service systems. In: Proceedings of the 38th International Conference on Software Engineering Companion, pp. 102–111. ACM (2016)
6. Lou, J.G., Fu, Q., Yang, S., Xu, Y., Li, J.: Mining invariants from console logs for system problem detection. In: USENIX Annual Technical Conference (2010)
7. van der Aalst, W., et al.: Process mining manifesto. In: Daniel, F., Barkaoui, K., Dustdar, S. (eds.) BPM 2011. LNBIP, vol. 99, pp. 169–194. Springer, Heidelberg (2012). doi:10.1007/978-3-642-28108-2_19
8. Xu, W., Huang, L., Fox, A., Patterson, D., Jordan, M.I.: Detecting large-scale system problems by mining console logs. In: Proceedings of the ACM SIGOPS 22nd symposium on Operating systems principles, pp. 117–132. ACM (2009)

Quantifying the Isolation Characteristics in Container Environments

Chang Zhao[1], Yusen Wu[1], Zujie Ren[1(✉)], Weisong Shi[2], Yongjian Ren[1], and Jian Wan[3]

[1] Hangzhou Dianzi University, Hangzhou, China
chaos_zhch@163.com, yusen.wu08@gmail.com, renzj@hdu.edu.cn,
yongjian.ren@infocore.cn
[2] Wayne State University, Detroit, USA
weisong@wayne.edu
[3] Zhejiang University of Science and Technology, Hangzhou, China
wanjian@zust.edu.cn

Abstract. In recent years, container technologies have attracted intensive attention due to the features of light-weight and easy-portability. The performance isolation between containers is becoming a significant challenge, especially in terms of network throughput and disk I/O. In traditional VM environments, the performance isolation is often calculated based on performance loss ratio. In container environments, the performance loss of well-behaved containers may be incurred not only by misbehaving containers but also by container orchestration and management. Therefore, the measurement models that only take performance loss into consideration will be not accurate enough. In this paper, we proposed a novel performance isolation measurement model that combines the performance loss and resource shrinkage of containers. Experimental results validate the effectiveness of our proposed model. Our results highlight the performance isolation between containers is different with the issue in VM environments.

Keywords: Containers · Performance isolation · Isolation measurement models

1 Introduction

Containers enable new ways to run applications by containerizing applications and services, making them portable, extensible, and easy to be transferred between private data centers and public clouds. However, containers suffer from a poor performance isolation as they share both OS kernels and physical servers. And in container environments, the life cycle and resources of containers are controlled by the container orchestrations. Therefore, the performance isolation measurement model in VM environments, is inapplicable for container environments.

© IFIP International Federation for Information Processing 2017
Published by Springer International Publishing AG 2017. All Rights Reserved
X. Shi et al. (Eds.): NPC 2017, LNCS 10578, pp. 145–149, 2017.
DOI: 10.1007/978-3-319-68210-5_17

In this paper, we proposed a comprehensive performance isolation measurement model that combines the performance loss and resource shrinkage of containers. The advantage of this model is that if the resource occupied by each container varies, the model can express the resource change, as well as the performance change. We conducted a group of performance evaluation experiments to validate the effectiveness of our proposed model.

2   Related Work

Performance isolation is one of the desirable features in virtualized environments [1]. In the field of traditional VMs, many research effort has been conducted to improve the performance isolation between VMs. Gupta *et al.* [2] developed a XEN-based monitoring system to monitor CPU utilizations of each VM, and dynamically schedule the resource allocation of CPU shares to enhance isolation. Shi *et al.* [3] proposed in a smart EdgeOS, the performance isolation might be more complicated than which in a distributed system. Therefore, a well designed control access mechanism should be added to the service management layer in the EdgeOS.

We noticed a few research works on performance isolation measured designed for traditional virtual machines [4]. These works often use the performance loss ratio to measure the isolation, which works on the assumption that the resource capacity of each virtualized machine is static. While for containers, the cause for performance losses for a container may not only due to the interference by misbehaving containers, but also the decrease of resources. Therefore, the existing models for VMs are inapplicable in container environments.

3   Performance Isolation Model

3.1   A Model Combining Performance Loss and Resource Shrinkage

Suppose there are two servers with same capacity, S_1 and S_2. Both of them host two containers, S_1 hosts container A_1 and B_1, and S_2 hosts containers A_2 and B_2. The configurations of all the four containers are same. Both B_1 and B_2 are misbehaving containers. Suppose A_1 and A_2 suffer same performance loss ratio, such as twenty percent. Meanwhile, the resource consumed by A_1 decreases a considerable portion, and A_2 does not. The isolation of S_1 should be better than the one of the S_2, because A_1 consume less resources to achieve a specific performance.

As shown in the following model 1, the performance isolation is associated with P_{loss} and R_{skg}. P_{loss} represents the performance loss degree of the containers, R_{skg} represents the resource shrinkage degree of the containers, and the larger value of P_{loss} and R_{skg} means the slower drop of the corresponding metrics. Through this model 1, we can normalize the performance isolation degree to the range of $[0,1]$.

$$I = f(P_{loss}, R_{skg}) = \frac{(1 + \beta^2) * P_{loss} * (1 - R_{skg})}{\beta^2 P_{loss} + (1 - R_{skg})} \tag{1}$$

The β in the formula 1 represents the scale factor used to adjust the weight of performance loss degree and resource shrinkage degree. A large β means that the performance loss is emphasized, while a small β means the resource elasticness is emphasized. By default, we can set β equal to 1.

3.2 Quantifying Performance Loss

In a well-isolated container system, the performance increasing of misbehaving containers does not affect the performance of other containers, as the green line shown in Fig. 1. In a no isolation container system, as the performance of misbehaving containers increasing, the performance of the well-behaving containers will drop linearly as the red line shown. And performance increasing of misbehaving containers is the same as the performance loss of the well-behaving containers.

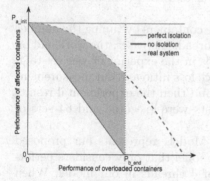

Fig. 1. Isolation curve including perfect isolation, no isolation and real system isolation. (Color figure online)

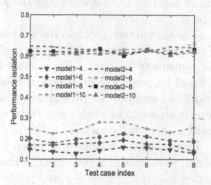

Fig. 2. Performance isolation with different workload of well-behaving containers.

However, in an actual container system, the performance of the well-behaving containers shows a downward trend in the curve, as the blue dotted line in Fig. 1. Thus we found that the blue dotted line closer to the green line and the shadow area is larger, the performance loss degree is better. We use the function $P_a = f(P_b)$ to represent the blue curve, then we define the calculation formula of the P_{loss} as the formula 2. For the model 1, we can also use the formula 2 to calculate R_{loss}.

$$I = \frac{\int_0^{P_{b\_end}} f(P_b)dP_b - P_{b\_end} * P_{a\_init}/2}{P_{b\_end} * P_{a\_init}/2} \tag{2}$$

4 Validation of the Model

4.1 Methodologies

In the experiment, well-behaving containers run SQL operations with a stable rate, while the workloads in misbehaving containers are gradually increased. To put workloads on these containers, we deploy MySQL database and use Sysbench benchmarks to generate SQL workloads.

4.2 Validation and Model Comparison

The workload in well-behaving containers have great influence on the performance isolation. When the workload on well-behaving containers is low, misbehaving containers can preempt the resources from well-behaving containers and impact the performance of well-behaving containers. In this case, the performance interference between containers is obvious and the performance isolation is poor.

The experiment controls the workload of the containers by tuning the number of threads of Sysbench. When the number of threads increases, the workload on the containers increases. The number of threads in the experiment was set to 4, 6, 8 and 10, respectively. We use the performance loss ratio and our measurement model to calculate the performance isolation, and then the experimental results were compared. In each case, eight experiments were executed and 64 sets of performance statistics were collected.

Experimental results are shown in Fig. 2. Model1 represents our proposed model, and model2 represents the traditional model that only considers performance loss ratio. Model-4 means the result of 4 threads in our model. When the workload in well-behaving containers changes, it is hard to accurately reflect the changes of the performance isolation. While for our model, the results for each group present obvious intervals, and demonstrate the distinct degrees of the performance isolation under the different workloads.

5 Summary

In this work, we presented an early-stage research work on the isolation in containers. We hope this work can motivate the container community to further address some open problems, such as resource scheduling among containers and workload-aware container orchestration. For more details, please refer to the extend version of this work [5].

Acknowledgement. This research is supported by the NSF of China (No. 61572163). Weisong Shi is in part supported by National Science Foundation (NSF) grant CNS-1563728.

References

1. Krebs, R.: Performance Isolation in Multi-Tenant Applications. PhD thesis, Karlsruhe Institute of Technology (2015)
2. Gupta, D., Cherkasova, L., Gardner, R., Vahdat, A.: Enforcing performance isolation across virtual machines in Xen. In: van Steen, M., Henning, M. (eds.) Middleware 2006. LNCS, vol. 4290, pp. 342–362. Springer, Heidelberg (2006). doi:10.1007/11925071_18
3. Shi, W., Cao, J., Zhang, Q., Li, Y., Xu, L.: Edge computing: vision and challenges. IEEE Internet Things J. **3**(5), 637–646 (2016)
4. Walraven, S., Monheim, T., Truyen, E., Joosen, W.: Towards performance isolation in multi-tenant SAAS applications. In: Proceedings of the 7th Workshop on Middleware for Next Generation Internet Computing, p. 6. ACM (2012)
5. Zhao, C., Wu, Y., Ren, Z., Shi, W., Ren, Y., Wan, J.: Quantifying the isolation characteristics in container environments. Technical report No. MIST-TR-2017-010, Wayne State University (2017). http://www.cs.wayne.edu/~weisong/papers/MIST-TR-2017-010.pdf

CSAS: Cost-Based Storage Auto-Selection, a Fine Grained Storage Selection Mechanism for Spark

Bo Wang[1], Jie Tang[2(⊠)], Rui Zhang[1,3], and Zhimin Gu[1]

[1] Beijing Institute of Technology University,
Beijing 100081, People's Republic of China
[2] South China University of Technology University,
Guangzhou 510641, People's Republic of China
cstangjie@scut.edu.cn
[3] Yan'an University, Yan'an 716000, People's Republic of China

Abstract. To improve system performance, Spark places the RDDs into memory for further access through the caching mechanism. And it provides a variety of storage levels to put cache RDDs. However, the RDD-grained manual storage level selection mechanism can not adjust depending on computing resources of the node. In this paper, we firstly present a fine-grained automatic storage level selection mechanism. And then we provide a storage level for a partition based on a cost model which fully considering the system resources status, compression and serialization costs. Experiments show that our approach can offer a up to 77% performance improvement compared to the default storage level scheme provided by Spark.

Keywords: Big data · Spark · Storage level selection · Optimize

1 Introduction

To balance volume and speed, Spark [1] provides five flags to mark storage level, corresponding to whether use disk, memory, offHeap, serialization and replication. However, the storage level selection mechanism of Spark has the following two problems: Firstly, storage level of a RDD is set by programmers manually, by default storage level is MEMORY_ONLY which the RDD can only be cached in memory. Experiments show that there are significant performance differences among different storage level. A reasonable storage level decision results in performance improvements; A wrong decision can lead to performance degradation or even failure inversely. Secondly, RDD-grained storage level selection mechanism may lead lower resource utilization. In Spark, the same cached RDD uses the same storage level, on the contrary, different RDDs may use different storage levels. While a RDD is divided into several partitions which have different size and locate in different executors. Some partitions of a RDD may be computed

© IFIP International Federation for Information Processing 2017
Published by Springer International Publishing AG 2017. All Rights Reserved
X. Shi et al. (Eds.): NPC 2017, LNCS 10578, pp. 150–154, 2017.
DOI: 10.1007/978-3-319-68210-5_18

on executors which have enough free memory, and others will be pended on executors which have not enough free memory on contrary.

In this paper, we propose a fine-grained storage level selection mechanism. Storage level is assigned to a RDD partition, not RDD, before it cache. And storage level selection of a RDD partition is automatically basing on a cost model which takes fully account of memory of the executor and various computing costs of the partition.

2   Design and Implementation

2.1   Overall Architecture

CSAS (Cost-based Storage Auto-Selection) can wisely select a Storage-level, based on future costs, for a partition before it is to be cached. The overall architecture, shown as Fig. 1, consists of three components: *(i)Analyzer*, which lies in the driver, provides the function of analyzing the DAG structure of the application to obtain the RDDs which will be cached and their execution flows; *(ii)Collections*, one in each executor, are used to collect real-time information, such as creation time, (De)serialization time of each RDD partition, during the task running; *(iii) Storagelevel Selectors*, also one in each executor, are arbiters for decision which storage level will be used by RDD partition when they will be cached.

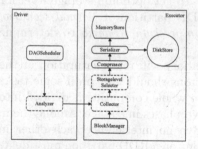

Fig. 1. Overall architecture of CSAS.

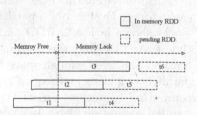

Fig. 2. RDD execution model.

2.2   Analyzer

As mentioned above, *Analyzer* obtains dependencies of RDDs and RDDs that will be cached according to DAG constructed by DAG Scheduler. There are two types of RDDs, called cache RDDs and non-cache RDDs. When computes on a RDD, it is necessary that all RDDs it depends are ready. If there are RDD(s) absent, the absences need to be created firstly. For non-cache RDDs, they are computed each time; For cache RDDs, they are got from memory or disk or both through CacheManager according of storage level after first computing. So we need to obtain the interdependencies among cache RDDs. In this paper, we use LCS's DFS algorithm [3] to get the ancestor cache RDDs of a RDD and the creating path of each cache RDD. At last, all these informations are recorded and are used to compute create cost of a RDD in *Collector*.

2.3 Collector

Informations that A *collector* collect are listed in the followings:

Create Cost: Time spends on computing a RDD partition after all ancestor cache partitions are ready, denoted as C_{create}.

(De)Serialization cost: Time takes on serialize or deserialize a RDD partition, denoted as C_{ser} or C_{deser}.

(De)Compression cost: Time takes on compress or decompress a RDD partition, denoted as C_{comp} or C_{decomp}.

Disk cost: Time takes on I/O on Disk, denoted as C_{disk}.

When (De)Serialization cost of a RDD partition is absent, we need estimate it using its cost per MB data [3], denoted as SPM and DSPM. When (de)serialization cost is unknown for a RDD partition, we estimate its (de)serialization cost according by the size of the partition and SPM or DSPM of corresponding RDD respectively. (De)Compression cost is also estimated using the same way.

According the above definition, we can calculate cache cost of a RDD partition in different scenarios, denoted as C_{cache}. To get optimum storage level for each partition, we compute cache cost of a RDD partition of *Normal scenario*, *Serialization scenario*, *Disk scenario* and *Compression scenario* to determine each storage level flag of a partition.

As shown in Fig. 2, RDD partitions in memory will reach saturation at the time t. At this time, the pending RDD partitions should wait until some tasks finished and freed enough space to run. So the whole computing is divided into parallel computing and sequence computing two phases in a stage. Among them, computing operations on RDD partitions have no interference each other in parallel computing phase. In contrast, operations on a RDD partition must delay until another computing finished in sequence computing phase. The moment that sequence computing phase begins is after the first finish task in parallel computing phase has released its memory. Thus, the worst case caching cost in stage i can be concluded in Eq. 1:

$$C_{wccc}^i = max\{C_{cache}^1, ..., C_{cache}^m\} + \sum_{(k=1)}^{(n-m)/m} maxC_{cache}^k \qquad (1)$$

where n is the number of total RDD partitions will be cached in the future of this stage; m is the number of RDD partitions computing in parallel; $maxC_{cache}^k$ is one of the top $(n-m)/m$ max cache cost among RDD partitions in sequence computing phase. The second half is the sum of top $(n-m)/m$ cache cost among RDD partitions in sequence computing phase.

2.4 Storagelevel Selectors

Storage level selector in this executor evaluates an appropriate storage level for the partition based on worst case caching cost of various scenarios before a RDD partitiòn is to be cached. Algorithm 1 shows the storage level selection strategy for a cache RDD partition is determined by the values of worst case caching cost among various scenarios under the current memory circumstance. All costs used in algorithm 1 are caculated based on Eq. 1.

Algorithm 1. Cost-based Storage Level Selection

```
function StorageLevelSelection
Input: Cms_regular, Cms_serialize, Cms_compress, Cms_disk,
 unroll_size, free_size
Output: StorageLevel
  useMemory = true
  deserialized, useDisk, Compress = false
  if(Cms_regular > Cms_serialize)then
.   deserialized = true
  endif
  if(Cms_regular > Cms_disk)then
    useDisk = true
  endif
  if((Cms_compress < Cms_serialize)
&&(Cms_compress < Cms_disk < 0))then
      Compress = true
  endif
  if(unroll_size > free_size)then
    useMemory = false
  endif
  if(!useMemory)then
    useDisk = true
  endif
  return StorageLevel
endfunction
```

3 Performance Evaluations

The experiment platform includes a cluster with three different nodes, one as both master and executor and the remaining only act as executors. And we adopt HDFS for storage, each partition has one replications. The datasets are generated by BigDataBench [4]. We use WordCount and KMeans two benchmarks in our experiments. For the convenience of test, we have two RDD cache for wordcount, respectively textFileRDD and flatMapRDD. The size of the two RDDs is about nine times difference. All data are normalized based on CSAS execution time.

Figure 3 shows the difference of performance between CSAS and Spark native system which under different cache storage levels. It shows that there is a huge difference in execution time under different storage levels in native Spark. And CSAS can reduce 66.7% time compared to M_M which are the default scheme in Spark.

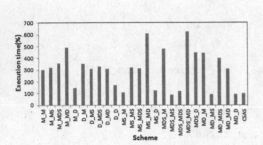

Fig. 3. Overall performance.

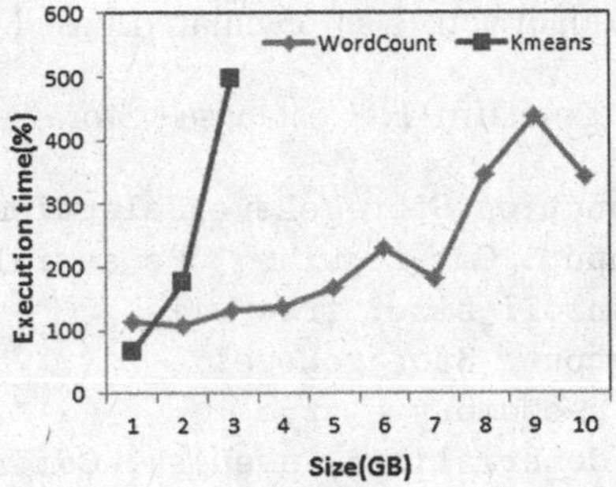

Fig. 4. Performance in different data sizes.

Figure 4 shows the compare of performance between CSAS and Spark native system which under different input sizes. In the experiment, we set all cache RDDs' storage level to MEMORY_ONLY. For WordCount, CSAS can reduce 8.1–77.2% time compared to M_M in different input sizes. And for Kmeans, Spark fails when input size bigger than 4 GB during using the default storage level, but CSAS can work well.

Acknowledgments. Jie Tang is the corresponding author of this paper. This work is supported by South China University of Technology Start-up Grant No. D61600470, Guangzhou Technology Grant No. 201707010148 and National Science Foundation of China under grant No. 61370062.

References

1. Zaharia, M., Chowdhury, M., Das, T., Dave, A., Ma, J., McCauley, M., Franklin, M.J., Shenker, S., Stoica, I.: Resilient distributed datasets: a Fault-tolerant abstraction for in-memory cluster computing. In: Proceedings of the 9th USENIX conference on Networked Systems Design and Implementation, San Jose, CA, p. 2 (2012)
2. Choi, I.S., Yang, W., Kee, Y.S.: Early experience with optimizing I/O performance using high-performance SSDs for in-memory cluster computing. In: Proceedings of IEEE International Conference on Big Data (Big Data 2015) (2015)
3. Geng, Y., et al.: LCS: an efficient data eviction strategy for spark. Int. J. Parallel Program., pp. 1–13 (2016)
4. BigDataBench. http://prof.ict.ac.cn/BigDataBench/

An In-Depth Performance Analysis of Many-Integrated Core for Communication Efficient Heterogeneous Computing

Jie Zhang and Myoungsoo Jung$^{(\boxtimes)}$

Computer Architecture and Memory Systems Laboratory,
School of Integrated Technology, Yonsei University, Seoul, South Korea
{jie,mj}@camelab.org

Abstract. Many-integrated core (MIC) architecture combines dozens of reduced x86 cores onto a single chip to offer high degrees of parallelism. The parallel user applications executed across many cores that exist in one or more MICs require a series of work related to data sharing and synchronization with the host. In this work, we build a real CPU+MIC heterogeneous cluster and analyze its performance behaviors by examining different communication methods such as message passing method and remote direct memory accesses. Our evaluation results and in-depth studies reveal that (i) aggregating small messages can improve network bandwidth without violating latency restrictions, (ii) while MICs can execute hundreds of hardware cores, the highest network throughput is achieved when only $4 \sim 6$ point-to-point connections are established for data communication, (iii) data communication over multiple point-to-point connections between host and MICs introduce severe load unbalancing, which require to be optimized for future heterogeneous computing.

Keywords: Manycore · Communication · Accelerator · Parallel programming · High performance computing · Heterogeneous computing

1   Introduction

In the past few years, many-core integrated (MIC) architecture has be employed for accelerating the heterogeneous computing [5]. Typically, a MIC architecture chip has dozens of reduced x86 cores, which can provide massive parallelism. Parallel user applications, which are executed across different cores of MIC(s), can share data or collaborate to compute with each other by using user-level communication systems, such as massage passing interface (MPI) [2] or open computing language (OpenCL) [6]. For the modern MIC designs, these user-level communication systems in practice are built upon a symmetric communication interface, referred to as *SCIF*, which is a kernel component of manycore platform software stack. Even though there are many prior studies that perform the user-level optimizations for efficient manycore communication [4], little attention has been paid to the low-level communication methods for MICs.

© IFIP International Federation for Information Processing 2017
Published by Springer International Publishing AG 2017. All Rights Reserved
X. Shi et al. (Eds.): NPC 2017, LNCS 10578, pp. 155–159, 2017.
DOI: 10.1007/978-3-319-68210-5_19

In this work, we build a real MIC-accelerated heterogeneous cluster that has eight main processor cores and 244 physical MIC cores (61 cores per MIC device) and characterize the performance behaviors on the heterogeneous cluster, which are observed by the low-level communication methods. Specifically, we evaluate the latency and bandwidth of the cluster using two different strategies: (i) *massing passing* and (ii) *remote memory access* (RMA). While the massage passing establish a pair of message queues for exchanging short, latency-sensitive messages, RMA enables one process to remotely access the memory of target process it connected to. In this paper, we explore a full design space of MICs with those two the message passing and RMA communication methods by taking into account a wide spectrum of system parameters, including different datapath configurations, various data page and message sizes, as well as different number of threads, ports and connection channels.

2   Background

In this section, we briefly explain how MIC devices communicate with the host through the user-level APIs supported by the software stack. In heterogeneous cluster, each separate multiprocessor (i.e., host and MICs) is regarded as a node. The software stack of MIC architectures provides a common transport interface, which is referred to as *symmetric communication interface* (SCIF) [1], to establish a point-to-point communication link to connect a pair of processes on either different nodes or in the same node. The APIs supported by the SCIF user mode library can be categorized as a set of connection APIs, messaging APIs, and remote memory access (RMA) APIs. Figure 1 demonstrates how two processes can connect with each other over SCIF APIs. As shown in Fig. 1a, the connection APIs provide a socket-like hand-shaking procedure (e.g., `scif_open()`, `scif_bind()`, `scif_listen()`, `scif_connect()`, and `scif_accept()`) to set up connections [7]. The messaging APIs support a two-sided communication between connected processes by implementing message queues (c.f. Fig. 1b). Messages can be sent and received via the commands `scif_send()` and `scif_recv()`.

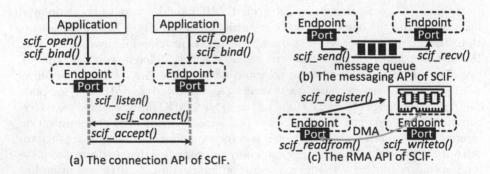

Fig. 1. Communication APIs of SCIF interface.

On the other hand, the RMA APIs are responsible for transferring a large bulk of data. As shown in Fig. 1c, it first maps a specific memory region of a local process to the address space of target process through a memory registration API, `scif_register()`. It then leverages read/write APIs, `scif_readfrom()` and `scif_writeto()`, to access remote data.

3 Empirical Evaluation and Analysis

Message-based Communication Method. Figure 2 illustrates the performance of MIC message passing mechanism by employing different number of producer/consumer threads within single connection channel or establishing multiple connection channels. Specifically, "XPYC" indicates X producer threads

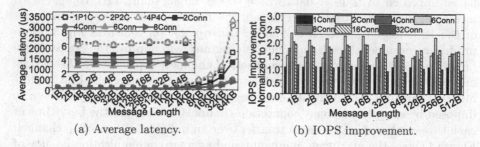

(a) Average latency.   (b) IOPS improvement.

Fig. 2. Performance improvement of message passing with multiple connection channels.

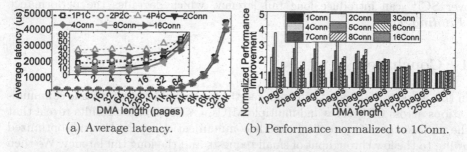

(a) Average latency.   (b) Performance normalized to 1Conn.

Fig. 3. Performance improvements of RMA with connection channels.

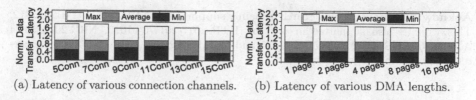

(a) Latency of various connection channels.   (b) Latency of various DMA lengths.

Fig. 4. Max, min, and average communication latencies of each thread under various connection channel and DMA length configurations.

and Y consumer threads are employed for a single connection channel, while "XConn" means X connection channels are established with a single producer thread and a single consumer thread per connection channel. From the results, we can conclude that, it improves communication throughput without introducing extra latency penalty, if one can aggregate multiple small-size messages to 512B (*Finding 1*). Multiple producer and consumer threads are unable to improve the communication throughput of single point-to-point connection channel (*Finding 2*). One can also observe that properly establishing multiple point-to-point connection channels can significantly improve the performance (*Finding 3*).

RMA-based Communication Method. Figure 3 shows the performance of RMA by employing multiple producers-consumers or setting up multiple channel connections. From this figure, we conclude that it is better to leverage message-based approach to transfer data whose size is larger than 512B, compared to messaging based approach, even though the minimum data access granularity of the RMA-based approach is 4 KB (*Finding 4*). As shown in Fig. 3, more producer/consumer threads unfortunately cannot help improve the performance (*Finding 5*). In addition, more connection channels can improve the performance, but four connection channels are sufficient to achieve the best performance (*Finding 6*). To figure out the reason behind the poor performance imposed by establishing many connection channels, we analyze the busy time of each thread which performs data transfer over an individual connection channel. Figure 4 shows the maximum, minimum, and average communication latency of each thread with different number of connection channels and different transfer data size. Based on the results, we can conclude that the communication over SCIF can introduce long tail latency, which degrades the performance (*Finding 7*).

4   Conclusion

In this work, we evaluated and analyzed the performance of inter-node communications across CPU cores and multiple MICs. Our evaluation results reveal that the performance of current inter-node communication methods is sub-optimized owing to the low throughput of small requests and the long tail latency. We then provide seven system-level findings with an in-depth performance analysis.

Acknowledgement. This research is mainly supported by NRF 2016R1C1B2015312. This work is also supported in part by IITP-2017-2017-0-01015, NRF-2015M3C4 A7065645, DOE DE-AC02-05CH 11231 and MemRay grant (2015-11-1731). The corresponding author is M. Jung.

References

1. IMI Core. Symmetric communications interface (scif) user guide. Intel Std., Rev. 0.8 (2012)
2. Gropp, W., et al.: A high-performance, portable implementation of the mpi message passing interface standard. Parallel Comput. **22**(6), 789–828 (1996)
3. Intel, Intel Xeon Phi 7120A (2014). https://ark.intel.com/products/80555
4. Potluri, S., et al.: Efficient inter-node mpi communication using gpudirect rdma for infiniband clusters with nvidia gpus. In: ICpp, pp. 80–89. IEEE (2013)
5. Saule, E., Kaya, K., Çatalyürek, Ü.V.: Performance evaluation of sparse matrix multiplication kernels on Intel Xeon Phi. In: Wyrzykowski, R., Dongarra, J., Karczewski, K., Waśniewski, J. (eds.) PPAM 2013. LNCS, vol. 8384, pp. 559–570. Springer, Heidelberg (2014). doi:10.1007/978-3-642-55224-3_52
6. Stone, J.E., et al.: Opencl: a parallel programming standard for heterogeneous computing systems. Comput. Sci. Eng. **12**, 66 (2010)
7. Xue, M., Zhu, C.: The socket programming and software design for communication based on client/server. In: PACCS, pp. 775–777. IEEE (2009)

Author Index

Printed in the United States
By Bookmasters